Tick...Tick...

Hear that clock ticking? It's the countdown to the AP Statistics Exam, which will be here before you know it. Whether you have a year to go or just one day, this is the time to start maximizing your score.

The Exam Is Just a Few Months Away!

Don't worry—you're still ahead of the game. However, it is important that you stop delaying and begin preparing now. Follow **The Big Picture: How to Prepare Year-Round** (page 235) to make the most of your time so you'll be ready on test day. This section gives you strategies to put into place up to a year before you take the exam.

Actually, I Only Have a Few Weeks!

Even if you're down to the last few weeks before the exam, you still have plenty of time for a full review. To make the best use of your time, turn to **The Main Course: Comprehensive Strategies and Review** (page 21), where you'll find **Comprehensive Strategies for Multiple-Choice Questions** (page 25) to help you ace the multiple-choice questions and **Comprehensive Strategies for Free-Response Questions** (page 33) for advice on approaching open-ended questions. **The Diagnosis: How Ready Are You?** (page 43) includes a diagnostic exam that allows you to identify areas of weakness so that you can address them. You should also review all the in-depth subject review chapters (beginning on page 91) for an overview of the big topics usually covered on the AP Statistics Exam. As you work through this information, keep track of the concepts, facts, and ideas about which you need more information. Use the **practice exams** (beginning on page 249) to increase your comfort with both the format and content of the exam.

Let's Be Honest. The Exam Is Tomorrow and I'm Freaking Out!

No problem! Review the **Introduction** (page ix), **About the Exam** (page x), and **The Essentials: A Last-Minute Study Guide** (page 1), so you know what to expect when you arrive to take the exam and have some ideas as to how to approach the test questions. Then, take at least one **practice exam** (beginning on page 249). Don't worry about your score—just focus on getting familiar with the exam. Before you go to bed, review the **Quick Exam-Taking Tips** (page 7) once more. It'll walk you through the day ahead.

Relax. Make the most of the tools and resources in this review guide, and you'll be ready to earn a top score.

My Max Score

AP STATISTICS

Maximize Your Score in Less Time

Amanda Ross, PhD,
and Anne Collins

 sourcebooks **edu**

Published by Sourcebooks, Inc.
P.O. Box 4410, Naperville, Illinois 60567-4410
(630) 961-3900
Fax: (630) 961-2168
www.sourcebooks.com

Library of Congress Cataloging-in-Publication Data

Ross, Amanda
    My max score AP statistics : maximize your score in less time / Amanda Ross, PhD and Anne Collins.
        pages cm
    1.   Statistics—Examinations—Study guides. 2.   Advanced placement programs (Education)—Examinations—Study guides. 3. Statistics—Examinations, questions, etc. I. Collins, Anne M. II. Title.
    QA276.2.R67 2013
    519.5076—dc23
                            2012037734

Printed and bound in the United States of America.
VP 10 9 8 7 6 5 4 3 2 1

Also Available in the My Max Score Series

AP Exam Study Aids

AP Biology

AP Calculus AB/BC

AP English Language and Composition

AP English Literature and Composition

AP European History

AP U.S. Government and Politics

AP U.S. History

AP World History

SAT Subject Test Study Aids

SAT Biology E/M Subject Test

SAT Literature Subject Test

SAT Math 1 and 2 Subject Test

SAT U.S. History Subject Test

SAT World History Subject Test

ASVAB Study Aids

ASVAB: Armed Services Vocational Aptitude Battery

Contents

Introduction

Everyone comes to the AP Statistics Exam from a different place. For some, it's the one AP exam of their high school career; for others, it's just one exam of many. Some students have focused on it all year, supplementing their classwork with extra study and practice at home. Other students haven't been able to devote the time they would like—perhaps other classes, extracurricular activities, after-school jobs, or family obligations have gotten in the way. But wherever you're coming from, this book can help! It's been designed to provide maximum assistance no matter where you are on your study path.

You'll find that this book has been divided into three sections: a last-minute study guide to use in the days before the exam; a comprehensive review for those with more than a week to prepare; and a long-term study plan for students preparing well in advance.

Think of each section as full of suggestions rather than a rigid prescription. Feel free to pick and choose the pieces you find most helpful from each section. Of course, if you have time, we recommend that you review *everything*—and take as many practice exams as you can, as many times as you can.

Whether you have a day to cram or a year to study at leisure, here are some things you should know before diving into the exam. For starters: What is the AP Statistics Exam, and what does it cover?

About the Exam

The AP Statistics Exam is a two-part exam. In Section I, you will have 90 minutes to complete 40 multiple-choice questions on a variety of topics. In Section II, you will have 60 minutes to complete 4 to 6 free-response questions. Each free-response question should take you about 12 minutes to complete. Additionally, Section II includes one longer investigative task, which you have 30 minutes to complete. The questions in this section typically cover the following topic areas:

- Exploring data (describing patterns and departures from patterns)
- Sampling and experimentation (planning and conducting a study)
- Anticipating patterns (producing models using probability and simulation)
- Statistical inference (estimating population parameters and testing hypotheses)

When your exam is graded, Section I and Section II will be given equal weight in determining your score.

What's Included

According to the College Board, the concepts covered on the AP Statistics Exam break down as follows:

SUBJECT	PERCENTAGE OF QUESTIONS
Exploring data: Describing patterns and departures from patterns	20–30%
Sampling and experimentation: Planning and conducting a study	10–15%
Anticipating patterns: Exploring random phenomena using probability and simulation	20–30%
Statistical inference: Estimating population parameters and testing hypotheses	30–40%

Exam Scoring

As you probably already know, AP exams are graded on a scale of 1 to 5. Most colleges offer college credit for a score of 5, a few offer credit for a 4, and a very few offer credit for a 3. No college gives credit if you score a 1 or 2. If you know the school you're likely to attend, it's a good idea to speak with your guidance counselor or to contact the admissions office directly to find out what score you need to earn college credit at that institution.

AP SCORE	QUALIFICATION
5	Extremely well qualified
4	Well qualified
3	Qualified
2	Possibly qualified
1	No recommendation

Unfortunately, there are no hard-and-fast rules to follow to guarantee a score of 5. However, the following chart gives you a general idea of the percentage of AP Statistics exam-takers who scored in each range in 2010 and 2011.*

AP SCORE	2010	2011
5	13%	12%
4	22%	21%
3	24%	25%
2	18%	18%
1	23%	24%

*NOTE: These numbers are estimates based on statistical information provided by the College Board. See www.collegeboard.com for more information.

Naturally, you want to be among the elite percentage who score a 4 or 5 on this exam, right? And with this material in hand, you should feel confident in your ability to achieve that score. Put this material to its intended use, so you'll have not only a strong understanding of the key concepts being tested but also ample opportunity to practice tried-and-true testing strategies.

Beyond the material in this book, an additional AP Statistics Exam is available to you on our website, mymaxscore.com. That site includes practice exams for other AP subjects as well.

Good luck!

THE ESSENTIALS: A LAST-MINUTE STUDY GUIDE

So, it's a night or two before the exam and you just don't feel ready. Should you panic? Absolutely not! This is the time to take a deep breath and finish your final preparations. If you've been taking an AP Statistics class or preparing in other ways throughout the year, you should be just about at your goal. All you need to do is calm your nerves by breathing deeply, refresh your mind by reviewing a few key strategies, and get your belongings together for test day. It's not too late to maximize your score!

First, remember that being anxious is just a waste of your energy. You can let your nerves paralyze you, or you can get into a better frame of mind by focusing your thoughts and energies on the things you can do now. Focusing is more likely to bring you success than worrying about how nervous you feel. Guide your energy into positive activities that leave you feeling prepared.

Second, if you're testing soon, you don't have a lot of time available, so it's important to make the most of the time you do have. Find a location where you have privacy to study in peace, such as your bedroom (good) or the library (even better, if your house is a busy one with too many distractions available to you). Tune out the world by turning off your telephone, your computer, and all of your other electronic gadgets. Stop texting, quit surfing the Internet, and turn off the music. Ask your family and friends not to disturb you unless it's really important. Close your door (or park yourself in a library cubicle) and get ready.

Step 1: Review the Exam-Taking Tips

If it's been a while since you've considered the exam setup, or if you're just not sure where to start, take a few minutes to review the first section of the book (that means you should also go back to the **Introduction** on page ix before going forward to the **Quick Exam-Taking Tips** on page 7). If you have only a few days, take time to carefully review the **Comprehensive Strategies for Multiple-Choice Questions** (page 25) and **Comprehensive Strategies for Free-Response Questions** (page 33) in **The Main Course: Comprehensive Strategies and Review** (page 21). The strategies covered in that section are tried-and-true; they can go far toward giving you a real boost in your score.

Step 2: Examine the Big Ideas

If you don't have time for a full content review, at least take the time to look over the basics. We've compiled these for you in **Big Ideas in Statistics** (page 13). This section outlines the concepts, themes, and ideas you'll encounter in both the multiple-choice and the free-response sections of the exam. If you have time, continue to the chapter reviews as well.

Step 3: Take a Practice Exam

One of the most effective ways to really get to know any exam is to take a practice exam, preferably one that has been specifically designed to mimic the exam in question. In this book, you'll find two complete practice exams (in addition to the diagnostic exam). Plus, a third practice exam is available at mymaxscore.com at no extra charge.

When taking practice exams, it's important to pretend you're really taking the exam. That means you should test in a quiet area and move from Section I to Section II on the preestablished time schedule. Use the answer keys provided to see how well you're likely to do if a similar question is asked on the actual exam. When reviewing your responses, watch for common themes or trends and identify areas that seem to need improvement. Once you know where you need the most help, review the appropriate sections in this book or go back to your class notes or textbook for more detail.

The Night Before: Gather Your Materials

The last thing you want to do the morning of the exam is rush around trying to find everything you need. Use this checklist to gather everything you need beforehand. Put together a backpack or small bag with these items (and anything else you might need). Have this bag ready so that you can grab it and go in the morning.

- You will need proof of identity (especially if you're testing at a school other than your own), so bring your photo ID. Place this in an easy-to-locate side pocket or zippered compartment so you can get your hands on it quickly when entering the exam site.

- Do you know your school code? This is especially important if you're testing in a school other than your own. Make sure you ask for this information from your AP administrator or guidance counselor beforehand. Write it on a piece of paper and place that paper in your bag along with your photo ID.

- Pack several sharpened pencils, a nonsmudging eraser, and several black or blue pens. Although you can use erasable pens if you like, you should make sure they aren't going to leave marks on the answer sheet. The multiple-choice section is graded by computer, so smudging can affect your results. That's why it's so important to make sure none of your erasers will leave marks. Also, note that while there *should* be a pencil sharpener available in the testing room, it's probably not a bad idea to pack a portable sharpener, just in case.

- Bring a graphing calculator with statistical capabilities. The College Board is particular as to the type of calculator allowed. Visit the College Board's website (www.collegeboard.com) for the most current information about allowed computational and graphic features. Minicomputers, pocket organizers, electronic writing pads, and calculators with QWERTY keyboards are not allowed in the exam room. You may not use your calculator's memory for storing notes.

- Plan to wear or bring a watch. (If your watch has any alarms, buzzers, or beepers, turn them off.)

- Include a small, easy-to-eat snack. Exam day is going to be long, and you may need nourishment. Choose a snack that's high in protein with a lower carbohydrate count. Avoid messy items like chocolate bars, as these can melt and get on your hands and desk. Avoid nuts, as they can trigger allergies in other testers. Some good choices might be an energy or protein bar or drink or an easy-to-eat piece of fruit such as a banana.

- Pack a bottle of water. You'll want something to drink at some point, and it's best to avoid substances with a lot of sugar or caffeine. Although you may think they'll give you energy, they're more likely to contribute to exam jitters—and you'll have enough of those on your own!

- Avoid packing items you can't take into the testing room. For example, cell phones, pagers, and other electronic devices (aside from your approved graphing calculator) are prohibited for a variety of reasons.

- Here's one important repeat: Try to pack only what you need.
  - Photo ID
  - School code

- ○ Pens, pencils, eraser, sharpener
- ○ Graphing calculator
- ○ Watch or timer
- ○ Snack and bottle of water

Exam Day: Tips

Here are some other tips for managing exam day.

- The night before the exam, *don't* stay up all night studying. At that point, you'll be as ready as ever! Instead, concentrate on getting a good night's sleep. It's more important to be rested and alert.
- Eat a light but satisfying meal in the morning. Protein-rich foods such as eggs, nuts, and yogurt are good choices, as they'll fill you up but won't give you a sugar or caffeine crash later. But don't eat too much—you don't want to be sluggish or uncomfortably full. If you must have coffee or another caffeinated beverage, that's fine. Just try not to overdo it.
- Dress in comfortable layers. The testing room might be too hot or too cool. You can't control the temperature, so you'll want to be able to adjust to it. Also, make sure your clothes are comfortable. Your newest outfit might be gorgeous, but the last thing you need during the exam is to feel annoyed by pants that are too tight or irritated by fabrics that feel itchy.
- Don't forget your backpack!
- Relax! Once you get to the testing room, take a few deep breaths and try to channel some of your energy into relaxation. Remind yourself that you know the material, you understand how the exam works, and you are ready to go. It's natural to be nervous, but it's better to save your energy for the mental task ahead.
- Once the exam begins, set everything else in your mind aside and focus on doing your best. You've done all you can to prepare. Time to make that preparation pay off!

Quick Exam-Taking Tips

Part I: Multiple-Choice Strategies

For the multiple-choice part of the exam, you'll be answering 40 questions in 90 minutes. That means you'll have just over two minutes to read and answer each question. That's two minutes to read and comprehend the question, analyze any associated chart or other data, and review all answer options to select the most appropriate response. Clearly, this part of the exam is going to go very quickly. But don't worry; you can be successful. You just need to understand how to approach these questions to maximize your score.

Here's a tip. Many test-prep "experts" recommend skipping through an exam to answer those questions you're sure about before going back through to answer those questions you're not sure about. However, we don't recommend that strategy to you, because too many test-takers waste an inordinate amount of time combing through the materials looking for questions they skipped. Additionally—and this is a very big "additionally"—skipping questions increases the chances that you'll fill out the answer sheet incorrectly. Finally, in recent years, the College Board has changed the way it scores the multiple-choice part of the exam; test-takers are no longer penalized for answering incorrectly. (The College Board says: *"Total scores on the multiple-choice section are based on the number of questions answered correctly. Points are not deducted for incorrect answers, and no points are awarded for unanswered questions.*") We recommend you flag items you're not sure of, so you can revisit them if you have time, but we don't think you should skip any questions. Read on.

Tip 1: Answer the question in your head.

Read each question or stem and answer it in your head before you actually look at the answer options. At times, answer choices are written in such a way as to distract you from the right answer. (That's why they're called "distracters.") However, if you have a good idea of the answer you seek before you read the distracters, you'll be less confused by those other options.

Tip 2: Pay attention to the words.

As you read the questions and answer choices, pay attention to the wording. Some questions will include words such as *NOT* or *EXCEPT*. The inclusion of these words radically changes the answer to the question. You're looking for the answer that is *not* true or does *not* apply. This might seem obvious, but it's actually quite easy to overlook these words when you're reading quickly.

Other questions might include qualifiers. A *qualifier* is a word or group of words that limits or modifies the meaning of another word or group of words. When a qualifier appears in a question, the correct response must reflect it. Some common qualifiers in exam questions include

- Likely, unlikely
- Apt to, may, might
- Always, never, often, sometimes
- Frequently, probably, usually, seldom
- Some, a few, a majority, many, most, much

Additionally, keep an eye out for double negatives, because (just as in math) two negatives make a positive. For example, *not uncommon* actually means *common*.

Watch for these words. As a general rule, you can immediately disqualify answer options that don't match up to the qualifier.

Tip 3: Read all the answer options.

Even when you're pretty sure of your answer, make sure you review all of the answer options before making your selection. Sometimes more than one answer may be correct; however, one choice will always be more correct than the others. Additionally, the answer you choose should completely address all parts of the question and reflect any qualifier worked into the question.

Tip 4: Elimination strategies are your friends.

You aren't penalized for guessing, but if you're going to guess, you should make every effort to find the correct answer. You can start by eliminating answer choices.

- Eliminate any answer you know is wrong.
- Eliminate options that seem unlikely or totally unfamiliar.
- Eliminate options that don't seem to fit grammatically with the stem/question.
- Give each answer option the "true–false" test and eliminate answer options that are false. Look for specific details that can make the statement false, such as a misstated fact or faulty reasoning.
- Watch for the inclusion of absolutes such as *all, only, always,* or *never.* These often signify incorrect responses (because an absolute can make an answer wrong, even if it might be right some portion of the time).
- Look for any paired statements that contradict each other (for example, option A might say, "The sky is green," while option B says, "The sky is blue"). One of the pair is frequently the correct answer.

The more answer choices you eliminate, the better your chances of finding the correct answer.

Finally, take a guess! If you're lost on a question or don't feel like you have enough time to analyze it as deeply as you'd like, just guess. Fill in an oval at random if you must. There's no penalty for guessing, and you might get lucky.

If you do guess, or if you're really torn about a question, flag that question in your exam booklet (or keep a running list on scrap paper of questions you want to revisit). Just remember to *answer the questions first*. Then if you have time, you can revisit those items after you've gone through the entire exam.

Tip 5: This is a repeat! Flag questionable answers.

Don't be afraid to mark up your exam booklet. While you need to keep your answer sheet clean and free from any stray markings, you can usually mark up the exam booklet as much as you want. Flag the questions you want to return to, or underline or otherwise mark any part of the question or answer option you think needs to be reviewed more carefully.

Tip 6: Be careful with the answer sheet!

Don't make mistakes when filling in your answers. Double-check to make sure your question and answer numbers correspond before you fill in the oval. Also, be sure you have penciled in the answer space completely and haven't left any stray pencil marks in other spaces.

Part II: Free-Response Strategies

For the free-response part of the exam, you'll be answering 4 to 6 questions in 60 minutes. That means you'll have about 12 minutes to read and respond to each free-response question. In addition, you'll have 30 minutes in which to respond to a lengthier investigative task. Don't let the free-response portion of the exam stress you out; this is your chance to show what you know. Read on for more helpful tips to help you maximize your score in the free-response section.

Tip 1: Read all the questions before you answer.

When you begin the free-response section, read all the questions before you start responding. Then, choose the questions that you're confident you can answer correctly and start with them. Continue solving the problems in an order that will allow you to receive your best score. In other words, save the questions that leave you scratching your head for last.

Tip 2: Show *all* your work.

As you respond to the problems, show all your work. You'll receive partial credit for partial solutions to problems. If you come up with the incorrect answer, you won't likely receive credit for correct thinking if the reviewer sees no evidence of your thought process on paper. Try to organize your answers as clearly and neatly as possible, showing the steps you took to reach your solution. If the reviewer has trouble following your reasoning, you are less likely to receive credit for it. If you make a mistake in your work, draw an "X" through it. Don't waste time trying to completely erase incorrect work.

Tip 3: Pay attention to units.

As you work through a problem, remember to record units for any calculations that require them. Keeping track of units as you work will help you ensure that your final answer is expressed correctly. If you don't record units for an answer that requires them—or if you record the wrong units—you may lose points, even if the rest of your work and your answer are correct.

Tip 4: Solve each part of a problem.

Many free-response questions have multiple parts, and each part requires a different response. Therefore, you should try to solve each part. Each part is scored separately, so it's possible to earn credit on two of the three or four parts of a problem, even if you solve one part incorrectly.

Tip 5: Avoid the "scattershot" approach.

As you work through the free-response section, avoid using what the College Board calls the "scattershot" approach. The scattershot approach is writing multiple equations in response to a problem and crossing your fingers that you identify the correct one somewhere in the mix and can earn partial credit. The reviewers who score your exam may actually deduct points for including unnecessary information in your response.

Big Ideas in Statistics

We're not going to lie to you: The AP Statistics Exam is no walk in the park. It's a tough test that requires a significant commitment from you. You're only going to get one real opportunity to ace AP Statistics, unlike some of the other examinations you'll take in your high school career. (Well, you *can* take the exam more than one time, but because it's only offered once a year, that's not really practical.) And even if you're quite familiar with other AP examinations, this exam can feel intimidating because the material is complex.

Here are quick summaries of the most important "big ideas" or concepts in AP Statistics. Your study should focus on four key areas:

- Exploring data—describing patterns and departures from patterns
- Sampling and experimentation—planning and conducting a study
- Anticipating patterns—exploring random phenomena using probability and simulation
- Statistical inference—estimating population parameters and testing hypotheses

Exploring Data

Exploration of data is part of descriptive statistics and inferential statistics. Data may be represented or summarized with graphs, tables, other diagrams, and equations. Such displays reveal patterns, correlations, normality, and differences in distribution.

Univariate data represent only one variable and may be shown through visual models including stem-and-leaf plots, bar graphs, histograms, and frequency plots. With such representations, the frequency of data values (or intervals of data values) may easily be determined. Modifications to these representations may be used to compare univariate data. For example, a back-to-back stemplot may be used to compare values in two different data sets.

Bivariate data represent two variables and may be represented using a scatterplot. A scatterplot shows the correlation between two variables; this correlation may or may not be linear. Correlations may be positive or negative, or they may not exist. The linear correlation of data is represented by the least-squares regression line (line of best fit) and the correlation coefficient, r.

Categorical, or nominal, data represent categories that may be quantitatively coded. The frequencies of each may be calculated and compared. Such comparisons may be made using two-way frequency tables. Two-way tables represent marginal, joint, and conditional frequencies.

Questions about exploring data may test your abilities in the following areas:

1. Graphing univariate data using dotplots, stem-and-leaf plots, bar graphs, histograms, boxplots, and frequency plots and interpreting the representations.
   a. Examining and describing the shape, modality, skewness, kurtosis, and normality of each representation.
   b. Interpreting the center and spread of the data in the graphical distribution, including any extreme outliers.

2. Summarizing univariate data representations by calculating measures of center, spread, and position.
    a. Calculating measures of center of data—that is, the mean, median, and mode.
    b. Calculating measures of spread of data—that is, the range, interquartile range, standard deviation, and variance.
    c. Calculating measures of position—that is, quartiles, percentiles, and z-scores.
3. Comparing univariate data using representations such as dotplots, back-to-back stemplots, parallel boxplots, and double bar graphs.
    a. Comparing shapes of distributions.
    b. Comparing centers of the data.
    c. Comparing deviations of scores from the mean and median.
    d. Comparing the skewness of each graphical representation and any clusters of data.
4. Exploring bivariate data to determine the correlation between variables.
    a. Examining the degree of linear correlation between two variables, and calculating the correlation coefficient r.
    b. Estimating and calculating a least-squares regression line. Using the line to make predictions between the variables.
    c. Creating a scatterplot that represents the correlation between two variables and explaining the correlation. Determining whether two variables represent no correlation, a positive correlation, or a negative correlation. Recognizing that a nonlinear correlation may exist.
    d. Creating and interpreting residual plots. Recognizing the influence of outliers on the correlation of data.
    e. Using various transformations, including logarithmic and power transformations, to achieve linearity when examining a correlation.

5. Exploring categorical or nominal data, including frequencies.
   a. Using frequency tables and bar graphs to explore and compare data.
   b. Identifying marginal and joint frequencies in a two-way table.
   c. Understanding the difference between frequencies and relative frequencies and identifying conditional relative frequencies in a two-way table.

Sampling and Experimentation

Experiments include various sampling techniques and types of experimentation. Data should be collected in a manner that promotes external validity. Measurement instruments should be designed in a manner that reveals internal validity and reliability. The method of analysis is contingent on several factors, including the type of data collected—that is, the type of variables (nominal, ordinal, interval, or ratio), the research questions to be answered, and the sample size involved.

Questions about sampling and experimentation may test your abilities in the following areas:

1. Understanding the types, purposes, and characteristics of various data collection methods.
   a. Defining and comparing experimental and nonexperimental research.
   b. Defining and comparing a census and a sample.
2. Creating surveys for dissemination.
   a. Considering whether the survey will involve parameters or statistics. Describing types of random sampling.
   b. Considering sources of sample bias and bias in surveys.
   c. Determining appropriate questions and overall design of effective, nonbiased surveys.
   d. Recognizing the facets that make a survey (or other instrument) valid and reliable.

3. Planning an effective experiment.
    a. Understanding the various types of randomized designs.
    b. Understanding and differentiating between the control group and treatment group(s). Choosing appropriate data collection methods and types of analyses.
    c. Considering bias in various aspects of an experiment, including unaccounted factors.
    d. Recognizing the components necessary for valid replications of a study.
    e. Generalizing the results of the sample to the population and recognizing any limitations in generalizability.

Anticipating Patterns

Patterns are inherent in probabilities and are represented in distributions of data. For example, experimental trials result in outcomes, and probability reveals patterns in those outcomes. As the number of trials increases, the experimental probability of an experiment mirrors the theoretical probability. In addition, patterns are part of probability distributions, including the binomial distribution and normal distribution. Sampling distributions represent another pattern—as the number of samples increases, the sampling distribution approaches the normal distribution. These patterns allow you to make predictions and estimations.

Questions about anticipating patterns may test your abilities in the following areas:

1. Computing and interpreting various probabilities.
    a. Understanding and comparing experimental and theoretical probability.
    b. Understanding how the Law of Large Numbers relates to theoretical probability.
    c. Understanding, calculating, and applying the expected value of an experiment.

    d.   Computing simple probabilities and connecting them to relative frequencies.

    e.   Recognizing independent, dependent, and mutually exclusive events, and using these definitions to appropriately find the probabilities of the union or intersection of probabilities.

    f.   Calculating conditional probabilities using given data, probabilities, or frequency tables.

    g.   Using the binomial distribution to calculate probabilities.

2.   Understanding alternative ways of representing sums and differences of independent random variables and stating conditions for independence of random variables.

    a.   Using the conditions for independence of random variables to explain when the variables x and y are independent.

    b.   Calculating the mean for sums and differences of independent random variables. Explaining how the expected value is related to the mean.

    c.   Calculating variability associated with the sums and differences of independent random variables.

3.   Understanding the concept of the normal distribution and sampling distributions of means and proportions.

    a.   Understanding the underlying concept of the normal distribution. Relating and comparing the measures of central tendency for a normal distribution to that of a nonnormal distribution.

    b.   Recognizing a normal distribution in graphical form. Connecting the representation of the distribution to the overarching idea stated in the Central Limit Theorem.

    c.   Using a table of normal distribution to determine the area under the normal-distribution bell curve that is a certain number of standard deviations above or below a given mean.

    d.   Understanding the concept of sampling distributions of a mean and proportion.

Statistical Inference

Test statistics and confidence intervals may be used to determine significance of models and goodness of fit. A null hypothesis may state that no difference exists between a sample mean and a population mean or that no difference exists between two sample means. With categorical variables, a null hypothesis may state that no difference exists between the frequencies of two or more categories of data. Distributions—including the z-distribution, t-distribution, and chi-square distribution—may be used to test for significant difference. With large sample sizes, however, confidence intervals are often used to support significant findings. Confidence intervals of a mean (or a proportion) or a difference between means (or proportions) represent the upper and lower limits of a population mean.

Questions about statistical inference may test your abilities in the following areas:

1. Understanding the foundational ideas of test statistics and hypothesis testing, computing various standardized scores, interpreting probabilities, and connecting these to the number of standard deviations above or below the mean.

   a. Understanding the basic concepts of hypothesis testing, including p-values, level of significance, degrees of freedom, null and alternative hypotheses, directional and nondirectional hypotheses, margin of error, and Type I and II errors.

   b. Understanding the concept of a t-distribution, calculating a t-value, and using a t-distribution table to determine the p-value and significance.

   c. Understanding the concept of a z-distribution and calculating a z-value. Using a z-distribution table to determine the p-value and significance.

2. Understanding the idea of and need for confidence intervals and computing confidence intervals for various situations.

    a.   Using a confidence interval to determine whether a sample mean (or proportion) is significantly different from a population mean (or proportion).

    b.   Using a confidence interval to determine whether two sample means (or proportions) are significantly different.

    c.   Understanding the concepts of point estimate, interval estimate, parameters, and margin of error.

3.   Conducting regressions and chi-square tests and understanding the concept of power.

    a.   Calculating the correlation coefficient r, as well as rho. Determining significance when conducting a regression.

    b.   Understanding the foundational concepts of a chi-square distribution and test, including assumptions and types of variables allowed. Determining significance using chi-square tables.

    c.   Understanding the concept of power and ways to calculate the sample size needed to produce a predetermined power.

THE MAIN COURSE: COMPREHENSIVE STRATEGIES AND REVIEW

Take a deep breath and try to relax. You still have a few weeks before the exam, so you have plenty of time to study before the big day. Then follow this plan to prepare yourself:

- Start by reading the comprehensive strategies for attacking both multiple-choice problems and free-response problems on pages 25 to 42.

- Then take the **Diagnostic Exam** that begins on page 45. The Diagnostic Exam will help you get used to the types of questions on the AP Statistics Exam. As you go through the answers, you can pinpoint areas where you may need to focus your studies.

- Review all the key statistics topics by working through the **Review** portion of this book, which begins on page 91. Pay special attention to topics covered earlier in the school year, as well as any areas of weakness you identified in the Diagnostic Exam.

- Take at least one more practice exam (there are two in this book) before test day. You can also find a third practice exam on our website at mymaxscore.com.

- The night before the exam, review **The Essentials: A Last-Minute Study Guide** on pages 1 to 20, including the **Quick Exam-Taking Tips** (page 7) and the **Big Ideas in Statistics** (page 13).

- Pack your materials for the next day, get a good night's sleep, and you'll be ready to maximize your score.

How the Exam Is Scored

Fifty percent of your exam score is based on the multiple-choice section. The other 50 percent is based on the free-response section. Multiple-choice questions are computer-scored. You earn 1 point for each correct response. You earn no points for a skipped question. In the past, a quarter of a point was deducted for each incorrect response, but this has changed, and students no longer lose any points for incorrect responses.

Free-response questions are scored by college faculty and expert AP teachers. These folks use scoring standards developed by college and university faculty who teach introductory statistics courses. The questions are scored holistically, which means the entire response is analyzed as a whole. Scorers make judgments about the overall quality of the response and assign a score of 0 through 4. These scores are based on a rubric, which provides guidance about assessing both statistical knowledge and communication of ideas. When evaluating statistical knowledge, scorers analyze the concepts and techniques you used to reach the correct solution to a problem. When evaluating the communication of ideas, scorers consider your explanation of what you did and why, and any conclusions you drew. The rubric used by the scorers breaks down as follows:

SCORE	STATISTICAL KNOWLEDGE	COMMUNICATION
4	Complete understanding of the problem's statistical components	Clear, organized, and complete explanation
3	Substantial understanding of the problem's statistical components	Clear explanation that may lack in organization or completeness
2	Developing understanding of the problem's statistical components	Some explanation of what was done and why but explanation may be vague or difficult to interpret
1	Minimal understanding of the problem's statistical components	Minimal or unclear explanation of what was done and why
0	No understanding of the problem's statistical components	No explanation

Students' scores on the free-response questions are added to their scores on the multiple-choice section, which results in a composite score. This score is then matched to a score on AP's five-point scoring scale, which is as follows:

AP SCORE	QUALIFICATION
5	Extremely well qualified
4	Well qualified
3	Qualified
2	Possibly qualified
1	No recommendation

Colleges and universities across the country grant college credit, placement, or both for top scores on AP exams. However, each college and university has its own credit and placement policies, which determine the score a student must receive to qualify for credit and/or placement.

Comprehensive Strategies for Multiple-Choice Questions

Four different types of multiple-choice questions appear on the AP Statistics Exam: straightforward questions, word problems, graph/chart-based questions, and multiple-choice within multiple-choice questions. The next few sections provide in-depth information on each of these question types. Before diving into these strategies, however, take a few minutes to review some of the basic question-answering strategies and techniques mentioned on pages 7 to 12.

As highlighted in the **Quick Exam-Taking Tips** on page 7, there are some important general strategies that you should keep in mind when answering questions on the AP Statistics Exam. Utilizing these basic strategies on exam day will help you answer questions as efficiently and accurately as possible. These strategies include the following:

1. **Answer the question before looking at the choices.** Whenever you begin a new question, read the stem carefully and take a moment to try to answer it in your head before you look at the answer choices. In many cases, the answer choices are specifically designed to distract you from finding the correct answer and can easily confuse or mislead you. If you answer the question in your head before you look at the choices, you'll start out with an idea of what the correct answer might be, and you'll be less likely to get confused by incorrect choices.

2. **Read all answer choices.** If you have read and answered the question in your head, you might be tempted to zero in on the answer choice that most closely resembles your own answer. Though that answer may be correct, you should always read through all the answer choices before you make your selection. Reading through the answer choices is critical because the obvious answer isn't always the correct answer. Some questions may require you to choose between several correct answers. In such cases, you have to select the *most* correct choice or the choice that does the best job of answering the question completely. No matter the question, reading through all the answer choices will help lead you to the best possible choice.

3. **Watch out for key words.** The wording of questions on the AP Statistics Exam is often precise, so you will need to read carefully to ensure that you understand exactly what each question is asking. Some questions may also use words such as *NOT* or *EXCEPT*, which totally change the meaning of a question and can lead you to choose the wrong answer choice.

   Some questions may also use modifiers, which are words or phrases that limit or modify the meaning of another word or phrase. On an exam, a modifier may attract your attention to an answer choice that may be correct under certain circumstances but not others.

   Finally, watch out for double negatives. Double negatives occur when two negative words are used together to create a phrase with a positive meaning. For example, the double negative phrase *not unlike* actually means *like* or *similar to*.

4. **Make use of elimination strategies.** Although you are not penalized for guessing on the AP Statistics Exam, it's still a good idea to do whatever it takes to find the correct answer. The best way to accomplish this is to eliminate as many incorrect answer choices as possible.

   The first answer choices you can eliminate are those you know are wrong. In most instances, you can also eliminate choices that seem unlikely to be correct or are totally unfamiliar.

Another way to eliminate incorrect answer choices is by using the "true–false" test. Read through the answer choices and look for any details that might suggest which ones are wrong. When you use the "true–false" test, keep an eye out for misstated facts or faulty reasoning.

Often, questions and answer choices that use absolutes, such as *all*, *always*, *only*, or *never*, give clues as to which answer choices you can eliminate, since applying an absolute to a correct statement can make the statement incorrect in some cases. For example, "You can hear birds sing only in the spring or summer" is wrong because, although birds do sing in the spring and summer, it is also possible to hear them sing at other times of the year.

Look for contradictory paired statements when reading through the answer choices, as these can also help you identify choices to eliminate. If you encounter a set of answer choices where Choice A is "The sweater is red" and Choice B is "The sweater is white," you can likely assume that one of these choices is correct and the other can be eliminated.

Specific Multiple-Choice Question Types

The multiple-choice section of the AP Statistics Exam contains a variety of multiple-choice question types. While many of the questions on the exam are typical multiple-choice questions, others use a different approach and require you to use different techniques and strategies to arrive at the correct answer. This section will provide you with a brief overview of the different types of questions you will encounter on the AP Statistics Exam, as well as helpful tips on how to approach them.

Straightforward Questions

The straightforward question is a standard, multiple-choice question of the type found on many different exams. These questions usually appear in the form of a simple question or a basic statistics problem that you must solve. In other cases, a straightforward question may provide you with an incomplete sentence that you must complete using one of the answer choices (although this type of question is rare on the AP Statistics Exam).

When answering straightforward questions, keep two important strategies in mind:

1. **Be certain you understand the question.** Before you try to select the correct answer, it's important to make sure that you fully understand what the question is asking. Since many of the questions on the AP Statistics Exam use complex wording and technical terminology, you may need to read each question more than once to fully grasp its meaning. Once you are confident that you understand the question, read through the answer choices. Knowing exactly what you need to look for before you move on to the answer choices will give you a better idea of what the correct answer should be and which choices can be eliminated.

2. **Read all the answer choices.** You may sometimes find that more than one answer choice sounds correct. If this happens, remember to select the one that *best* answers the question. Choosing an answer that looks right at first glance without reading the others can easily lead to wrong answers, even when you know the correct answer.

Word Problems

Many of the multiple-choice questions on the AP Statistics Exam are word problems. These questions present brief scenarios (usually about a paragraph long) and ask you to solve a problem based on the information contained within the scenario. Some of these questions may include charts or graphs that provide additional information.

When answering word problems, keep these two important strategies in mind:

1. **Read the scenario carefully.** The word problems you encounter on the AP Statistics Exam are not simple questions. The scenarios are often complex and contain a considerable amount of information that you will have to read, interpret, and use to arrive at the correct answer. It is usually a good idea to read through each scenario more than once to make sure that you understand exactly what you have to do before you try to solve the problem.

2. **Write down important details.** You might find it helpful to write down important details or numbers in the exam booklet, which includes areas to use as scratch paper. Since these questions are often longer and more complicated than others, it may be easier to quickly jot down the key information you need to answer the question so that you can refer to it directly instead of searching through the scenario repeatedly.

Chart or Graph Questions

The AP Statistics Exam includes questions based on various types of charts and graphs. In most cases, you have to use these visual prompts to answer questions or solve problems. Some of these questions may be based on common types of charts and graphs, such as pie charts, line graphs, and bar graphs. Others may utilize simple tables. You'll also likely encounter boxplots, stem-and-leaf plots, and scatterplots.

While most chart or graph questions require the use of a single visual aid to find the correct answer, some questions may ask you to decide which type of chart, graph, table, or plot would be most appropriate for representing a given set of data.

When answering chart or graph questions, keep these two strategies in mind:

1. **Study the chart or graph first.** When faced with a chart or graph problem, always take time to examine the chart or graph before you start to read the question. Taking a moment to familiarize yourself with the chart or graph will help you better understand the question and what it is asking you to do. Since you can refer back to the chart at any time, you won't have to worry about remembering specific details, just the big picture. If you skip over the chart and head right to the question, you may find it more difficult to understand—which means you'll have to spend more time rereading before you can arrive at an answer.

2. **Look out for labels.** Charts and graphs on the AP Statistics Exam contain various labels that are critically important for understanding the data and for answering the question. When you answer a chart or graph question, make sure that you pay close attention to these labels and take them into consideration as you work toward a solution.

Multiple-Choice within Multiple-Choice Questions

Multiple-choice within multiple-choice questions are among the most unusual questions you'll encounter on the AP Statistics Exam. Although these questions generally aren't any more difficult than other types of questions, they are often more confusing.

Multiple-choice within multiple-choice questions contain some type of scenario or question followed by two separate lists. The first list, which immediately follows the question or scenario itself, consists of several choices identified by Roman numerals. One, several, or all of these choices may correctly answer the question. The list may look something like this:

I.   The randomly selected bottle has a significantly lower amount of juice than the average bottle.

II. The number of ounces of juice in the selected bottle is two standard deviations below the mean.

III. The number of ounces of juice in the selected bottle is three standard deviations below the mean.

IV. The randomly selected bottle does not have a significantly lower amount of juice than the average bottle.

The second list includes the answer choices that correspond to your answer sheet. Each of these choices contains a different combination of Roman numerals, which represent the choices in the first list. The answer choices for these questions may look something like this:

    A.   I and II
    B.   I and III
    C.   II and IV
    D.   III and IV
    E.   IV only

Your task is to select the choice that contains the correct answer. When answering multiple-choice within multiple-choice questions, keep this two-step strategy in mind:

1. **Mark the Roman numerals of all the choices that answer the question correctly.** When you encounter a multiple-choice within multiple-choice question, you can save time by circling the Roman numerals for all the choices that answer the question correctly. This will help you avoid going back and rereading these choices numerous times as you work your way through the answer choices.

2. **Look for the answer choice that matches the Roman numerals you circled.** Once you know exactly which Roman numerals answer the question correctly, look for the answer choice that contains those numerals and ignore the others.

Comprehensive Strategies for Free-Response Questions

The multiple-choice section of the AP Statistics Exam is followed by four to six free-response questions and an investigative task. Each question in the free-response section requires you to solve a problem and show all the work you did to arrive at your answer. The important thing to remember about these questions is that you will be graded not only on whether you answered correctly but also on the quality of your work.

Basic Free-Response Question Tips

In this section, you'll find a brief review of the basic free-response question tips mentioned on page 10, as well as some other important free-response strategies. To begin, let's review the tips you read earlier:

1. **Read ALL the questions first.** Before you begin answering questions in the free-response section, take a moment to read through all the questions. Once you have read them all, begin with the questions you feel most comfortable with and have the best chance of answering correctly. From there, continue answering the other questions in whatever order is most likely to earn you the best possible score, leaving the most difficult questions for last.

2. **Remember to show ALL your work.** This is *extremely* important. Remember that on the AP Statistics Exam, you are graded on the quality of your work, as well as on the validity of your answers. Even if you answer incorrectly, you can earn points for demonstrating your ability to reason and solve problems through your work. If you don't show your work, you'll lose out on the points you could receive for properly documenting your thought process.

   Also, when working through problems, remember that cleanliness counts. Messy work is more difficult for reviewers to interpret and, as a result, could lead to a lower score. Try to keep your work as clean as possible. If you make a mistake, cross it out with an "X" instead of using excessive scribbling to void the error. Don't worry about erasing things, either. Erasing mistakes only makes your paper messier and consumes time that could be used more wisely.

3. **Mind your units.** Many of the questions in the free-response section require you to solve problems that involve various units of measurement. When you are working on such problems, remember to use the appropriate units throughout your work and in your final answer. If you neglect to include units when you need to use them, or if you use the incorrect units, you can lose points, even if your answer is correct or your work is otherwise good.

4. **Solve each step of the problem.** In most cases, the problems in the free-response section will have multiple steps, each of which requires a different answer or solution. In addition, the answer you find for each step in the process may be an important component of the next step, so you'll need to solve each problem in the proper order. That said, however, even if you solve one step of a problem incorrectly, you can still get credit for the other steps, so it's very important that you answer each step of a problem carefully.

5. **Don't use the "scattershot" approach.** When you are working on free-response questions, it's best to avoid a strategy known as the

"scattershot" approach. This approach involves writing multiple equations in response to a problem and hoping that one of them is correct and worthy of credit. Though you may be able to find the correct answer this way, many reviewers will deduct points if you include too much unnecessary information in your work.

Free-Response Question-Answering Strategies

In addition to the basic tips above, you should also keep the following strategies and suggestions in mind when answering free-response questions on the AP Statistics Exam.

1. **Define symbols correctly.** Many of the most common mistakes on the AP Statistics Exam are a result of students' failure to correctly define symbols in their work. It's important to remember not only to be careful to use the correct symbols in your work but also to be sure that you define exactly what those symbols mean. For instance, when solving a problem, you may be tempted to write something like "$\mu = 56$" as an answer. Although this answer may be correct, you might make a mistake somewhere in your work because you have not defined what μ means. To correct this issue, clarify what μ represents by stating, "$\mu = 56$, where μ is the mean age of the residents of Fulton Street." Clearly defining the symbols you use in your work will help you remember what each one means and prevent you from making any mistakes that might result from getting them mixed up.

   You should also be sure that you are using the correct symbols when you are solving problems with a calculator. Many calculators use symbols and formats that are different from those commonly used in statistics, so it's very important to make sure that the symbols and format you are using in your work are appropriate for the exam. Do not copy what you see on your calculator screen.

2.   **Write clearly and precisely.** When faced with free-response questions, many students feel unsure about how long or short their answer should be and end up writing either much more than is necessary or far too little. Remember that quality is more important than quantity. All you need to do is answer the question clearly and precisely. Make sure that your response answers the question completely, but don't go overboard. Writing more than you need just to fill up the space you are given can result in a response that contains a lot of irrelevant or incorrect information that could cost you points.

In addition, don't begin writing until you have thoroughly collected your thoughts and know what you want to write. Although it may seem like a good idea to begin writing as quickly as possible to save time, this strategy can lead to the inclusion of irrelevant or incorrect information that could hurt your score. Always think through the question and develop a clear response in your mind before you start to write.

Finally, when you are interpreting the results of a statistical procedure, remember to write as clearly as possible and to avoid using general statements that do not speak to the context of the question. In other words, you shouldn't write something such as "The null hypothesis is rejected." Instead, explain exactly why the hypothesis was rejected in the context of the question.

3.   **Don't round your answers.** Though you may need to round your answers in some cases, it is usually best to avoid rounding too much, especially in the middle of a calculation. If you round your answers at each step of a calculation, you run the risk of ultimately arriving at the wrong final answer. The only answer you should normally round is the final answer itself, if necessary. If you do need to round your answer, round to two decimal places, except in probability questions, which will usually require you to round to four decimal places.

Strategies for Specific Types of Free-Response Questions

The AP Statistics Exam includes several different types of free-response questions. The following are some strategies for answering each of the various types.

Graphical Data Questions

Some questions on the AP Statistics Exam require you to create graphical representations of various data. When you encounter such a question, you need to know how to create graphs, plots, and other visual representations of data correctly.

One of the most common mistakes students make when creating graphs or plots is failing to properly label and scale the axes. The axes are a pivotal part of any graph or plot, and any mistakes in labeling them can cause a misrepresentation of data that can, in turn, lead to mistakes in other work based on that data.

Whenever you create any sort of graph or plot, make sure that all your data is labeled correctly and displayed in the appropriate format.

Planning Studies Questions

Planning studies questions are often especially difficult to answer because they usually involve nonformulaic answers and require you to use specific statistics vocabulary. When answering planning studies questions, the best strategy is to familiarize yourself with the concept being tested and write a precise answer that uses the vocabulary associated with that concept in the context of the question. Also, be particularly careful to avoid using the "scattershot" approach with these questions, as planning studies questions are the ones for which many students are most likely to employ this tactic.

Probability Questions

Probability questions on the AP Statistics Exam are the most like typical math problems. These questions usually require you to show only that you know how to solve a particular problem correctly. When answering these questions, there are several things to keep in mind.

First, always begin by stating what formula you are going to use to solve the problem. Once you have stated the formula, you can plug in the values from the problem and begin to solve it.

Since many of these questions require you to solve a problem over a series of steps, be sure to show all of your work for each step. This is particularly important because your score for these problems will be based not only on your final answer, but also on the thread of reasons that runs throughout your work. In other words, a mistake in one step does not automatically disqualify the entire answer from consideration, even if the final answer is ultimately incorrect. You can still receive points if your work shows that you followed a constant line of reasoning all the way through, regardless of the mistake.

Also, your response should always reflect the context of the question. When you solve a probability question, remember to include the context of the question in your response, along with the mathematical equations you used to arrive at your answer.

Finally, before you move on to the next question, make sure that your answer is actually logical. Sometimes, you may arrive at an answer and just assume that it's correct so that you can get to the next question. If you take a moment to review your solution, you may find that your solution isn't a logical response to the question. Just in case, it's always a good idea to quickly review the reasonability of your answer before you move on.

Inference Questions

Most inference questions require you to use hypothesis testing to find a solution. When you are tackling these types of questions, there are a number of important things you should remember to include in your response.

First, include a clear statement of a set of hypotheses. You also need to carefully define any notation you'll be using.

Next, identify the test procedure and statistic. Be careful to use standard statistical notation and not the calculator form, as mentioned earlier.

Additionally, identify and check the validity of your assumptions. Assumptions are an important part of any statistical model. The assumptions associated with a particular statistical model provide its underlying structure and justify the procedures used within the model. If your assumptions are incorrect, your work may yield incorrect answers. Unfortunately, you won't always be able to directly assess the accuracy of your assumptions, so you'll need some other way to determine their validity. Often, the best way to test an assumption is to plug in a related condition based on your sample data. If you arrive at a plausible result, you can probably assume that your assumption is valid.

Finally, as with other questions, show all your work, including all the steps you took to find your answer, and state your results in the context of the question.

The Investigative Task

The final free-response question on the AP Statistics Exam is an investigative task. This question is quite different from the others on the exam and requires some extra attention. The primary difference between the investigative task and the other questions is that the investigative task will probably be comparatively unfamiliar to you. In fact, the investigative task is specifically designed to be unfamiliar to exam-takers.

The purpose of the investigative task is to make you use the concepts you have learned to answer a type of question you have never seen before. In many cases, the task will be related to a concept that you haven't encountered before but that you should be able to interpret and solve using skills you have learned from other areas of statistics.

Since the investigative task is meant to be unfamiliar, there is, unfortunately, little you can do to prepare for it. Your best option is to review investigative tasks from old exams to get a feel for how they work and what you might be expected to do. Remember, however, that what was included in previous investigative tasks may not accurately reflect exactly what you'll encounter with the investigative tasks that appear on present or future AP Statistics Exams.

When you take the AP Statistics Exam, there are two main things you should keep in mind concerning the investigative task:

1. **Complete the investigative task first.** It may not be a good idea to put off the investigative task until last, even though it is the last question on the exam. By the time you reach the end of the exam, you'll be tired. Since the investigative task requires you to think creatively and use your imagination, you may want to tackle it while you are still fresh and thinking clearly.

2. **Don't panic.** Although you'll almost certainly find yourself in unfamiliar territory with the investigative task, it can be solved. Don't be intimidated. All you need to do is use what you know about statistics and think calmly and creatively. Worrying too much will only make your job harder to do.

The Diagnosis:
How Ready Are You?

Diagnostic Exam

This part of your book includes a full-length diagnostic exam. This exam has been designed to help you practice for the AP Statistics Exam and identify areas of weakness, ultimately helping you to improve your score. After taking the diagnostic exam, you might realize you are spending too much time with each question or that you are not reading the questions closely enough. You might discover that you consistently struggle with certain types of questions or with questions that address specific topics or ideas. All of these issues are resolvable. However, to identify them, it is essential that you complete the diagnostic exam in an environment that closely mimics the actual testing environment.

Therefore, you should follow these guidelines:

- Block out a full three-hour time period to take the diagnostic exam. Stay within this allotted time frame. Stop testing at the end of three hours.

- Select an environment that is quiet, with a minimal amount of distraction, such as a quiet room in your home, at your school, or in the local library.

- Turn off your cell phone and your computer. Ask family and friends to avoid disturbing you during the testing period.

- While taking the exam, have *only* the examination and answer key open. Don't use other resource materials! Even though you may be tempted, looking up the answers will hinder your progress. You're only cheating yourself.

- As you take the exam, have a highlighter available. Use it to quickly mark any term or concept that seems unfamiliar to you. Later, you can use this information in your studies.

- Finally, follow the instructions provided.

Once you have completed the examination, assess your score by checking your answers against the key at the end of this section. More information about assessing your performance is provided in that section.

Good luck!

Diagnostic Exam

Statistics

SECTION I

Time—90 minutes

40 questions

Directions: Solve each of the following problems. After examining the answer choices, select the best solution to the problem. No credit will be given for anything written in the exam book. Do not spend too much time on any one problem.

1. Aaron records the number of laps he swims each week during a 20-week period as follows:

$$61, 73, 57, 94, 85, 53, 92, 60, 93, 49,$$
$$75, 63, 67, 73, 100, 46, 76, 43, 60, 80$$

Which of the following graphs represents a cumulative frequency plot for the number of laps he swam?

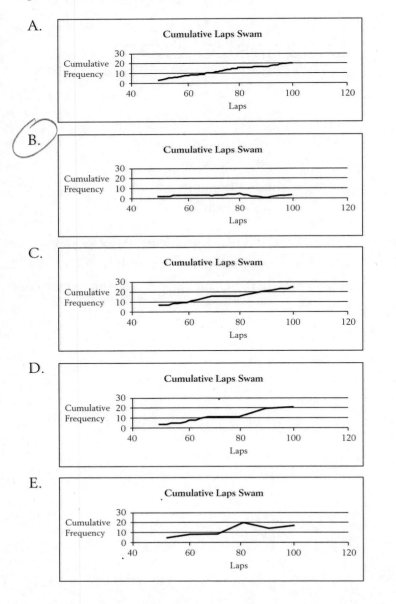

A.

B.

C.

D.

E.

2. Abby uses a random number generator to generate the data that follows:

25, 52, 31, 34, 41, 45, 33, 35, 31, 43, 57, 56, 29, 55, 56, 23, 58, 46, 60, 44, 39, 25, 55, 33, 55, 31, 44, 38, 38, 26

Which of the following boxplots correctly represents the data?

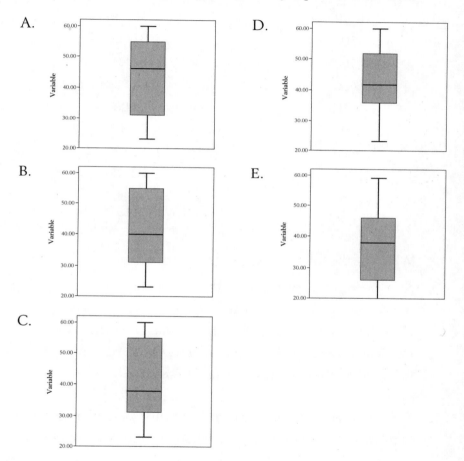

A.

D.

B.

E.

C.

3. Kevin records his monthly consulting income for a period of two years. The data is shown in the following table.

MONTH	CONSULTING INCOME	MONTH	CONSULTING INCOME
1	$1,750	13	$3,800
2	$2,200	14	$2,800
3	$3,100	15	$3,150
4	$4,500	16	$1,700
5	$3,250	17	$2,200
6	$2,000	18	$4,800
7	$1,900	19	$4,950
8	$5,500	20	$1,375
9	$3,800	21	$2,500
10	$2,750	22	$3,600
11	$3,950	23	$3,800
12	$4,025	24	$4,000

Which of the following statements is true?

A. The mode is greater than the median only.

B. The mode is greater than the mean and median.

C. The mean is greater than the median and mode.

D. The mean is greater than the mode only.

E. The mode is greater than the mean only.

4. Suppose a data set has a mean of 120 and a standard deviation of 15. How many standard deviations below the mean is a score of 85?

A. $1\frac{2}{3}$

B. 2

C. $2\frac{1}{3}$

D. $2\frac{1}{2}$

E. $2\frac{2}{3}$

5. Dr. Allen records his students' final averages as follows:

85, 69, 72, 80, 76, 56, 76, 96, 87,

56, 91, 72, 65, 76, 85, 79, 88, 62

Which of the following best represents the standard deviation of the scores?

A. 10.2
B. 10.8
C. 11.6
D. 12.2
E. 12.6

6. What is the interquartile range of the data represented by the following stem-and-leaf plot?

Stems	Leaves
2	0, 5, 5, 6
3	0, 2, 5, 5, 7, 8
4	2, 5, 7
5	0, 4, 5, 5, 8, 9
6	1, 2, 6
7	2, 2, 2, 3, 6, 7, 8, 9

A. 29
B. 31
C. 33
D. 35
E. 37

7. The following boxplots summarize data.

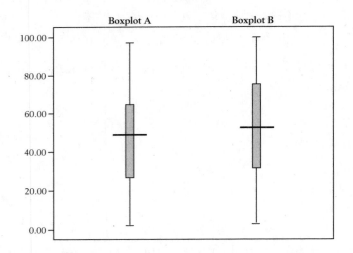

Which of the following statements about the boxplots is true?

A. Boxplot A shows more variability about the center and a greater
    cluster of values below the median.
B. Boxplot B shows more variability about the center and a greater
    cluster of values below the median.
C. Boxplot A shows more variability about the center and a greater
    cluster of values above the median.
D. Boxplot B shows more variability about the center and a greater
    cluster of values above the median.
E. Boxplots A and B show the same variability.

8. What is the best estimate of the correlation coefficient of the line of best fit in the scatterplot that follows?

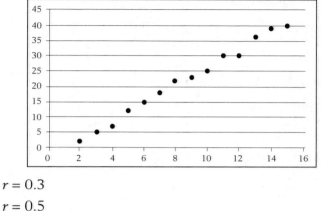

A. $r = 0.3$
B. $r = 0.5$
C. $r = 0.7$
D. $r = 0.9$
E. $r = 1.0$

9. What is the best representation of the equation of the least-squares regression line for the following scatterplot?

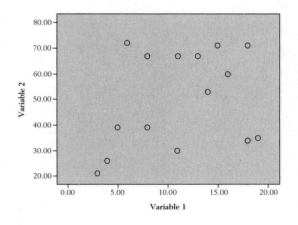

A. $y = 0.09x + 7$
B. $y = 4.9x + 25$
C. $y = 2.9x + 30$
D. $y = 5.09x + 10$
E. $y = 3.2x + 44$

10. The correlation coefficients for five different data sets are shown below. Which of the correlation coefficients represents the strongest linear relationship?

 A. $r = -0.8$
 B. $r = -0.4$
 C. $r = 0.3$
 D. $r = 0.5$
 E. $r = 0.7$

11. The following table provides values for x and y.

x	y
2	91
8	56
2	68
17	75
9	38
18	93
18	22
7	25
8	30
13	59
1	83
14	17
16	64
5	25
15	48

Which of the following best represents the correlation coefficient r?

A.   0.02
B.   0.08
C.   0.12
D.   0.16
E.   0.20

12. Which of the following choices represents a residual plot of the x- and y-values shown in the following table?

x	y
2	54
6	64
6	51
8	62
1	61
2	74
4	75
10	75
8	64
7	72
9	52
9	70
9	59
10	51
10	53

A.

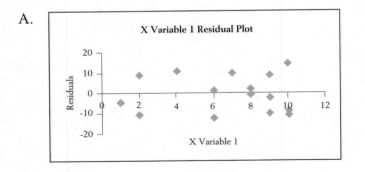

B.

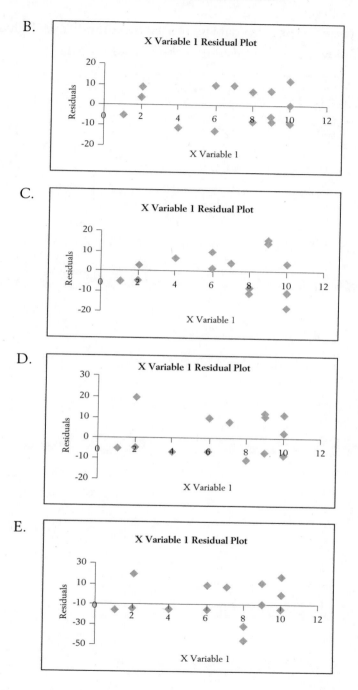

C.

D.

E.

13. Dr. Wilson transforms some data by using a logarithmic transformation. The following is a scatterplot of the transformed data.

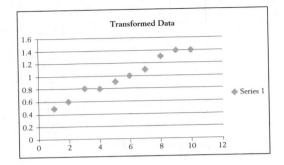

Which of the following tables represents the original data?

A.

x	y
1	3
2	4
3	6
4	6
5	8
6	11
7	14
8	20
9	24
10	28

D.

x	y
1	6
2	9
3	10
4	12
5	14
6	16
7	19
8	21
9	23
10	25

B.

x	y
1	5
2	7
3	12
4	15
5	19
6	25
7	28
8	30
9	33
10	35

E.

x	y
1	4
2	5
3	9
4	6
5	10
6	13
7	16
8	22
9	28
10	30

C.

x	y
1	2
2	4
3	8
4	8
5	12
6	14
7	16
8	18
9	20
10	24

14. Which of the following represents a study in which every member of a population must be included?

    A.   Census
    B.   Experiment
    C.   Observation
    D.   Survey
    E.   Quasi-experiment

15. Angela chooses members of her sample by choosing every fifteenth person on a list. What method of random sampling is she using?

    A.   Simple random sampling
    B.   Stratified random sampling
    C.   Cluster sampling
    D.   Systematic random sampling
    E.   Snowball sampling

16. Robert uses two classrooms as the two groups in his study. Students may not be moved between the groups. Which of the following best describes the type of sampling bias pertinent to his study?

    A.   Undercoverage bias
    B.   Convenience sample bias
    C.   Voluntary response bias
    D.   Response bias
    E.   Census bias

17. Margaret wishes to limit the effects of confounding variables on the outcome of her study. Which of the following approaches does not limit the role of confounding variables?

    A.   Blinding or double-blinding
    B.   Randomization of subjects
    C.   Usage of a census
    D.   Usage of matched pairs
    E.   Usage of a control group

18. Which of the following statements is true?

I.   An instrument may be valid but not reliable.
II.   If an instrument is valid, then it is reliable.
III.   An instrument may be reliable but not valid.
IV.   If an instrument is reliable, then it is valid.

    A.   I and II
    B.   I, II, and III
    C.   II and III
    D.   II and IV
    E.   IV only

19. Eric spins a spinner with six equally spaced sections labeled 1 to 6. If he spins the spinner 120 times, how many times can he expect to get an even number?

    A.   20
    B.   40
    C.   60
    D.   80
    E.   100

20. A bag contains four red marbles, eight blue marbles, and six yellow marbles. What is the probability that Noel draws a red marble, replaces it, and then draws a yellow marble?

    A. $\frac{5}{9}$

    B. $\frac{4}{51}$

    C. $\frac{88}{153}$

    D. $\frac{2}{27}$

    E. $\frac{7}{9}$

21. A hat contains five blue cards, nine orange cards, and four red cards. What is the probability that Fred draws an orange card, does not replace it, and then draws another orange card?

    A. $\frac{4}{17}$

    B. $\frac{1}{4}$

    C. $\frac{9}{34}$

    D. $\frac{2}{7}$

    E. $\frac{4}{9}$

22. Tiana spins a spinner with eight equally spaced sections labeled 1 to 8 and flips a coin. What is the probability that she spins a number greater than 5 or gets tails?

    A. $\frac{1}{4}$

    B. $\frac{3}{16}$

    C. $\frac{1}{2}$

    D. $\frac{7}{8}$

    E. $\frac{3}{4}$

23. The following table provides data about the genders and political parties of the citizens in a town.

	REPUBLICAN	DEMOCRAT	INDEPENDENT	TOTAL
Male	180	160	80	420
Female	140	160	100	400
Total	320	320	180	820

What is the probability that a citizen is a male or a Democrat?

   A. $\dfrac{37}{41}$

   B. $\dfrac{7}{29}$

   C. $\dfrac{29}{41}$

   D. $\dfrac{3}{37}$

   E. $\dfrac{3}{29}$

24. A bag contains nine blue marbles, three red marbles, and six yellow marbles. Suppose Erica draws three marbles from the bag. Which of the following best represents the expected value for the number of yellow marbles she draws from the bag?

   A.   0.76

   B.   0.82

   C.   0.90

   D.   0.94

   E.   0.99

25. Jared rolls a die 25 times. Which of the following best represents the probability of getting five sixes?

   A.   0.002

   B.   0.112

   C.   0.142

   D.   0.182

   E.   0.224

26. A consultant writes grant proposals. Approximately 8% of her proposals contain errors. In a random sample of 25 of her proposals,
what is the probability that at least three will contain errors?

A.   0.23
B.   0.28
C.   0.32
D.   0.37
E.   0.41

27. Given two random variables, A and B, which of the following equations verifies the independence of A and B?

A. $P(A \cap B) = P(A) \cdot P(B)$
B. $P(A \cap B) = P(A) + P(B)$
C. $P(A \cap B) = P(A) + P(B) - P(A \text{ and } B)$
D. $P(A \cap B) = P(A) \cdot P(B) - P(A \text{ and } B)$
E. $P(A \cap B) = P(A) \cdot P(B) - P(A \text{ or } B)$

28. The class mean on a mathematics test is 80, with a standard deviation of 15. Assuming the scores are normally distributed, which
of the following represents the range of scores that represent the
middle 95% of the scores?

A.   25–70
B.   35–125
C.   40–115
D.   50–110
E.   60–120

29. Given a normal distribution, which of the following best represents the area under the curve that is more than two standard deviations above the mean?

    A. 2%
    B. 3%
    C. 6%
    D. 7%
    E. 9%

30. Suppose a population has a mean of 90. Which of the following statements is true?

    A. The mean of the sampling distribution will be approximately 90.
    B. The mean of the sampling distribution will be 10.
    C. The mean of the sampling distribution will be 0.
    D. The mean of the sampling distribution will be approximately 45.
    E. The mean of the sampling distribution will be approximately 60.

31. A population has a mean of 185 and a standard deviation of 15. What is the z-score for an individual score of 170?

    A. −1
    B. −1.5
    C. −2
    D. −2.5
    E. −3

32. Jennifer scores a 90 on her statistics test. The class average is 82, with a standard deviation of 5. Using a level of significance of 0.05, which of the following statements is true?

A. Jennifer's score is significantly higher than the class average, as evidenced by a p-value of 0.0548.

B. Jennifer's score is not significantly higher than the class average, as evidenced by a p-value of 0.0548.

C. Jennifer's score is significantly higher than the class average, as evidenced by a p-value of 0.0495.

D. Jennifer's score is not significantly higher than the class average, as evidenced by a p-value of 0.0495.

E. Jennifer's score is significantly higher than the class average, as evidenced by a p-value of 0.0385.

33. A company sells cartons of milk, claiming 8 ounces in each carton with a standard deviation of 0.1 ounce. If a randomly selected carton contains 7.7 ounces of milk, which of the following statements can be accurately made?

I. The randomly selected carton has a significantly lower amount of milk than the average carton.

II. The number of ounces of milk in the selected carton is two standard deviations below the mean.

III. The number of ounces of milk in the selected carton is three standard deviations below the mean.

IV. The randomly selected carton does not have a significantly lower amount of milk than the average carton.

A. I and II
B. I and III
C. II and IV
D. III and IV
E. IV only

34. Suppose a sample of 16 randomly selected bottles reveals a mean of 11.4 ounces, with a standard deviation of 0.5 ounces. If the bottling company claims a mean of 11.8 ounces, which of the following represents the *t*-value?

    A. −2.8
    B. −3.2
    C. −3.4
    D. −3.6
    E. −3.8

35. A random sample of 36 boxes of cereal is selected. The mean number of ounces of cereal is 19.9, with a standard deviation of 0.1 ounces. If the cereal company claims a mean of 20 ounces, which of the following statements is true?

I.   The null hypothesis of no difference should be rejected.
II. The null hypothesis of no difference should not be rejected.
III. The *t*-value is −6.
IV. The *p*-value is less than 0.001.

    A. I and III
    B. I and IV
    C. I, III, and IV
    D. II and III
    E. III only

36. A coffee shop introduces a new beverage size, which is supposed to contain 32 ounces of coffee. The standard deviation is 0.9. From a random sample of 25 of the beverages, the sample mean is found to be 31.7. Which of the following statements is true?

A. There is a significant difference in the number of ounces of coffee found in the sample beverages, with a p-value less than 0.01.

B. There is a significant difference in the number of ounces of coffee found in the sample beverages, with a p-value less than 0.05.

C. There is not a significant difference in the number of ounces of coffee found in the sample beverages, with a p-value greater than 0.05 and less than 0.1.

D. There is not a significant difference in the number of ounces of coffee found in the sample beverages, with a p-value greater than 0.1.

E. There is a significant difference in the number of ounces of coffee found in the sample beverages, with a p-value less than 0.001.

37. In a peer-reviewed journal, the following numbers of mixed-methods articles were published over the last four years.

YEAR	NUMBER OF MIXED-METHODS ARTICLES
1	6
2	8
3	7
4	10

During the previous four years, the percentages of mixed-methods articles per year were 20%, 22%, 24%, and 25%, respectively. The journal publishes 30 articles per year. Which of the following statements is true?

I.   There is not a significant difference between the numbers of mixed methods articles published over the last four years, as compared to the previous four years.
II. There is a significant difference between the numbers of mixed methods articles published over the last four years, as compared to the previous four years.
III. The chi-square statistic is greater than 0.5.
IV. The p-value is less than 0.01.

    A. I and III
    B. I, III, and IV
    C. II and III
    D. II and IV
    E. III only

38. When comparing number of voters in a particular county over the past 5 years to the expected number of voters, the resulting chi-square statistic is 5.3. Which of the following is the best estimate for the p-value?

A. 0.25
B. 0.45
C. 0.50
D. 0.65
E. 0.85

39. Suppose a researcher wants to calculate the power for finding a difference of 10 points between a sample mean and a population mean. If the population mean is 80, the population standard deviation is 15, and the sample size is 30, which of the following best represents the power for detecting a difference when using a level of significance of 0.05?

A. 0.875
B. 0.935
C. 0.955
D. 0.985
E. 0.999

40. A company claims a box of crackers contains 18 ounces in each box. The population standard deviation is 0.2 ounces. In a random sample of 50 boxes, the sample mean is determined to be 17.8. Which of the following best represents a 95% confidence interval for the actual number of ounces in each box?

A. (17.7, 17.9)
B. (16.8, 17.8)
C. (17.8, 18.2)
D. (16.8, 18.2)
E. (18.2, 18.4)

END OF SECTION I

Statistics
SECTION II
Time—90 minutes

6 questions

Part A

Time—About 60 minutes

Questions 1–5

Directions: Show all your work. Indicate clearly the methods you use, because you will be scored on the correctness of your methods as well as on the accuracy and completeness of your results and explanations.

1. Decide which group shows more variation in the back-to-back stemplot that follows. Justify your answer.

Freshmen		Sophomores
0, 5	1	0, 4, 2, 2, 6, 6, 8
3, 4, 6, 7	2	0, 1, 8
2, 5, 6, 9, 9	3	0, 4, 5, 5
5, 9	4	1
0, 0, 0, 1, 3, 7	5	2, 3, 5, 6, 7, 7, 8
0, 4, 5, 8, 9	6	1
3, 3, 4, 7	7	0, 0, 1, 4, 6
6	8	4, 4
0	9	

2. The means of 30 random samples are shown below:

    20, 20, 20, 20, 20, 20, 20, 20, 20, 21, 21, 21, 21, 21, 21,
    22, 22, 22, 22, 23, 23, 23, 23, 23, 24, 24, 24, 24, 24, 24

    (a) What is the best approximation for the mean of the population, or μ? Justify your answer.
    (b) Discuss the appearance of the distribution of the means of the sampling distribution.
    (c) What deductions may be made based on the given means of the random samples? Be specific.

3. A weight-loss manufacturer claims to include 12 ounces of liquid in each weight-loss shake. A random sample of 40 bottles reveals a mean of 11.9 ounces, with a standard deviation of 0.1 ounces.

   (a) Is the company's claim legitimate? Explain.
   (b) Which distribution did you use? Why?
   (c) What is the margin of error for a 95% confidence level? Describe the process used to arrive at the margin of error.

4. This year, a total of 1,000 students applied to each of the honor societies shown in the following table. (Thus a total of 3,000 student applications were reviewed across the three honor societies.) The number of college students admitted to three different honor societies is shown below:

HONOR SOCIETY	NUMBER OF STUDENTS ADMITTED
Kappa Delta Pi	60
Phi Kappa Phi	110
National Honor Society	95

In the past, 5% of students have been admitted to Kappa Delta Pi, 10% have been admitted to Phi Kappa Phi, and 8% have been admitted to the National Honor Society.

   (a) Is there a significant difference between the number of students accepted to each honor society this year and the number of students typically accepted? Explain.
   (b) How do the degrees of freedom impact the outcome of the analysis? Be specific.

5. A beverage-making company claims to include 16 ounces of soda in each bottle. It also claims a standard deviation of 0.2 ounces. A random sample of 30 bottles shows a mean of 15.9 ounces per bottle.

    (a) Calculate a 95% confidence interval. Explain the process used.
    (b) Decide if you agree with the company's claim. Explain.
    (c) Would your decision change if you used a 90% confidence interval? Justify your answer.

END OF PART A

Statistics
SECTION II
Part B
Time—About 30 minutes
Question 6

Directions: Show all your work. Indicate clearly the methods you use, because you will be scored on the correctness of your methods as well as on the accuracy and completeness of your results and explanations.

6. The Statistics final exam scores and Algebra final exam scores for the same random group of 16 students are shown below:

STATISTICS	65	87	83	79	73	64	73	79
	68	90	65	95	90	93	86	92
ALGEBRA	76	86	88	71	66	93	100	97
	81	76	75	80	78	99	88	90

(a) Create a scatterplot of the data and describe the overall appearance of the graph.

(b) Find the least-squares regression line and discuss the correlation coefficient r.

(c) Discuss the significance of the correlation. Provide an approximate p-value.

(d) Explain any connection between the resulting p-value and the correlation coefficient.

(e) Should an Algebra score be predicted for a given Statistics score? Explain.

END OF DIAGNOSTIC EXAM

Diagnostic Exam Answers and Explanations

Section I: Multiple-Choice Questions

1. A	21. A
2. B	22. D
3. B	23. C
4. C	24. E
5. C	25. D
6. E	26. C
7. D	27. A
8. D	28. D
9. A	29. A
10. A	30. A
11. C	31. A
12. A	32. B
13. A	33. B
14. A	34. B
15. D	35. C
16. B	36. B
17. C	37. A
18. C	38. A
19. C	39. C
20. D	40. A

ANSWER EXPLANATIONS

1. **A.** Using intervals of 41–50, 51–60, 61–70, 71–80, 81–90, and 91–100, with the upper bin limits represented, the frequencies were 3, 4,

3, 5, 1, and 4, respectively, with cumulative frequencies of 3, 7, 10, 15, 16, and 20. Choice A correctly represents these cumulative frequencies.
Difficulty level: Medium

2. **B.** The lower extreme is 23, the upper extreme is 60, the median is 40, the first quartile is 31, and the third quartile is 55. Choice B correctly represents these values. Since the data set has an even number of values, the median is equal to the average of the two middle values of the data set when arranged in ascending order. The first quartile is the median of the lower half of the values, and the third quartile is the median of the upper half of the values.
Difficulty level: Medium

3. **B.** The mode is 3,800, the mean is 3,225, and the median is 3,200. Thus, the mode is greater than the mean and the median.
Difficulty level: Easy

4. **C.** To determine the number of standard deviations a score is below the mean, a z-score must be calculated. The formula for finding a z-score is $z = \frac{X - \mu}{\sigma}$, where z represents the z-score, X represents the score, μ represents the population mean, and σ represents the population standard deviation. Substituting the score of 85, population mean of 120, and standard deviation of 15 gives: $z = \frac{85 - 120}{15}$, or $z = -2\frac{1}{3}$. Thus, the score is $2\frac{1}{3}$ standard deviations below the mean.
Difficulty level: Medium

5. **C.** The standard deviation represents the deviation of a set of scores from the mean. The formula for finding the standard deviation is $s_x = \sqrt{\frac{\sum (X - \overline{X})^2}{N - 1}}$. The mean of the scores is approximately 76.2. Deviation of the scores from the mean can be written as 8.8, −7.2, −4.2, 3.8, −0.2, −20.2, −0.2, 19.8, 10.8, −20.2, 14.8, −4.2, −11.2, −0.2, 8.8, 2.8, 11.8, and −14.2. The squares of the deviations can be written as: 77.44, 51.84, 17.64, 14.44, 0.04, 408.04, 0.04, 392.04, 116.64, 408.04, 219.04, 17.64, 125.44, 0.04, 77.44, 7.84, 139.24, and 201.64. These

squares sum to 2,274.52. Dividing this sum by 17 (sample size of 18 minus 1) gives approximately 133.8. The square root of this quotient is approximately 11.6.

Difficulty level: Medium

6.   **E.** The first quartile is 35, and the third quartile is 72. Thus, the interquartile range is equal to the difference between the two values, or 37. The first quartile is equal to the median of the lower half of the scores, or the eighth value when the values are arranged in ascending order. The third quartile is equal to the median of the upper half of the scores, or the twenty-third value when the values are arranged in ascending order.

Difficulty level: Medium

7.   **D.** Boxplot B shows data that are more spread out around the center than boxplot A. Notice that the data between the median and the upper quartile in boxplot B encompass a larger range than the data between the median and the upper quartile in boxplot A. The range between the medians and lower quartiles in the two boxplots are comparable. In addition, most of the scores are clustered above the median in boxplot B.

Difficulty level: Medium

8.   **D.** The degree of correlation may range from -1 to $+1$. The closer an r-value is to -1 or 1, the stronger the linear relationship. Since this scatterplot reveals a strong linear relationship, the r is best estimated as 0.9.

Difficulty level: Easy

9.   **A.** The least-squares regression line is the calculated line that passes through the points in a scatterplot and reveals the minimum error associated with the prediction. In this case, the correct choice for the least-squares regression line may actually be determined using a visual approach. The line that best represents the correlation of the data would appear to have a slope of 1 or less. In other words, the slope of the line $y = x$ can be seen as reasonably passing through these points. Thus, the slope of 0.09 is a reasonable estimate. In addition, the y-intercept will not be much larger than 0; thus 7 is a good estimate for the y-intercept.

Thus, the equation $y = 0.09x + 7$ is the best estimate for the least-squares regression line. The slopes for Choices B through E are much too steep for the least-squares regression line. The actual equation may be calculated using a manual formula or by entering the data into a graphing calculator and choosing the LIN(REG) function.

Difficulty level: Hard

10. **A.** The strength of linearity for any relationship is determined by the proximity of the correlation coefficient to either −1 or 1. The distance is measured in terms of absolute value. Thus, a correlation coefficient of −0.8 shows a stronger linear relationship than a correlation coefficient of 0.7.

Difficulty level: Easy

11. **C.** The data may be entered into a graphing calculator or Excel spreadsheet. Using the LIN(REG) function of a graphing calculator will yield the summary statistics, including the *r*-value. Using Excel, the *r*-value may be determined by using the Data Analysis Add-in to compute a regression. The resulting "Multiple R" is the correlation coefficient.

Difficulty level: Medium

12. **A.** The least-squares regression line is approximately $y = -0.5x + 66$. The residuals may be determined by evaluating the line for various *x*-values and subtracting the predicted *y*-values from the actual *y*-values. Thus, evaluation of the line for the *x*-values of 1, 2, and 4 gives predicted *y*-values of 65.5, 65, and 64. Subtraction of 65.5 from the actual *y*-value of 61 (the *y*-value for an *x*-value of 1) equals −4.5. Subtraction of 65 from the actual *y*-values of 54 and 74 (the *y*-values for *x*-values of 2) equals −11 and 9. Subtraction of 64 from the actual *y*-value of 75 (the *y*-value for an *x*-value of 4) equals 11. Thus, the correct residual plot should include the points (1, −4.5), (2, −11), (2, 9), and (4, 11). Choice A correctly includes these points.

Difficulty level: Hard

13. **A.** The given scatterplot represents data that has been transformed by taking the logarithm of each *y*-value. Taking the logarithm of each

y-value in the table for answer A, we find approximately 0.5, 0.6, 0.8, 0.8, 0.9, 1.0, 1.1, 1.3, 1.4, and 1.4, which matches the scatterplot.

Difficulty level: Hard

14. **A.** A census is a survey or other experiment in which the population constitutes the sample. In other words, every member of a population is studied or included.

Difficulty level: Easy

15. **D.** When every *n*th member is selected from a list, the procedure is referred to as systematic random sampling. Simple random sampling provides every member of a population an equal opportunity for being chosen. Stratified random sampling and cluster sampling involve dividing the population into groups and then randomly selecting participants from the groups or randomly selecting participants from a specified cluster or group.

Difficulty level: Easy

16. **B.** Since he is using intact classrooms of students as the two groups, and students cannot be randomly assigned to groups, he is using a convenience sample. Thus, the study will include convenience sample bias.

Difficulty level: Easy

17. **C.** Usage of an entire population does not limit the effects of confounding variables because those variables are included in either a population or sample. Confounding variables are those variables that may contribute to certain changes in outcomes but are not part of the intervention itself. Examples include age, gender, number of years of teaching, and so on. Blinding groups, randomly assigning participants, or matching groups limits the effects of outside variables.

Difficulty level: Medium

18. **C.** If an instrument is valid, then it is also considered to be reliable. If an instrument measures what it is supposed to measure, one can assume the instrument will yield consistent results. Conversely, an instrument may be reliable but not be valid. In other words, the instrument may

produce consistent results on questions that do not measure what they are supposed to measure.

Difficulty level: Medium

19. **C.** The theoretical probability of spinning an even number is $\frac{3}{6}$ or $\frac{1}{2}$. Thus, he can expect the spinner to land on an even number $\frac{1}{2} \cdot 120$ times, or 60 times.

Difficulty level: Easy

20. **D.** The probability of events A and B, or $P(A \text{ and } B)$, is equal to the product of the two probabilities. Since the first marble is replaced, the events are independent. Thus, the sample space will not change with the second draw. The probability may be written as $\frac{4}{18} \cdot \frac{6}{18}$, which reduces to $\frac{2}{27}$.

Difficulty level: Medium

21. **A.** The probability of events A and B, or $P(A \text{ and } B)$, is equal to the product of the probability of A and the probability of B, given A, written as $P(A \text{ and } B) = P(A) \cdot P(B|A)$. Since the first card is not replaced, the events are dependent. Since event B involves a draw of the same-colored card, the number of possible outcomes and the total sample space will each decrease by 1. Thus, the probability may be written as $\frac{9}{18} \cdot \frac{8}{17}$, which reduces to $\frac{4}{17}$.

Difficulty level: Medium

22. **D.** The probability of events A or B, or $P(A \text{ or } B)$, is equal to the sum of the two probabilities. Since the events are mutually exclusive, the probability may be represented as $P(A \text{ or } B) = P(A) + P(B)$. Therefore, the probability she spins a number greater than 5 or gets heads may be represented as $\frac{3}{8} + \frac{1}{2}$, or $\frac{7}{8}$.

Difficulty level: Medium

23. **C.** The probability of the nonmutually exclusive events A or B, or $P(A \text{ or } B)$, can be written as $P(A \text{ or } B) = P(A) + P(B) - P(A \text{ and } B)$. Thus, the probability a citizen is a male or a Democrat can be represented as $\frac{420}{820} + \frac{320}{820} - \frac{160}{820}$, which reduces to $\frac{29}{41}$.

Difficulty level: Medium

24. **E.** The expected value is equal to the sum of the products of each x-value and the corresponding probabilities. The following table can be used to represent the x-values and probabilities of each. The x-values represent the possibilities of drawing a yellow marble. Since only three marbles are drawn, she may get zero, one, two, or three yellow marbles.

x	f(x)
0	$\dfrac{\binom{6}{0}\binom{12}{3}}{\binom{18}{3}} \approx 0.27$
1	$\dfrac{\binom{6}{1}\binom{12}{2}}{\binom{18}{3}} \approx 0.49$
2	$\dfrac{\binom{6}{2}\binom{12}{1}}{\binom{18}{3}} \approx 0.22$
3	$\dfrac{\binom{6}{3}\binom{12}{0}}{\binom{18}{3}} \approx 0.02$

The expected value may be written as $E(X) = (0 \cdot 0.27) + (1 \cdot 0.49) + (2 \cdot 0.22) + (3 \cdot 0.02)$, or $E(X) = 0.99$.

Difficulty level: Hard

25. **D.** The BINOMPDF function of a graphing calculator may be used to calculate the probability of obtaining a discrete number of outcomes. The function may be entered into a graphing calculator as BINOMPDF(n, ϖ, x), where n represents the number of trials, ϖ represents the probability of success in each trial, and x represents the number of successes. Thus, the given problem may be represented as BINOMPDF(25, 0.17, 5), which is approximately 0.182. The probability he gets five sixes in 25 rolls is approximately 0.182 or 18.2%.

Difficulty level: Hard

26. **C.** The BINOMCDF function of a graphing calculator may be used to calculate the probability of a range of values. The function may be written as $P(x \geq 3) = 1 - P(x \leq 2)$. This may be entered into the graphing calculator as $1 - $ BINOMCDF$(25,.08,2)$ which is approximately 0.32. Thus, the probability at least three proposals will contain errors is 0.32 or 32%.
  Difficulty level: Hard

27. **A.** Two random variables are independent if the intersection of the variables is equal to the product of the probabilities of the random variables. Thus, $P(A \cap B) = P(A) \cdot P(B)$ verifies that A and B are independent.
  Difficulty level: Medium

28. **D.** In a normal distribution, 95% of the scores fall within ± 2 standard deviations. Two standard deviations below the mean of 80 equals 50 (that is, $80 - 15 - 15$). Two standard deviations above the mean of 80 equals 110 (that is, $80 + 15 + 15$). Thus, 95% of the scores in the middle of the distribution fall between 50 and 110.
  Difficulty level: Medium

29. **A.** To find the proportion under the curve that is more than two standard deviations above the mean, a standard normal distribution table may be used. Since the z-score is equal to 2, the smaller portion value given for this area will show the area of the curve more than two standard deviations from the mean. The table shows this value to be 0.0228, or approximately 2% of the area under the curve.
  Difficulty level: Medium

30. **A.** The mean of a sampling distribution is close to that of the population mean. Therefore, a sampling distribution completed from a population with a mean of 90 will show an approximate mean of 90 as well. A sampling distribution is the plotting of means of n samples within a population.
  Difficulty level: Easy

31. **A.** A z-score is equal to the ratio of the difference between the population mean and the sample score to the population standard deviation. This relationship can be written as $z = \dfrac{X - \mu}{\sigma}$. Substituting the individual

score of 170 for X, the population mean of 185 for μ, and the population standard deviation of 15 for σ gives $z = \dfrac{170 - 185}{15}$, or $z = -1$.

Difficulty level: Medium

32. **B.** The z-score is $z = \dfrac{(90 - 82)}{5} = 1.6$. The p-value for a z-score of 1.6 is 0.0548. Since this p-value is greater than the level of significance of 0.05, her score is not significantly different from the class average.

Difficulty level: Medium

33. **B.** The z-score is $z = \dfrac{(7.7 - 8)}{0.1} = -3$. Thus, the randomly selected carton has an amount of milk that is three standard deviations below the mean. The p-value for a z-score of 3 (the sign of the integer only determines the direction above or below the mean) is 0.0013. For a level of significance of 0.05 (or 0.01, for that matter), the p-value is lower than the level of significance. Thus, the randomly selected carton of milk does have a significantly lower number of ounces of milk than the average carton.

Difficulty level: Medium

34. **B.** The formula for a t-value is $t = \dfrac{\bar{x} - \mu}{\left(\frac{s}{\sqrt{n}}\right)}$, where $\bar{x}$ represents the sample mean, μ represents the population mean, s represents the sample standard deviation, and n represents the sample size. Substituting a sample mean of 11.4, a population mean of 11.8, a sample standard deviation of 0.5, and a sample size of 16 gives $t = \dfrac{11.4 - 11.8}{\left(\frac{0.5}{\sqrt{16}}\right)}$, or $t = -3.2$.

Difficulty level: Medium

35. **C.** The t-value is $t = \dfrac{(19.9 - 20)}{\left(\frac{0.1}{\sqrt{36}}\right)} = -6$. The critical t-value for 35 degrees of freedom for a one-directional test is approximately 1.684. Since the absolute value of −6 is greater than the absolute value of 1.684, the null hypothesis should be rejected, thereby allowing a claim of significant difference. The p-value is actually less than 0.001, since the absolute value of −6 is greater than any of the given critical t-values for that number of degrees of freedom.

Difficulty level: Medium

36. **B.** In comparisons of a sample mean and population mean, the z-score is represented as $z = \dfrac{\overline{X} - \mu}{\left(\frac{s}{\sqrt{n}}\right)}$. The z-score is $z = \dfrac{(31.7 - 32)}{\left(\frac{0.9}{\sqrt{25}}\right)} =$ approximately -1.667. The p-value is approximately 0.0485, which is less than a significance level of 0.05. Thus, there is a significant difference between the number of ounces in the sample and the number of ounces claimed by the coffee shop.

   Difficulty level: Medium

37. **A.** The chi-square statistic can be represented as $\chi^2 = \dfrac{(6 - 6)^2}{6} + \dfrac{(8 - 6.6)^2}{6.6} + \dfrac{(7 - 7.2)^2}{7.2} + \dfrac{(10 - 7.5)^2}{7.5}$, or $\chi^2 \approx 1.1$. For 3 degrees of freedom, a chi-square statistic of 1.1 lies between probabilities of 0.75 and 0.9, while closer to 0.75. Since 0.75 is greater than the level of significance of 0.5, there is not a significant difference between the number of mixed-methods articles published over the last four years and during the previous four years.

   Difficulty level: Hard

38. **A.** For 4 degrees of freedom, a chi-square value of 5.3 lies between the probabilities of 0.5 and 0.25, although much closer to 0.25.

   Difficulty level: Easy

39. **C.** The power statistic, or δ, is equal to the product of the ratio of the difference in the sample and population means to the population standard deviation and the square root of the sample size, written as $\delta = d\sqrt{n}$, where $d = \dfrac{|\overline{X} - \mu|}{\sigma}$. Substituting the mean difference of 10 and population standard deviation gives $d = \dfrac{10}{15}$, or $d \approx 0.67$. Substituting the d-value and sample size into the formula for the power statistic gives $\delta = 0.67\sqrt{30}$, or approximately 3.65. Using the power table, the power is approximately 0.955 for a level of significance of 0.05.

   Difficulty level: Hard

40. **A.** A 95% confidence interval can be calculated using the formula $\overline{X} \pm z_{.025}\left(\frac{\sigma}{\sqrt{n}}\right)$. The confidence interval can be written as $17.8 \pm 1.96\left(\frac{0.2}{\sqrt{50}}\right)$, which is approximately 17.7 and 17.9. Thus, the 95% confidence interval may be written as (17.7, 17.9). In other words, the real number of ounces per box of crackers is likely between 17.7 and 17.9 ounces.

　　Difficulty level: Medium

Section II, Part A: Free-Response Questions

1. The sophomore group shows more variation. The freshman group is closer to a normal distribution than the sophomore group. In other words, the freshman group shows a frequency of scores that generally increases toward the median and then decreases at a comparable rate. On the other hand, the scores for the sophomore group are more sporadic, without a certain distribution pattern shown. The variation in the groups may also be compared by computing the standard deviations for each. The freshman group has an approximate standard deviation of 21, while the sophomore group has an approximate standard deviation of 24.

　　Difficulty level: Hard

2.

(a) The mean of the sampling distribution (or the mean of the random sample means) may be used to approximate the population mean, or μ. Thus, the population mean will likely be near 21.8, or the mean of the given sampling distribution.

(b) The graph of the sampling distribution of the means will be approximately normally distributed. Thus, plotting the means of the samples will show a relatively bell-shaped curve.

(c) As the number of random sample trials increases, the distribution will more closely approximate the normal distribution. Thus, as the number of random sample means increases, the overall mean, or the mean of the sampling distribution, will more closely approach the population mean. It may be deduced that the population mean is near 21.8.

If 1,000 random samples of size n are drawn, the population mean will still be near 21.8.

Difficulty level: Hard

3.

(a) The company's claim is not legitimate, because the difference between the number of ounces of liquid in each bottle in the sample and the number claimed by the company is significant, as evidenced by a p-value less than 0.001. The t-value is approximately -6.3, while the critical t-value for 39 degrees of freedom for a one-tailed test at a level of significance of 0.05 is approximately 1.685. Since the absolute value of the t-value is greater than the critical value, the null hypothesis should be rejected and a significant difference declared.

(b) A t-distribution should be used, since the population standard deviation, or σ, is not known.

(c) The margin of error is approximately 0.03, or 3%. Since the sample size is larger than 30, the following formula may be used, with 0.1 substituted for the population standard deviation: $E = z_{\frac{\alpha}{2}} \cdot \frac{\sigma}{\sqrt{n}}$. For a 95% level of confidence, the critical z-value of 1.96 should be used. Thus, the margin of error may be written as $E = 1.96 \cdot \frac{0.1}{\sqrt{40}}$, which is approximately 0.03.

Difficulty level: Hard

4.

(a) No, there is not a significant difference between the number of students accepted this year and the number accepted in the past: $\chi^2 = 5.8125$. For 2 degrees of freedom, the chi-square statistic falls between probabilities of 0.1 and 0.05. Since the probability is larger than 0.05, the null hypothesis should not be rejected.

(b) If there were one fewer honor society to compare, giving degrees of freedom of 1, the same chi-square statistic would yield a significant difference, with a p-value between 0.01 and 0.025.

Difficulty level: Hard

5.

(a) The confidence interval is approximately $(15.18, 16.62)$. The margin of error was calculated as $E = 1.96 \cdot \dfrac{0.2}{\sqrt{30}}$, which is approximately 0.72. Subtracting 0.72 from the sample mean of 15.9 and adding 0.72 to the sample mean of 15.9 gives the limits of the confidence interval.

(b) Yes, one can agree with the claimed population mean, because 16 is within the limits of the confidence interval.

(c) Yes, the decision would change to "not agree." Using a 90% confidence interval will result in nonagreement with the company's claim. The margin of error is approximately 0.06, which gives an approximate confidence interval of $(15.84, 15.96)$. Since 16 does not lie within those limits, it seems unlikely the claim is true.

Difficulty level: Hard

Section II, Part B: The Investigative Task

6.

(a)

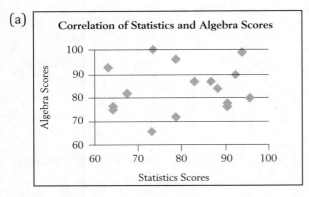

The graph does not show a linear pattern or relationship. Instead, the points are quite sporadic. The points do not seem to model a quadratic or power function either.

(b) The least-squares regression line is approximately $y = 0.2x + 71.5$. The correlation coefficient, r, is approximately 0.17, showing a very weak correlation between the Statistics and Algebra scores.

(c) The correlation is not significant, as evidenced by a p-value of approximately 0.54.

(d) The high p-value and low correlation coefficient both reveal data that are not linearly correlated. A high p-value reveals nonsignificance in correlation; a low correlation coefficient does the same.

(e) Since the data show a weak correlation, one score would not be used to predict another score. Substituting a value into the least-squares regression line would not produce a meaningful prediction, since the data are only weakly correlated.

Difficulty level: Hard

Using the Diagnostic Exam

Calculating Your Score

Calculating your composite score for the AP Statistics Exam isn't difficult. Follow the steps below to approximate your composite score.

Section I: Multiple-Choice Questions

1. Count *only* the items you answered correctly. Write that number here: _____

2. Perform the following calculation:

$$\frac{}{\text{Number Correct}} \times 1.2500 = \frac{}{\text{Weighted Section I Score}}$$
$$\text{(out of 40)} \qquad \text{(Do not round)}$$

Section II: Free-Response Questions

Question 1: $\dfrac{}{\text{(out of 4)}} \times 1.8750 = \dfrac{}{\text{(Do not round)}}$

Question 2: $\dfrac{}{\text{(out of 4)}} \times 1.8750 = \dfrac{}{\text{(Do not round)}}$

Question 3: $\dfrac{}{\text{(out of 4)}} \times 1.8750 = \dfrac{}{\text{(Do not round)}}$

Question 4: $\dfrac{}{\text{(out of 4)}} \times 1.8750 = \dfrac{}{\text{(Do not round)}}$

Question 5: $\dfrac{}{\text{(out of 4)}} \times 1.8750 = \dfrac{}{\text{(Do not round)}}$

Question 6: $\dfrac{}{\text{(out of 4)}} \times 3.1250 = \dfrac{}{\text{(Do not round)}}$

$\text{Sum} = \dfrac{}{\substack{\text{Weighted Section II Score} \\ \text{(Do not round)}}}$

COMPOSITE SCORE

$\dfrac{}{\substack{\text{Weighted} \\ \text{Section I Score}}} + \dfrac{}{\substack{\text{Weighted} \\ \text{Section II Score}}} = \dfrac{}{\substack{\text{Composite Score (Round} \\ \text{to nearest whole number)}}}$

This is your composite score. The College Board goes one step further and translates your composite score into a scaled score. The following is the score conversion chart for AP Statistics:

COMPOSITE SCORE RANGE	AP SCORE
63–100	5
49–62	4
37–48	3
29–36	2
0–28	1

It isn't necessary to take the extra step to translate your composite score to a scaled scored to see how well you'll perform. A high composite score (49–100) translates to a high scaled score (4 or 5). If you scored that well, congratulations! You're definitely ready to ace this exam. On the other hand, a low composite score (say, 36 or under) translates to a low scaled score (2, 1, or 0). Remember, many colleges and universities require students to receive *at least* a 3 on an AP exam to qualify to receive college credit for a course, and many require a score of 4 or 5.

Improving Your Score

How do you feel about your performance? Remember, the diagnostic examination in this book is meant to help you identify your weak areas and show you where you may need to improve in terms of either the content you are studying or your actual test-taking habits. Don't underestimate the importance of good test-taking habits; for standardized examinations such as this one, your approach is every bit as important as the knowledge you bring to the table.

Assess your performance *honestly*. Go back through the exam and review the questions you answered correctly, those you answered incorrectly, and those you skipped. Can you identify patterns or trends in your incorrect or missed answers? Did your mistakes result from a failure to read all of the answer options or from misreading the questions? Did you miss any core concepts? Also review the vocabulary terms you highlighted. Are these similar in nature or related to particular concepts or ideas? If you have time, follow up on this material. Close the gaps in your knowledge so they aren't a problem when you get to your actual exam.

Finally, how did you do with time? Did you run out of time? Were you rushing to finish within the allotted time period? Did you spend too much time on each individual question? Or did you fail to spend *enough* time? Remember, successful test-taking is as much about managing your time as it about understanding the content.

A Final Word about the Diagnostic Exam

Finally, don't feel too badly if you didn't do well on this diagnostic exam the first time through. After all, the entire point of this book is to give you the opportunity to identify areas for improvement and to give you the materials for practice. Use this book to test and retest, until you feel thoroughly comfortable with both the setup and the content of the examination.

Before moving on, head back to **The Main Course: Comprehensive Strategies and Review** (page 21) and review the test-taking strategies discussed there. Now that you've had an opportunity to take the practice exam, some of the test-taking strategies will make more sense to you. As you move forward, you'll be able to see more specifically how you can apply these strategies to your advantage.

Review Chapter 1:
Graphing Univariate Data and Interpreting the Representations

Part I: Graphing Univariate Data

Univariate data represent one variable. Frequency of such data values may be represented using various graphs or plots. Examples of univariate data include scores on a mathematics test, ages of students in a class, heights of employees, and number of hours of sleep various professionals get per night.

Dotplots

A dotplot is a graph of a number line with points plotted above appropriate values on the line. Each point corresponds to a value in a data set. For multiple occurrences of a value in a data set, a corresponding number of points are plotted to represent that value. The following dotplot represents a graph of the data set:

87, 79, 16, 39, 35, 65, 79, 96, 75, 19, 44, 96, 85, 85, 6, 30, 39, 77, 30, 79, 85, 30, 6, 59, 52, 39, 77, 79, 19, 44, 66, 79, 30, 44, 52, 52, 77, 79, 75, 39, 52, 75, 39, 65, 77, 77, 39, 52, 79, 39

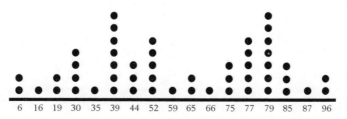

Stem-and-Leaf Plots

A stem-and-leaf plot may also be used to represent univariate data. The stem portion of the plot represents the leading digits, while the leaf portion represents the less significant digits. With data sets including only two digits, the tens digits represent the leading or most significant digits, while the ones digits represent the less significant digits.

The following diagram is an example of a stem-and-leaf plot:

Stems	Leaves
5	0, 2, 3, 4, 5, 8
6	0, 1, 3, 6
7	3, 6, 8
8	3, 3, 4, 7, 7, 8
9	1, 3, 5, 7, 9, 9

Bar Graphs

A bar graph represents the frequency of *nominal* or *interval* categories of a set of data. The set of data is univariate because it represents one variable with a certain number of categories. Bar graphs are used to represent frequency of *discrete* variables. Consider the following example:

Eric wants to represent the favorite poem genres of students in his class. (In this case, he will represent the frequency of *nominal* categories of data.) He first represents the data using the following table:

POEM GENRE	NUMBER OF STUDENTS
Narrative	7
Epic	5
Dramatic	4
Satirical	4
Lyrical	6
Other	8

The data represented in the table may be shown using the following bar graph:

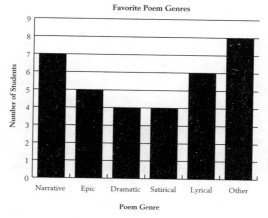

A bar graph can also be used to represent *interval data*. Consider the following example:

Monique wants to represent the number of students of different ages at her local high school. She records the data in the following table:

AGE	NUMBER OF STUDENTS
14	71
15	80
16	74
17	83
18 and up	62

She also represents the data with the following bar graph:

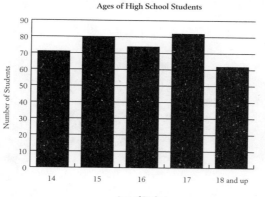

Histograms

Histograms are another way to represent frequency of data. Histograms can represent frequencies of infinitely many values that are included between discrete values. In other words, histograms may be used to represent continuous data, as well as any real-number data. Consider the following example:

A manager wishes to examine the total number of miles driven by his sales professionals over the last week. Since mileage can take on continuous values (5.8 miles may be driven), a histogram is appropriate. He records the miles driven by 30 of his employees as follows:

248.8, 375.0, 364.6, 385.2, 283.0, 352.3, 162.0,
62.9, 267.4, 104.7, 497.6, 592.7, 520.0, 115.3, 447.5,
348.0, 550.6, 575.2, 202.8, 597.0, 437.4, 560.9,
110.3, 558.7, 438.0, 340.0, 429.5, 393.5, 559.4, 81.6

The manager may create a histogram by first determining the size and number of the intervals to be represented on the x-axis. When deciding on these preliminary design components, he should first examine the minimum and maximum values. Since the minimum value is 62.9 and the maximum value is 597.0, an appropriate range for the histogram would be 50–600. A logical interval width is 50. The first interval will actually begin with 51. Thus, the following intervals may be used to represent the values on the x-axis:

51–100, 101–150, 151–200, 201–250, 251–300,
301–350, 351–400, 401–450, 451–500, 501–550, 551–600

The following histogram results:

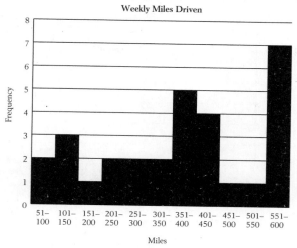

Frequency Plots

A *frequency plot* can be used to represent the same data as a histogram. A frequency plot, however, connects frequencies with a line instead of representing each frequency with separate bars. It is another representation that may be used to present continuous data. Consider the following scenario:

Juan wants to represent the frequencies of the ages of his employees within various age ranges. His employees' ages are as follows:

> 33, 46, 50, 37, 39, 27, 54, 54, 24, 30, 53, 60, 26,
> 39, 42, 35, 27, 48, 36, 54, 50, 53, 36, 45, 25, 48,
> 53, 41, 38, 26, 31, 28, 51, 42, 60, 23, 33, 32, 48, 41

A regular frequency plot may or may not include the intervals along the x-axis. The plot may show the upper limits of each interval.

The process for creating the frequency plot is the same as that used with a histogram. In place of bars, however, the frequency values are plotted and connected.

Cumulative Frequency Plots

A *cumulative frequency plot* represents the cumulative frequencies, as data for each subsequent interval range are added. While a frequency plot represents each distinct frequency within a given range of values, a cumulative frequency plot represents a running tally of all frequencies, as upper limits progress from left to right. For example, the sum of the frequencies for the first two upper limits will be used to represent the cumulative frequency of the second upper limit. The initial frequency of the first upper limit will remain the same. The sum of the first three upper limits will be used to represent the cumulative frequency of the third upper limit. This process continues for each upper limit along the x-axis. Each upper limit represents numbers up to and including that value. Consider again the example of the manager who wants to track miles driven by his sales professionals:

Suppose the manager wants to represent the cumulative number of employees driving up to (and including) a maximum numbers of miles.

To show this data, the manager needs a cumulative frequency plot such as the following:

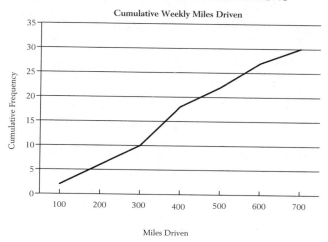

Notice that two employees drive up to 100 miles, five employees drive up to 150 miles, and six employees drive up to 200 miles. The histogram, which represents frequencies (or numbers of) employees driving within certain mileage intervals, may be used to check (and create) the cumulative frequency plot shown above. For example, notice that the first bar in the histogram represents two employees, whereas the sum of the first two bars represents a total of five employees. In other words, five employees drive a number of miles that is less than or equal to 150. Also, notice that the cumulative frequency plot shows a maximum cumulative frequency of 30 employees, or the total number of employees included. This reveals that 30 employees drive less than or up to the maximum number of 600 miles per week.

Boxplots

A *boxplot* is another graph used to represent univariate data. A boxplot concretely represents the median, first and third quartiles, and upper and lower limits of a data set. Consider the following data set:

60, 59, 91, 91, 69, 74, 91, 95, 56, 61, 87, 72, 74, 66, 52,
78, 54, 85, 58, 74, 72, 69, 91, 78, 72, 68, 88, 98, 64, 81

The first step in creating a boxplot is to identify the minimum and maximum data values. In this case, they are 98 and 52. These values will represent the whiskers of the plot.

The next step is to determine the *median* of the data set. The median may be determined by arranging the values in ascending order and finding the middle value, or the average of the two middle values in the case of an even number of values. In this case, since the sample size is even, the median will be equal to the average of the two middle values.

The data set can be rewritten as follows:

52, 54, 56, 58, 59, 60, 61, 64, 66, 68, 69, 69, 72, 72, **72**,
74, 74, 74, 78, 78, 81, 85, 87, 88, 91, 91, 91, 91, 95, 98

The two boldface values represent the two middle values, which have an average of $\frac{72 + 74}{2} = 73$. Thus, the median of the data set is 73. This value will be represented by a horizontal line at the value of 73.

The third step involves computing the first and third quartiles. The *first quartile* represents the median of the lower half of a data set, whereas the *third quartile* represents the median of the upper half of a data set. In other words, 25% of the values fall below the first quartile, while 75% of the values fall above it. Conversely, 75% of the values fall below the third quartile, while 25% of the values fall above it.

Thus, the first quartile will represent the median of the first 15 values. Since the number of values in the first half is odd, the median will be the middle value, or 64.

The third quartile will represent the median of the next 15 values. Again, the median will be the middle value. This value is 87.

The first and third quartiles will represent the endpoints of the box. The boxplot may now be drawn with a lower whisker at 52, an upper whisker at 98, a median at 73, a first quartile at 64, and a third quartile at 87. The boxplot should appear as follows:

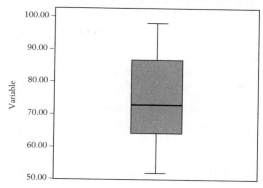

Part II: Interpreting Graphical Representations

The shape of a graphical representation of data may be described in terms of modality, normality, skewness, and kurtosis.

Modality

The *modality* of a distribution refers to the number of peaks in the graph. For example, a distribution with one peak is *unimodal*, whereas a distribution with two peaks is *bimodal*. A normal distribution is, of course, unimodal.

Normality

A *normal distribution* is a distribution that is symmetric and unimodal. The mean, median, and mode of a normal distribution are equivalent. The following graph represents a normal distribution:

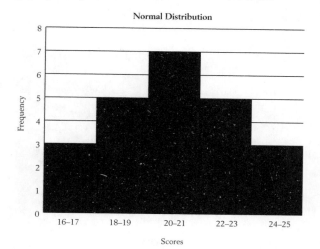

Skewness

When a distribution is *not* normal, it may be positively or negatively skewed. Such distributions are not symmetric. *Positively skewed distributions* show a greater number of lower scores or values. *Negatively skewed distributions* show a greater number of higher scores or values. In other words, a positively skewed distribution has a tail that points to the right, and a negatively skewed distribution has a tail that points to the left. It should be noted that skewed distributions have means that are pulled toward the extremes in the tail.

The following graphs show positively and negatively skewed distributions:

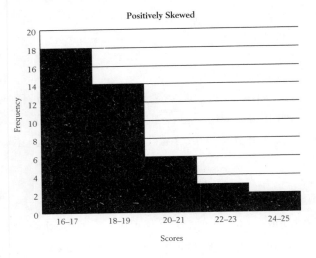

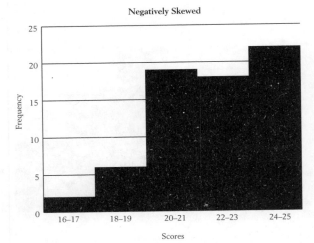

Kurtosis

Kurtosis refers to the steepness or flatness of a distribution. A normal distribution is *mesokurtic*. A *platykurtic* distribution is flatter, indicating a higher level of variability about the mean than a normal distribution. A *leptokurtic* distribution is steeper, indicating less variability about the mean than a normal distribution.

The following graphs represent platykurtic and leptokurtic distributions:

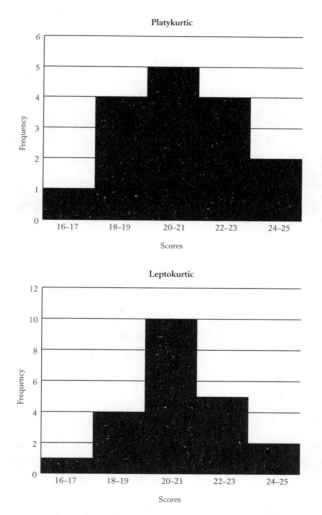

The center, spread, and outliers of a distribution may also be interpreted.

Center

The measures of center of a distribution are important. Measures of center include the mean, median, and mode.

The *mean* of a data set represents the average of the data set. The *median* is the middle value in a data set arranged in ascending order. The *mode* is the most frequently occurring value.

In a normal distribution, the mean, median, and mode will be at the same point (all falling at the middle of the distribution).

In skewed distributions, however, the measures of center will vary. For example, the mean of a positively skewed distribution will be higher than the median. Conversely, the mean of a negatively skewed distribution will be smaller than the median. (Recall that the mean of a skewed distribution is pulled toward the extremes.)

For normal and skewed distributions, the median will be at the center of the distribution. For this reason, the median is a better measure of central tendency when dealing with data with extreme outliers.

The mode of a distribution is the highest point on the graph.

Spread

The *spread* of a data set refers to the variability about the center. Measures of spread include range, interquartile range, variance, and standard deviation. Calculation of these measures will be covered in **Review Chapter 2: Summarizing Distributions of Univariate Data**. However, interpretations regarding the spread of a data set using only a graph are often necessary.

Given a graph of a normal distribution, it may be stated that scores are distributed symmetrically about the mean. In other words, the percentage of scores to either side of the mean either decreases or increases at the same rate. Thus, the spread of data is not great, which indicates the absence of extreme outliers.

A graph of a nonnormal distribution (or skewed distribution) will have varying degrees of spread or variability. The range depends on the values of the extreme outliers. The *interquartile range (IQR)*, which represents the range of the middle 50% of the scores, will be less variable since the extreme outliers aren't included. Spread may be determined by viewing the distance of scores from the mean.

Outliers

Outliers are scores that differ markedly from the mean. Outliers influence the mean but have no effect on the median. Outliers are represented by the tails of a distribution.

Review Questions

1. Create a stem-and-leaf plot for the following data set.

    16, 40, 39, 4, 38, 14, 35, 29, 42, 14, 29, 22, 19, 25, 20,
    31, 33, 48, 37, 41, 29, 43, 24, 33, 39, 1, 31, 29, 8, 16

2. Create a histogram using the following data.

    23, 33, 27, 35, 17, 40, 16, 10, 35, 40, 20, 34, 7, 9,
    8, 8, 39, 38, 3, 5, 13, 46, 23, 30, 38, 8, 25, 42, 29, 3

3. A fitness instructor records the number of sit-ups completed by her students during one class. Create a cumulative frequency plot for the number of sit-ups recorded below.

    74, 29, 34, 64, 33, 89, 71, 44, 91, 81, 15, 36, 50, 47, 85

4. Design a data set with 30 values. Use the data to create a boxplot.

5. Discuss the differences in the shape, center, and spread of normal and skewed distributions.

Answer Explanations

1.

Stems	Leaves
0	1, 4, 8
1	4, 4, 6, 6, 9
2	0, 2, 4, 5, 9, 9, 9, 9
3	1, 1, 3, 3, 5, 7, 8, 9, 9
4	0, 1, 2, 3, 8

2.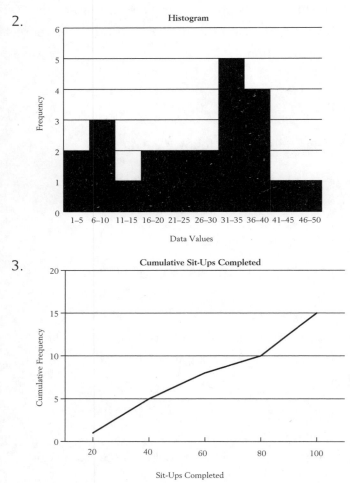

3.

4. Here is one sample data set:

29, 31, 48, 38, 36, 18, 28, 13, 46, 33, 37, 40, 35, 38, 36,
25, 42, 25, 13, 35, 37, 43, 40, 2, 48, 18, 12, 29, 42, 30

The boxplot for the data is shown below:

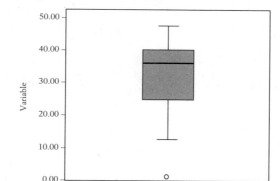

5.   A normal distribution has a bell-shaped curve. The frequency of values rises and falls at the same rate to either side of the center; therefore, the graph is symmetric. The center of the distribution is represented by the mean, median, and mode. All three measures of center fall at the same place. There is not a large spread in the data. Most of the values lie close to the mean.

Nonnormal distributions are not symmetric and may have more than one peak, be positively or negatively skewed, and appear either platykurtic or leptokurtic. The center of these distributions is best represented by the median, or middle value, of the data set. The mean is pulled toward the extremes in the tails of skewed distributions. There is more variability, or spread, in nonnormal distributions.

Review Chapter 2: Summarizing Distributions of Univariate Data

Measures of center, spread, and position of a set of univariate data values can be determined from the data set itself or from graphical representations of the data. In addition to the representations presented in this chapter, center and spread summary statistics may also be calculated using other univariate representations such as dotplots and frequency plots.

Extreme outliers heavily impact the mean, range, standard deviation, and variance of a data set. The median and mode are not affected by outliers. Thus, the median is a more stable statistic for representing the center of nonnormal data sets or data sets that are skewed.

Part I: Measures of Center and Spread

Measures of Center

The mean, median, and mode of a distribution represent the center of a data set. Consider the data set shown below:

18, 24, 18, 20, 46, 18, 49, 12, 18, 36, 49, 19, 21,
25, 39, 41, 43, 28, 27, 30, 18, 26, 31, 45, 46

The *mean* is an average of the scores, or the ratio of the sum of the scores to the number of scores in the data set. Thus, the mean of the preceding data set may be written as $\frac{474}{25}$, which equals 29.88.

For a data set with an odd number of values, the *median* is the middle value when data are arranged in ascending order. For a data set with an even number of values, the median is the average of the two middle values. The data set presented previously, written in ascending order, is as follows:

$$12, 18, 18, 18, 18, 18, 19, 20, 21, 24, 25, 26, 27,$$
$$28, 30, 31, 36, 39, 41, 43, 45, 46, 46, 49, 49$$

The data set has an odd number of values, so the median is the middle value. Thus, the median is 27.

The *mode* is the most frequently occurring score. In this case, the mode is 18.

Measures of Spread

The range, interquartile range, standard deviation, and variance represent the spread of a data set.

The *range* is equal to the difference between the maximum and minimum values in a data set. The range of the aforementioned data set is 37 (that is, 49 – 12).

The *interquartile range* of a data set is the range of the middle 50% of the values (the distance between Q1 and Q3). In other words, the interquartile range is the difference between the first and third quartiles of a data set.

To determine the interquartile range of the data set presented previously, the first and third quartile values must be determined first.

The first quartile is the median of the lower half of the scores. The third quartile is the median of the upper half of the scores. The lower and upper halves of the data set each contain 12 scores. Since 12 is an even number, the quartiles will be the average of the two middle values in each of the lower and upper halves.

The first quartile is the average of 18 and 19, or 18.5. The third quartile is the average of 41 and 43, or 42. Therefore, the interquartile range is 23.5 (that is, $42 - 18.5$).

The *standard deviation* of a data set represents the variability of the scores about the mean. The formula for standard deviation is $s_x = \sqrt{\dfrac{\sum (X - \overline{X})^2}{N - 1}}$. Stated simply, the standard deviation of a data set is equal to the square root of the ratio of the sum of the squared deviations of the scores to the difference of the number of scores and 1. This formula relates to the standard deviation for a sample.

For this data set, the sum of the squared deviations can be written as follows:

$$(18 - 29.88)^2 + (24 - 29.88)^2 + (18 - 29.88)^2 + (20 - 29.88)^2 +$$
$$(46 - 29.88)^2 + (18 - 29.88)^2 + (49 - 29.88)^2 + (12 - 29.88)^2 +$$
$$(18 - 29.88)^2 + (36 - 29.88)^2 + (49 - 29.88)^2 + (19 - 29.88)^2 +$$
$$(21 - 29.88)^2 + (25 - 29.88)^2 + (39 - 29.88)^2 + (41 - 29.88)^2 +$$
$$(43 - 29.88)^2 + (28 - 29.88)^2 + (27 - 29.88)^2 +$$
$$(30 - 29.88)^2 + (18 - 29.88)^2 + (26 - 29.88)^2 +$$
$$(31 - 29.88)^2 + (45 - 29.88)^2 + (46 - 29.88)^2$$

The sum of the squared deviations can next be written as follows:

$$(-11.88)^2 + (-5.88)^2 + (-11.88)^2 + (-9.88)^2 + (16.12)^2 +$$
$$(-11.88)^2 + (19.12)^2 + (-17.88)^2 + (-11.88)^2 + (6.12)^2 +$$
$$(19.12)^2 + (-10.88)^2 + (-8.88)^2 + (-4.88)^2 + (9.12)^2 +$$
$$(11.12)^2 + (13.12)^2 + (-1.88)^2 + (-2.88)^2 + (0.12)^2 +$$
$$(-11.88)^2 + (-3.88)^2 + (1.12)^2 + (15.12)^2 + (16.12)^2$$

After squaring the deviations, the sum can be written as follows:

$$141.13 + 34.57 + 141.13 + 97.61 + 259.85 + 141.13 +$$
$$365.57 + 319.69 + 141.13 + 37.45 + 365.57 + 118.37 +$$
$$78.85 + 23.81 + 83.17 + 123.65 + 172.13 + 3.53 +$$
$$8.29 + 0.01 + 141.13 + 15.05 + 1.25 + 228.61 + 259.85$$

The sum of the squared deviations equals 3,302.53. (Note: This is an estimate due to rounding of the squared deviations.)

Thus, the standard deviation for this data set can be written as $s_x = \sqrt{\dfrac{3,302.53}{24}}$ or $\sqrt{137.61}$, which equals approximately 11.7.

The standard deviation may also be calculated using a graphing calculator. After entering the data set into a list, the standard deviation can be calculated by choosing 2STAT and then choosing STDDEV, under MATH. This method shows the same standard deviation of approximately 11.7.

The *variance* is equal to the square of the squared deviation, or approximately 137.61. In other words, the variance is equal to the ratio of the sum of the squared deviations of the scores to the difference of the number of scores and 1. Stated another way, the variance is the value under the radical, prior to taking the square root.

The variance may be calculated using a graphing calculator by following the same steps as those for standard deviation but choosing VARIANCE instead.

Part II: Representations and Calculations of Center and Spread

Boxplots

A boxplot is a graph that can be used to estimate the median, range, and interquartile range of a data set. A boxplot clearly marks the median and the first and third quartiles of the data. The upper and lower extreme scores are also identified.

The following boxplot represents the distribution of miles driven per day by various sales professionals at a health insurance company:

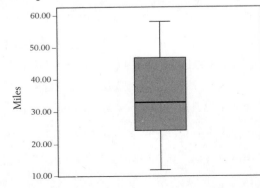

In the boxplot, the median is marked by the thick black line located inside the box. The median can be estimated as approximately 33 miles. The minimum number of daily miles appears to be approximately 12, while the maximum number of miles is approximately 57. The first quartile, which represents the median of the lower half of the values, appears to be approximately 21 miles. The third quartile, which represents the median of the upper half of the values, appears to be approximately 46.

Therefore, the following can be stated: "The center of the data appears to be 33 miles per day. The data do not show a large variability, as approximately equal clusters of scores fall above and below the median. Fifty percent of the miles driven per day fall between 21 miles and 46 miles. In other words, 25% of the mileages fall between 12 miles and 21 miles. Also, 25% of the mileages fall between 46 miles and 57 miles."

The data is not skewed in either direction.

The scores are actually as follows:

28, 56, 44, 23, 18, 39, 49, 22, 18, 46, 38, 19, 42,
48, 32, 33, 17, 12, 48, 45, 33, 22, 18, 46, 46

Thus, the median is exactly 33 miles. The lower extreme is 12 miles, while the upper extreme is 56 miles. The first quartile is 20.5, while the upper quartile is 46. The original estimates from the diagram alone are very close to the actual values for the center and spread.

Other Representations

Measures of center and spread also may be estimated from other graphical representations, including bar graphs, stem-and-leaf plots, and histograms.

Bar Graphs

A bar graph such as the following one can be used to determine all measures of center and spread for a given data set:

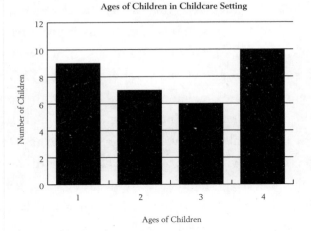

To determine the measures of center and spread, the bar graph must first be used to write the data set. Each frequency (number of children) indicates the number of times each corresponding age must be listed. The data set may be written as follows:

$$1, 1, 1, 1, 1, 1, 1, 1, 1, 2, 2, 2, 2, 2, 2, 2,$$
$$3, 3, 3, 3, 3, 3, 4, 4, 4, 4, 4, 4, 4, 4, 4, 4$$

The mean is equal to the sum of the scores, divided by 32 (the number of scores). Thus, the mean is $\frac{81}{32}$, or approximately 2.53.

Since the data set has an even number of values, the median is equal to the average of the two middle values. The data set must be listed in ascending order before the median is found. Thus, the median is equal to the average of 2 and 3, or 2.5.

The mode may be discerned without listing the data values. The mode is represented by the tallest bar. The tallest bar indicates that 10 children are age 4. Thus, the mode is 4.

The range is equal to the difference between the lowest and highest ages, or 3.

The first quartile is the middle value of the lower half of the scores, or 1. The third quartile is the middle value of the upper half of the scores, or 4. Thus, the interquartile range is 3. In this case, the interquartile range is the same as the range. Range and interquartile range are not usually the same, however.

The standard deviation can be calculated as shown previously: The sum of the squares of the differences from the mean is approximately 45.97. Thus, the standard deviation is $s_x = \sqrt{\dfrac{(x - \bar{x})^2}{n - 1}} = \sqrt{\dfrac{45.97}{31}}$, which is approximately 1.22.

The variance is approximately 1.48, which is the square of the standard deviation.

Stem-and-Leaf Plots

A stem-and-leaf plot can reveal the same information as a bar graph, since the representation can be used to list each data value. Consider the stem-and-leaf plot below:

Stems	Leaves
0	4, 6, 8
1	2, 6, 7, 7, 8, 9, 9
2	1, 2, 5, 8, 8
3	1, 2, 3, 4
4	4

The data can be listed as follows:

$$4, 6, 8, 12, 16, 17, 17, 18, 19, 19,$$
$$21, 22, 25, 28, 28, 31, 32, 33, 34, 44$$

Since the methods of calculation have already been shown, only the summary statistics are provided for this example:

Mean = 21.7

Median = 20

Mode = 17, 19, 28

Range = 40

Interquartile range (IQR) = 13

Standard deviation ≈ 10.28

Variance ≈ 105.59

Histograms

Since a histogram represents frequencies of intervals of data, the measures of center and spread may be estimated using the midpoint of each interval. Consider the following histogram:

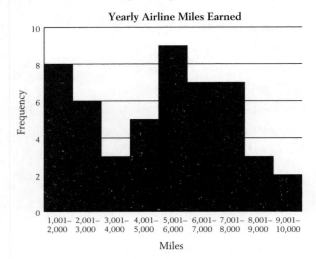

The data can be extracted from the histogram by representing each midpoint a number of times equal to the corresponding frequency. Since the data values will be estimates, the measures of center and spread will also be estimates. Thus, the data may be listed as follows:

1,500, 1,500, 1,500, 1,500, 1,500, 1,500, 1,500, 1,500, 2,500, 2,500, 2,500, 2,500, 2,500, 2,500, 3,500, 3,500, 3,500, 4,500, 4,500, 4,500, 4,500, 4,500, 5,500, 5,500, 5,500, 5,500, 5,500, 5,500, 5,500, 5,500, 5,500, 6,500, 6,500, 6,500, 6,500, 6,500, 6,500, 6,500, 7,500, 7,500, 7,500, 7,500, 7,500, 7,500, 7,500, 8,500, 8,500, 8,500, 9,500, 9,500

The measures of center and spread can be calculated as usual. The summary statistics are as follows:

Mean = 5,040 miles

Median = 5,500 miles

Mode = 5,500 miles

Range = 8,000 miles

Interquartile range = 4,000 miles

Standard deviation = 2,400.77 miles

Variance = 5,763,673.47 miles

Note: The mode of a histogram is represented by the highest bar, just as it is in a bar graph.

From the histogram, it can be discerned that the median, or middle of the data set, is 5,500. The data set appears to show a larger number of lower miles, which makes it negatively skewed. With a skewed distribution, the mean is pulled toward an extreme. Therefore, it makes sense that the mean is less than the median. The middle 50% of the scores appears to be between 3,500 and 7,500 miles, showing an IQR of 4,000.

Significant variability appears about the center of the data. Therefore, using the graph alone, we can expect that the standard deviation and variance will be fairly large.

Part III: Measures of Position

Measures of position indicate where certain values lie in a data set. These include quartiles, percentiles, and z-scores.

Percentiles

Percentiles represent the position at which x% of values fall below a certain value. We will discuss quartiles and deciles, but percentiles can correspond to any other percentage as well.

Quartiles represent quantities of 25% of data values and include the first quartile, the median, and the third quartile. Thus, the first quartile represents the position below which 25% of the values fall. The median represents the position below which 50% of the values fall and above which 50% of the values fall. The third quartile represents the position below which 75% of the values fall.

Measures of position include *deciles*, as well. Deciles represent multiples of 10% of data. That is, the first decile represents the position below which 10% of the values fall, the second decile represents the position below which 20% of the values fall, and so on. However, deciles are not as widely used as quartiles.

Z-Scores

For the purpose of this chapter, we will only discuss z-scores as related to position. A z-*score* is a standardized score that represents the number of standard deviations above or below a mean. Therefore, a z-score provides information about the position of a score relative to the center of the distribution. A z-score is equal to the ratio of the difference between the score and the mean and the standard deviation, written as $z = \frac{X - \mu}{\sigma}$, where X represents the score, μ represents the population mean, and σ represents the population standard deviation.

Consider a student that scores an 82 on an exam. If the class average is 90, with a standard deviation of 5 points, the z-score can be calculated as $z = \frac{82 - 90}{5}$, or -1.6. Thus, the student's score is 1.6 standard deviations below the mean of 90.

The use of a z-score for hypothesis testing is covered in Chapter 12.

Based on the yearly airline miles data given in the histogram presented on page 114, z-scores can be calculated for any particular number of miles. This calculation will reveal the number of standard deviations that a number of miles is above or below the average number of miles. For example, suppose an employee traveled 3,000 miles. This number of miles will be compared to the mean. The z-score can be written as $z = \frac{3,000 - 5,540}{2,400.77}$, which is approximately -1.06. Therefore, the following may be stated: "The quantity of 3,000 miles is approximately 1.06 standard deviations below the mean number of miles of 5,540."

Review Questions

1. Calculate the mean, median, mode, standard deviation, and variance for the following data set.

    12, 29, 31, 40, 22, 39, 34, 10, 15, 5, 4, 28, 37, 15,
    12, 5, 38, 24, 1, 12, 14, 4, 21, 26, 30, 7, 2, 2, 4, 7

2. Find the minimum value, maximum value, median, first quartile, and third quartile for the following data set.

    33, 26, 8, 37, 33, 17, 36, 40, 10, 11, 13, 21, 40, 34,
    2, 3, 2, 30, 26, 2, 33, 26, 26, 10, 12, 6, 21, 11, 25, 32

3. Briefly describe the procedure for calculating standard deviation.

4. Create a bar graph with a numerical independent variable. Find the mean, median, mode, range, IQR, standard deviation, and variance.

5. Create a set of 20 values. Find the z-score for one of the scores. Interpret the z-score.

Answer Explanations

1. The summary statistics are as follows:

$$\text{Mean} \approx 17.7$$

$$\text{Median} = 14.5$$

$$\text{Mode} = 12$$

$$\text{Standard deviation} \approx 12.8$$

$$\text{Variance} \approx 164.6$$

2. The summary statistics are as follows:

Minimum value = 2

Maximum value = 40

Median = 23

Q1 = 10

Q3 = 33

3. The differences of each score and the mean should be computed first. Next, those differences should be squared. Then, the sum of all squared differences should be found. Next, the sum of the squared differences should be divided by the difference of N (the sample size) and 1. Finally, the square root of this ratio should be found.

4.

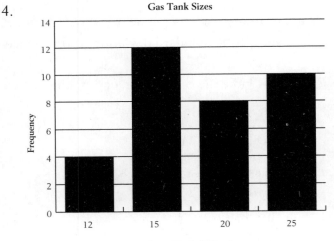

Gas Tank Sizes

Size of Tank (gallons)

Mean ≈ 18.8

Median $= 20$

Mode $= 15$

Range $= 13$

IQR $= 10$

Standard deviation ≈ 4.8

Variance ≈ 22.9

5.   A possible data set is:

1, 7, 25, 13, 18, 21, 30, 28, 30, 1, 15, 39, 39, 15, 18, 3, 28, 26, 37, 20

The mean is 20.7, and the standard deviation is approximately 11.9. The z-score may be found by using the formula $z = \frac{X - \mu}{\sigma}$. The z-score for 13 may be found by calculating $z = \frac{13 - 20.7}{11.9}$, which is approximately −0.65. Thus, the value of 13 is 0.65 standard deviations below the mean of 20.7.

Review Chapter 3: Using Graphs to Compare Univariate Data

Distributions of univariate data may be compared using representations such as dotplots, back-to-back stemplots, parallel boxplots, and double bar graphs.

Dotplots

Dotplots may be used to compare distributions of two or more data sets. The following dotplots represent frequencies of ages of students participating in two different college honor societies.

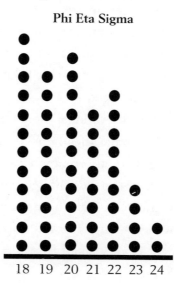

Phi Eta Sigma

18 19 20 21 22 23 24

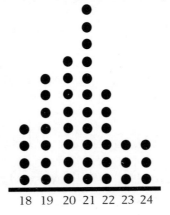

Comparing Shapes

The distribution for Phi Eta Sigma is positively skewed (i.e., the tail points to the right), with a higher number of younger students participating in the honor society. Therefore, the distribution for Phi Eta Sigma shows a cluster of students of lesser ages. The distribution for Pinnacle National Honor Society is close to normal, with frequencies of students increasing and then decreasing, as ages increase.

Comparing Centers and Deviations

The distribution for Phi Eta Sigma shows a center of approximately 20 to 21. (The actual mean and median are 20.2 and 20, respectively.) The frequencies of ages do not show much variation from the center. Notice most students' ages range from 18 to 22. The actual standard deviation for Phi Eta Sigma is approximately 1.7, which shows the ages are within two standard deviations of the mean.

The distribution for Pinnacle National Honor Society shows a center of approximately 21. (The actual mean and median are 20.7 and 21, respectively.) Since the ages are approximately normally distributed, it can be discerned that most of the student ages will be within two standard deviations from the mean. In fact, the standard deviation is actually about 1.7. Most students' ages range from 20 to 22.

Since the range of ages is very small (range = 6), there are not any outliers in either distribution.

In summary, the centers of the distributions are quite close, and the variability is the same. However, the shapes of the distributions differ in that one is skewed, while the other is approximately normal.

Back-to-Back Stemplots

Back-to-back stemplots may also be used to compare distributions of two or more data sets. Consider the back-to-back stemplot that follows:

CLASS A		CLASS B
1, 3, 5, 5, 6, 6, 7	5	2, 3, 3, 3, 4, 7, 8
1, 6, 9, 9	6	2, 9
6, 6, 8, 9	7	3, 4, 5, 5, 9
0, 2, 4, 4, 7, 8	8	2, 4, 5, 5, 7, 7, 9
3, 7, 8, 8	9	0, 2, 3, 7

Comparing Shapes

Neither distribution shows positive or negative skewness. Class A does not show a cluster of scores. Class B reveals a cluster of scores between 70 and 99. If the data for both classes were graphed, two peaks would result, with the peaks for both classes representing scores between 50 and 59 and 80 and 89. Neither class distribution is approximately normal. Refer to the following histograms.

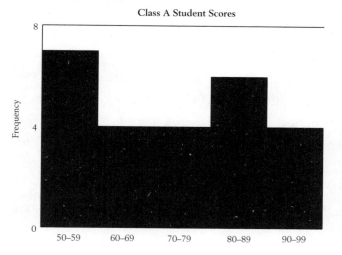

Class A Student Scores

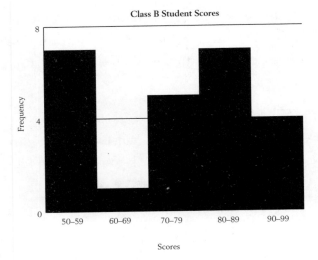

Class B Student Scores

Comparing Centers and Deviations

The distribution for class A shows a center of approximately 70 to 75. (The actual mean and median are 73.9 and 76, respectively.) The frequencies of scores do show variation from the center. The actual standard deviation for class A is approximately 15.4, which shows a high level of variability. With a normal distribution, approximately 99% of the scores fall within 3 standard deviations of the mean.

The distribution for class B shows the same approximate center. (The actual mean and median are 74.3 and 75, respectively.) The frequencies of scores again show variation about the mean and median. The standard deviation for class B is slightly less than that for class A, with a standard deviation of approximately 15. However, this standard deviation also reveals a very high level of variability.

The back-to-back stemplot alone, as well as the graphed histograms, reveals much variability about the center of the data, indicating a high standard deviation.

The ranges for each are comparable, with a range of 47 for class A and a range of 45 for class B.

In summary, the centers of the distributions are close, and both classes show much variability in scores. Neither distribution is approximately normal or skewed in one particular direction. With the nonnormal distributions, it can also be noted that neither class distribution shows symmetry.

Parallel Boxplots

The following parallel boxplots compare college student scores in two different statistics course sections, 301 and 302.

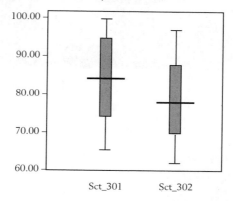

Comparing Shapes

Neither section distribution shows skewness in the middle 50% of the scores. When all scores are considered, however, section 302 appears to have a larger number of lower scores, which indicates positive skewness. With section 302, a noticeably larger cluster of scores falls above the third quartile than that shown for section 301. Neither distribution appears to be normal. The following histograms depict the same data as the boxplots above and are provided here as another reference for comparing the shapes of the two distributions. Notice that the nonnormality of each distribution is clearer from the histograms.

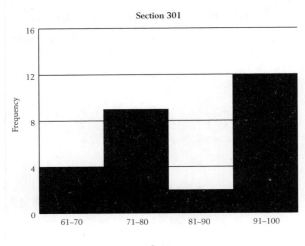

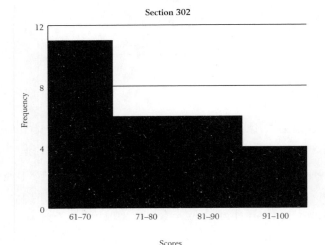

Comparing Centers and Deviations

The distribution for Section 301 shows a median of approximately 83, which is indeed the exact median. The scores seem to show quite a bit of variability about the center. The actual standard deviation for Section 301 is approximately 11.7, which shows a high level of variation.

The distribution for Section 302 shows a median of approximately 77. (The actual median is 77.5.) The scores again seem to show much variation about the center. In fact, the standard deviation is approximately 11.4. From the boxplots alone, one might be tempted to believe that Section 302 shows more variability and, therefore, a higher standard deviation. This assumption would be due to the larger number of scores falling between the third quartile and the maximum score. However, looking at the interquartile range (IQR) reveals something different. The IQR for Section 301 is approximately 21 (that is, 94 – 73); the IQR for Section 302 is approximately 19. The IQR for Section 302 shows a smaller range of scores falling in the middle 50% of the scores. Thus, the scores for Section 302 are slightly more clustered around the center, indicating a *lower* standard deviation.

The range for each section is the same (range = 36).

In summary, the center of Section 301 is higher than the center of Section 302 by approximately 6 points. It appears that students in Section 301 did better than students in Section 302. The variability about the center is about the same. However, the shapes of the distributions differ in that one is skewed while the other does not reveal a particular skewness. Neither distribution is normal.

Double Bar Graphs

Double bar graphs are another graphical representation for comparing univariate data. The following double bar graph compares the number of students of different ages participating in a production from two different high schools.

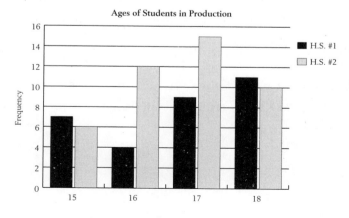

Comparing Shapes

The distribution of students' ages for H.S. #2 is more normally distributed than that for H.S. #1. The distribution of students' ages for H.S. #1 is negatively skewed, showing that a larger number of its students are older.

Comparing Centers and Deviations

The distributions for both high schools show a center of approximately 16 to 17. (The actual mean and median for H.S. #1 are 16.8 and 17, respectively. The actual mean and median for H.S. #2 are 16.7 and 17, respectively.) The frequencies of ages do not show much variation from the center. With the small range, a lower standard deviation is to be expected. The standard deviation is approximately 1.2 for H.S. #1 and approximately 1 for H.S. #2.

In summary, the centers of the distributions are quite close, and the variability is approximately the same. However, the shapes of the distributions differ in that one is skewed while the other is more normally distributed. In addition, H.S. #1 shows a larger number of older students, compared to total students.

Review Questions

1. Provide a data set with 25 values. Next, provide another data set with less variation about the mean. Graph the data sets using any graphical representation.

2. Explain what it means when one distribution is negatively skewed and another is approximately normal. What may be concluded from such shapes?

3. Compare the shapes, centers, and standard deviations of the data sets for the following dotplots.

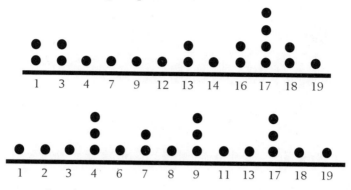

4. Compare the shapes, centers, and standard deviations of the data sets for the following boxplots.

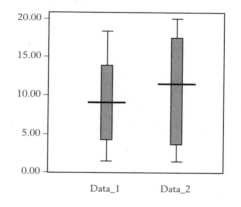

5. Compare the shapes, centers, and standard deviations of the data sets for the following back-to-back stemplot.

DATA SET A	STEM	DATA SET B
2, 2, 3, 5	0	1, 3, 6, 9, 9
2	1	1, 5, 5, 8, 9
1, 1, 3, 3, 6, 7	2	0, 3
3, 8	3	1
2	4	2, 5, 6
0, 0, 1, 3, 5	5	1, 1, 5, 8
0	6	

Answer Explanations

1. The following is a possible first data set:

$$47, 22, 44, 26, 1, 45, 15, 35, 10, 38, 41, 41, 14,$$
$$24, 24, 50, 21, 42, 47, 13, 22, 34, 15, 3, 29$$

The following is a possible less-variable data set:

$$11, 17, 24, 38, 36, 29, 9, 46, 41, 39, 39, 36, 12,$$
$$43, 25, 10, 41, 13, 18, 35, 46, 26, 26, 3, 16$$

The following are possible parallel boxplots that represent the data and spread:

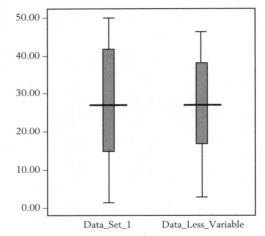

As can be discerned from the boxplots, the values in the less-variable data set are more closely clustered about the center, or median. Both data sets have a median of 26. Data set 1, however, has a standard deviation of approximately 14.5; the boxplot on the right (the less-variable set) has a standard deviation of approximately 13.2.

2. When a distribution is negatively skewed, it is not symmetric or normal. The data are skewed left (the tail points to the left) and, therefore, include a larger number of higher values. A normal distribution is symmetric and has a mean, median, and mode all located at the same point. As the values increase, the frequencies increase and then decrease at the same rate. With negatively skewed data, the mean is pulled toward the lower extreme. Thus, the mean is less than the median.

3. Neither distribution is normal. The first dotplot seems to be negatively skewed with more high scores. The second dotplot shows three peaks. The first dotplot seems to have a center between 12 and 13, while the second one seems to have a center around 9. In fact, the data in the first dotplot has a mean of 11.75 and a median of 13.5. The data in the second dotplot has a mean of 9.75 and a median of 9. The second dotplot seems to show slightly less variability about the mean. However, both seem to show much variability, indicating a high standard deviation. The standard deviation for the data in the first dotplot is approximately 6.3, while the standard deviation for the data in the second dotplot is 6.

4. The boxplot on the left appears to be approximately normal, while the boxplot on the right is negatively skewed with a larger number of lower scores. The center of the boxplot on the left is less than the center of the boxplot on the right. The median of the boxplot on the left appears to be 9, while the median of the boxplot on the right appears to be 12. The boxplot on the right is more variable than the one on the left, which indicates a higher standard deviation. The actual standard deviations are 5.7 for the one on the left and 7 for the one on the right.

5. Data set A shows a median of 26.5, while data set B shows a median of 19.5. Neither data set is normal or skewed in one direction. If it were not for the four values in the 50 range, it could be said that data set B was positively skewed. Each data set shows more than one peak and much variability about the mean. The actual standard deviations for both data sets are approximately 19.

Review Chapter 4:
Exploring Bivariate Data

The correlation, or relationship, between two variables may be determined using scatterplots, least-squares regression lines, and correlation coefficients. Patterns in bivariate data may be used to make predictions using the line of best fit as a model. The majority of this chapter focuses on linear correlations, but be aware that not all correlations are linear. For nonlinear correlations, transformations may be used to achieve linearity for interpretive and predictive purposes.

Types of Correlations

Bivariate data may show a positive correlation, a negative correlation, or no correlation. For data showing some correlation, the correlation may be perfect, strong, or weak. With a perfect correlation, either negative or positive, the line used to make predictions is the actual line through the points. In reality, perfect correlations are very rare. The strengths of correlations range from -1 to 1, where r represents the correlation. In this text, Pearson's correlation coefficient, r, will be used in exact calculations.

The scatterplots on the following pages represent types of correlations.

Positive Correlation

With a positive correlation, the y-values increase as the x-values increase.

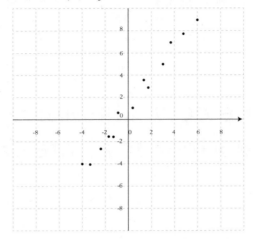

Negative Correlation

With a negative correlation, the y-values decrease as the x-values increase.

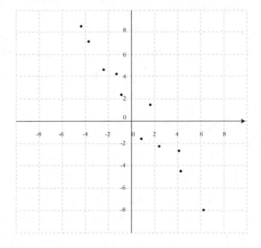

No Correlation

When there is no correlation between two variables, no evident pattern exists. No linear correlation is indicated by an r-value of 0.

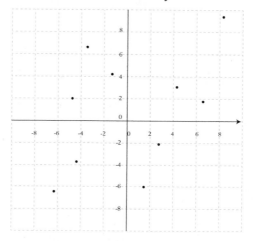

Perfect Correlations

A perfect correlation is one in which the least-squares regression line is the actual line passing through the points. In other words, the points represent solutions of the line. With a perfect negative correlation, the coefficient of correlation is $r = -1$. With a perfect positive correlation, the coefficient of correlation is $r = 1$.

The first scatterplot that follows represents a perfect positive correlation. The least-squares regression line for this data is $y = 2x + 1$. The second scatterplot that follows represents a perfect negative correlation. The equation for the least-squares regression line is $y = -3x + 2$.

In reality, very few, if any, correlations are actually perfect.

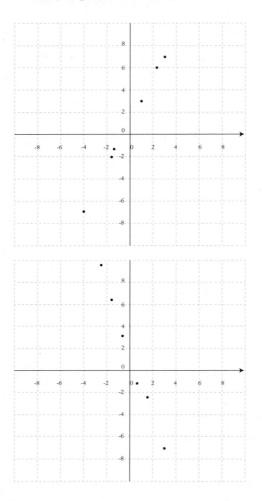

Strong Correlations

Strong correlations are correlations that are close to −1 or +1. For example, a correlation of $r = 0.8$ or 0.9 depicts a strong positive correlation. Likewise, a correlation of $r = -0.8$ or -0.9 depicts a strong negative correlation.

A strong correlation shows little deviation of data points from the least-squares regression line. In other words, the margin of error is small.

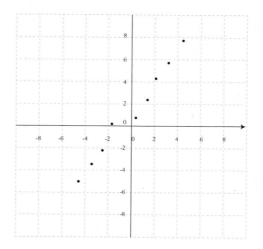

Weak Correlations

Weak correlations are correlations that are closer to 0. For example, a correlation of $r = 0.1$ or 0.2 depicts a weak positive correlation. Likewise, a correlation of $r = -0.1$ or -0.2 depicts a weak negative correlation.

A weak correlation shows a large deviation of data points from the least-squares regression line. With a weak correlation, the estimation of data points with a line of best fit includes a greater margin of error.

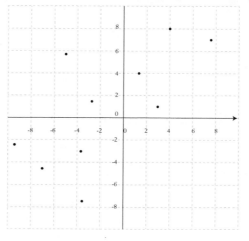

Calculating Correlation Coefficients

Pearson's correlation coefficient, r, measures the strength of a linear relationship. In the types of correlations previously discussed, visual estimates of r were given for nonperfect correlations. The exact value of r can be calculated using the following formula:

$$r = \frac{n(\sum xy) - (\sum x)(\sum y)}{\sqrt{(n\sum x^2 - (\sum x)^2)(n\sum y^2 - (\sum y)^2)}}$$

Consider the data given in the following table:

x	y
3	9
2	5
6	8
7	2
10	12
14	18
16	20

Columns for xy, x^2, and y^2 may be added to compute r using the formula:

x	y	xy	x²	y²
3	9	27	9	81
2	5	10	4	25
6	8	48	36	64
7	2	14	49	4
10	12	120	100	144
14	18	252	196	324
16	20	320	256	400

A summation row can then be added:

x	y	xy	x²	y²
3	9	27	9	81
2	5	10	4	25
6	8	48	36	64
7	2	14	49	4
10	12	120	100	144
14	18	252	196	324
16	20	320	256	400
58	**74**	**791**	**650**	**1,042**

The sums and sample size, $n = 7$, may be substituted into the formula for Pearson's r:

$$r = \frac{7(791) - (58)(74)}{\sqrt{(7(650) - (58)^2)(7(1042) - (74)^2)}}$$

This simplifies to $r \approx 0.85$. Thus, the correlation coefficient is approximately 0.85, which indicates a strong correlation.

The correlation coefficient can also be calculated using either a graphing calculator or an Excel spreadsheet.

Using a calculator, the values of x and y must first be entered into two separate lists. Next, choose VARS, then EQ, and next r. Press Enter.

Using an Excel spreadsheet, enter the x- and y-values into two separate columns, choose Regression, and find the Multiple R.

Estimating Least-Squares Regression Lines

A least-squares regression line can be estimated by drawing a line that passes through the points, while minimizing the average standard error, or average deviations from the line. After drawing the estimated line, use two points lying close to the line to determine the slope of the line. This slope and the estimated y-intercept (where the line crosses the vertical axis) may be used to write an estimated least-squares regression line.

For example, consider the following scatterplot. (Note: This is the same scatterplot that appears in the positive correlation section.)

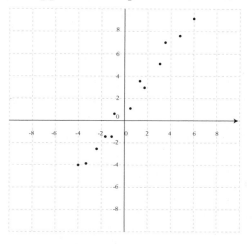

An estimated line with a y-intercept of approximately 1 would seem to be a good fit for the data points. The slope of the line will reasonably range from 1 to 2. A slope of 1.5 and y-intercept of 1 give the line $y = 1.5x + 1$, which seems to be a good estimate for the data. The following graph shows the estimated least-squares regression line.

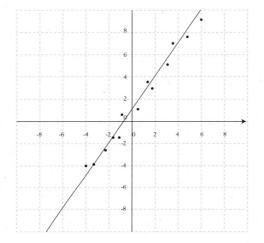

Notice that the points do not show much deviation from the fitted line. The estimated line appears to be a good fit for the data. Therefore, it is reasonable to use this line to predict other data points.

Suppose the y-value for an x-value of 10 needs to be predicted. The value can be determined by evaluating the estimated least-squares regression equation for an x-value of 10. Doing so gives the following: $y = 1.5(10) + 1$, or $y = 16$. Therefore, based on the trend in the data points shown in the scatterplot, one can reasonably predict that an x-value of 10 corresponds to a y-value of 16.

The following scatterplot represents the correlation of salary and years of teaching experience of a random sample of 15 teachers who teach in different school districts.

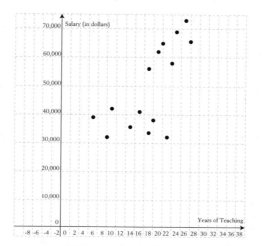

The line drawn in the following graph passes through the middle of the points and seems to minimize deviations from the line.

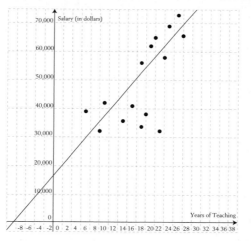

This line has a y-intercept of approximately 17,000. Using two points close to the line, the slope may be estimated. Using the points (28, 65,500) and (24, 58,000), the estimated slope can be calculated as follows:

$$m = \frac{y_2 - y_1}{x_2 - x_1}$$

$$m = \frac{58,000 - 65,500}{24 - 28}$$

The slope is approximately 1,857. Thus, a reasonable estimate for the least-squares regression line is $y = 1,857x + 17,000$.

Calculating Least-Squares Regression Lines

Using the scatterplot shown in the previous section, the actual least-squares regression line may also be calculated, either manually or with a graphing calculator.

The data points for the scatterplot shown in the previous section are as follows: (11, 42,000), (19, 33,700), (28, 65,500), (7, 39,000), (15, 35,500), (19, 56,000), (22, 65,000), (23, 32,000), (27, 23,000), (21, 62,000), (17, 41,000), (24, 58,000), (20, 38,000), (25, 69,000), and (10, 32,000).

The least-squares regression line is written as $y = mx + b$, where $m = r\left(\dfrac{SD_y}{SD_x}\right)$ and $b = \overline{Y} - m\overline{X}$.

Substituting an r-value of 0.68, a standard deviation for y of 14,948.95, a standard deviation for x of 6.24, a mean for y of 49,446.67, and a mean for x of 19.2, the following can be written:

$$m = 0.68\left(\frac{14{,}948.95}{6.24}\right), \ b = 49{,}446.67 - 1{,}629(19.2)$$

Thus, the least-squares regression line can be written as $y = 1{,}629x + 18{,}170$. This line is not precise, due to rounding of the values of the variables.

The least-squares regression line can be determined using a graphing calculator by choosing STAT, CALC, and then LINREG after entering the x- and y-values into two separate lists.

Doing so gives the following least-squares regression line: $y = 1{,}649.8x + 17{,}770.2$. This line is quite close to the line derived via manual calculation.

Making Predictions

Suppose one wanted to predict a teacher's salary after 40 years of teaching. The least-squares regression line of $y = 1{,}649.8x + 17{,}770.2$ can be used to make the prediction. Substituting an x-value of 40 into the equation gives the following: $y = 1{,}649.8(40) + 17{,}770.2$, or $y = 83{,}762.2$.

Nonlinear Correlations

Some correlations are nonlinear. In other words, the trendline that best fits the data is not a line. Instead, it may be a curve.

Consider the data in the following table:

x	y
−7	110
−3	18
−1	5
1	6
4	36
6	80
8	140
10	200
13	360
17	545

The data from the table are plotted on the following graph:

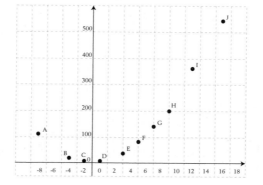

The data plotted in the graph resemble a parabola. A straight line could be fitted to the data, but it would not provide a trendline that models the data as closely as a curve does.

The following graph was created in Excel and shows a trendline of power 2, or a quadratic. Notice how closely the trendline models the data.

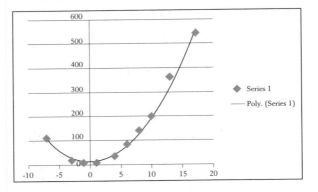

The nonlinear correlation for the parabola is approximately $r = 0.998$, indicating a very strong polynomial correlation.

The data may also be fitted with a line.

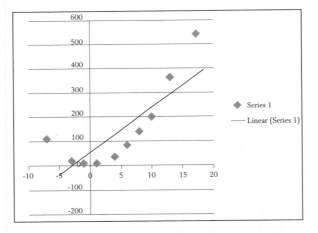

The scatterplot shows much more deviation of the data points from the trendline. The r-value for the linear trendline is approximately 0.81. Thus, a quadratic curve best fits the data.

Transformations to Achieve Linearity

A nonlinear correlation may be transformed to achieve linearity. For example, the data points from the preceding section may be transformed using power and logarithmic transformations, among others, to reveal data that may be more accurately modeled with a linear trendline.

Power Transformations

Power transformations raise the values of the x- or y-variable to some specified exponent, or power. Suppose the original y-values given for the data in the preceding section are raised to the second power. In other words, the transformed y-values will equal y^2.

The following transformed data would result.

x	y
−7	12,100
−3	324
−1	25
1	36
4	1,296
6	6,400
8	19,600
10	40,000
13	129,600
17	297,025

The transformed data from the table have been plotted on the following graph:

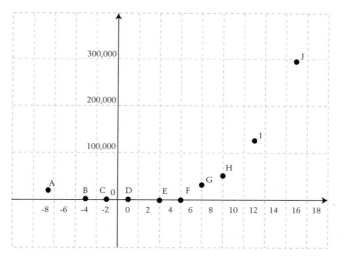

Using Excel, a linear trendline may be fitted to the data, and a diagram such as the following would result:

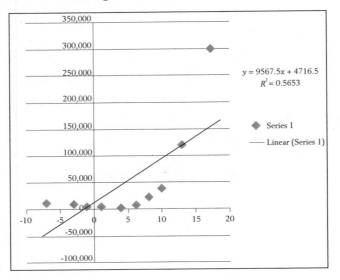

The r-value for the transformed data, fitted with a linear trendline, is approximately 0.75, which is actually slightly less than the r-value given for the original data fitted with a linear trendline.

Perhaps, however, a different power transformation would yield better results. We can now try transforming the x-values instead by raising all x-values to a power of 2. Doing so results in the following:

x	y
49	110
9	18
1	5
1	6
16	36
36	80
64	140
100	200
169	360
289	545

The data are plotted as follows:

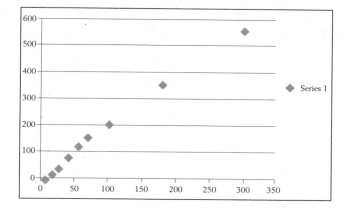

The fitting of a linear trendline is shown as follows:

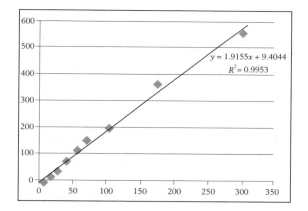

The data now show an r-value of approximately 0.998 when fitted with a linear trendline. This r-value is much higher than the r-value found for the original data fitted with a linear trendline. With this second power transformation, we have achieved linearity.

Why did this work? Recall that the original data looked like a parabola, corresponding to a quadratic relationship where y is proportional to x. Thus when we square the x-values and compare them to the y-values, we have an approximately linear relationship, as we discovered with the second power transformation we performed.

Logarithmic Transformations

The data also may be transformed by taking the logarithm of each y-value or by taking the logarithm of the x- and y-values. The following table represents the original x-values from the preceding examples and the logarithm of each original y-value.

x	y
−7	2.04
−3	1.26
−1	0.70
1	0.78
4	1.56
6	1.90
8	2.15
10	2.30
13	2.56
17	2.74

The transformed data are plotted on the following graph:

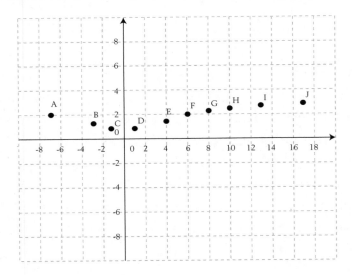

Notice that the positive integer data points appear to be more linear. However, the r-value for the transformed data is actually lower than the original data fitted with a linear trendline. In this case, the logarithmic transformation did *not* reveal a more linear relationship. The following diagram shows a linear trendline fitted to the transformed data.

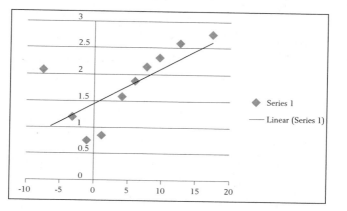

The trendline shown in the graph is represented by the equation $y = 0.0663x + 1.481$, with an r-value of approximately 0.70.

Since the transformed data did not reveal a higher r-value when fitted with a linear trendline, the next step is to take the logarithm of both the x- and y-values. Doing so gives the data shown in the following table. A logarithm of a negative number may not be calculated; therefore, the table includes only those points with positive x-values.

x	y
0	0.78
0.60	1.56
0.78	1.90
0.90	2.15
1	2.30
1.10	2.56
1.23	2.74

The data from the table are plotted in the following graph:

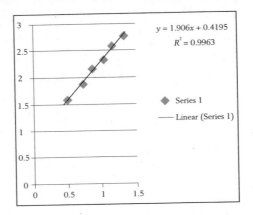

Now, the data show an r-value of approximately 0.998, which was the same r-value given for the data fitted by the quadratic trendline. The transformed data has now achieved linearity.

Residual Plots

Residuals represent the difference between predicted y-values and actual y-values. The predicted y-values can be determined by evaluating the least-squares regression line for various x-values.

Consider the data in the following table:

x	y
2	−5
0	−11
4	5
6	12
8	20
10	22
13	33
15	40
18	50
22	55
25	50
30	90
35	100
38	102
46	125

The plotted data are shown in the following graph:

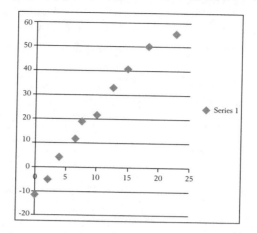

The least-squares regression line is $y = 3.1092x - 8.37$. The line may be estimated as $y = 3.1x - 8.4$. Evaluating the line for all x-values gives the predicted values shown in the table that follows:

x	PREDICTED y
2	-2.2
0	-8.4
4	4
6	10.2
8	16.4
10	22.6
13	31.9
15	38.1
18	47.4
22	59.8
25	69.1
30	84.6
35	100.1
38	109.4
46	134.2

The residuals equal the difference between the predicted y-values and the actual y-values. Thus, the predicted y-values are subtracted from the actual y-values. The following table represents this information:

x	y	PREDICTED y	DIFFERENCE (RESIDUALS)
2	−5	−2.2	−2.8
0	−11	−8.4	−2.6
4	5	4	1
6	12	10.2	1.8
8	20	16.4	3.6
10	22	22.6	−0.6
13	33	31.9	1.1
15	40	38.1	1.9
18	50	47.4	2.6
22	55	59.8	−4.8
25	50	69.1	−19.1
30	90	84.6	5.4
35	100	100.1	−0.1
38	102	109.4	−7.4
46	125	134.2	−9.2

Plotting the x-values and residuals gives the following residual plot:

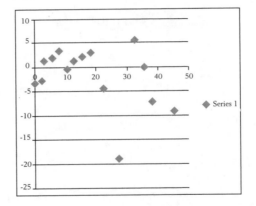

This plot may be verified by creating a residual plot in Excel using the original x- and y-values. The residual plot may be created by choosing a Regression from Data Analysis and clicking Residual Plots. Doing so gives the following:

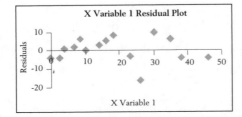

The residual plot, created in Excel from the original data points, is very close to the one derived manually; slight differences are due to the rounding of the least-squares regression line.

Review Questions

1. Create a scatterplot of a strong, negative correlation. Estimate the correlation coefficient.

2. Calculate Pearson's correlation coefficient using the data in the following table.

x	y
-3	-6
-2	-3
0	5
3	10
6	20
9	35
12	45
15	50
18	60
20	84

3. Provide an estimate of the least-squares regression line using the following scatterplot. Describe the procedure used to arrive at the estimated line.

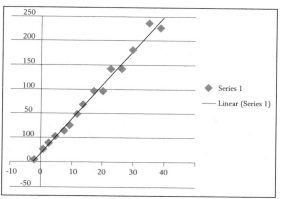

4. Use a logarithmic transformation to achieve linearity of the data in the following table. Provide a table of the transformed data. Show the scatterplot of the transformed data with the linear trendline and the *r*-value of the linear trendline.

x	y
–3	15
–1	–5
1	1
3	20
6	75
10	200
12	275
14	452
17	550
20	790
24	1,160

5. Create a data set with ten ordered pairs. Show the residual plot.

Answer Explanations

1.

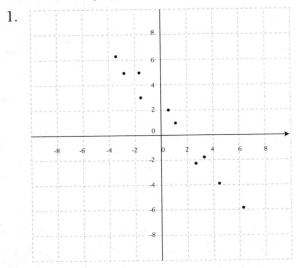

The correlation coefficient should be around $r \approx -0.9$. The actual correlation coefficient is approximately -0.99.

2. $r \approx 0.986$

3. An estimated least-squares regression line is $y = 5x + 2$. The y-intercept appears to be slightly above the origin (0). Thus, a y-intercept of 2 is appropriate. Using two of the points on the line, namely (18, 100) and (34, 185), the slope can be written as $m = \dfrac{185 - 100}{34 - 18}$, which is approximately 5.3. Substituting the estimated slope and y-intercept into the slope-intercept form of an equation gives the estimated least-squares regression line $y = 5x + 2$.

4. The transformed data are represented in the table below. Both the x- and y-values were transformed by taking the logarithm of each. Only the positive integers are included.

log x	log y
0	0
0.48	1.30
0.78	1.88
1	2.30
1.08	2.44
1.15	2.66
1.23	2.74
1.30	2.90
1.38	3.06

The scatterplot is as follows:

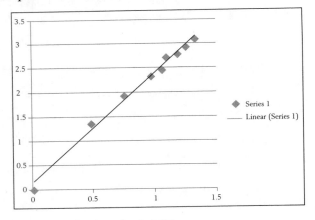

The *r*-value is approximately 0.997.

5. A possible data set with ten ordered pairs is shown below:

x	y
−5	−30
−3	−25
−1	−12
3	20
6	30
9	45
12	75
16	95
20	100
22	138

The residual plot for this data is as follows:

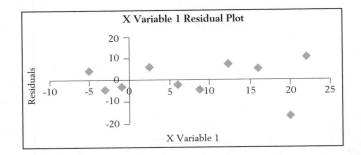

Review Chapter 5:
Exploring Categorical Data

Bar Graphs

As explained in earlier chapters, bar graphs may be used to represent frequencies of categories of data. The data may be *nominal* in nature, or it may be *interval*, which means that each category represents a discrete numerical value. This section covers nominal data.

Suppose students' preferences for state trips are obtained and represented in the following bar graph:

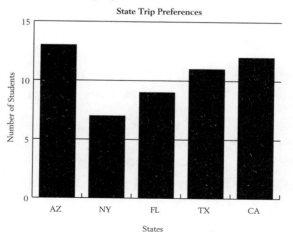

From the bar graph, it can be discerned that a trip to Arizona is preferred by most students, and a trip to New York is preferred by the fewest students. Thus, the modal category is Arizona. The mean and median are nonsensical when examining nominal data.

Suppose two different groups of students were surveyed to compare preferences for state trips. This data is graphed as follows:

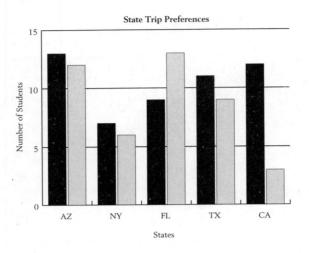

The bar graph shows that most students in the second group (in gray) preferred Florida. The fewest students in this group preferred California. Thus, the modal category for this group of students is Florida. New York ranks next to last in preference.

One-Way Frequency Tables

Frequency tables may be used to explore or compare categorical data.

The frequencies represented in the preceding bar graph may be represented in a one-way frequency table. A one-way frequency table represents data for one variable.

The data can be represented according to frequencies of each category—each state, in this case. Thus, the following frequency table may be created:

STATE	FREQUENCY
AZ	13
NY	7
FL	9
TX	11
CA	12

The frequency table reveals the same modal category of Arizona.

One-Way Relative Frequency Tables

A relative frequency represents the ratio, or proportion, of a frequency for a particular category to the total frequencies. The state preferences data may be represented by the following relative frequency table:

STATE	RELATIVE FREQUENCY (RATIO)
AZ	0.25
NY	0.13
FL	0.17
TX	0.21
CA	0.23

The relative frequencies may also be converted to percentages and represented as follows:

STATE	RELATIVE FREQUENCY (PERCENTAGE)
AZ	25%
NY	13%
FL	17%
TX	21%
CA	23%

The sum of the relative frequencies, or percentages, should equal 100%. The sum of the relative frequencies in the table on the preceding page equals 99% due to rounding.

Two-Way Frequency Tables

Two-way frequency tables are used to compare frequencies of data for two variables.

Consider the following two-way frequency table:

	MATH	SCIENCE	HISTORY	LITERATURE	ART	TOTAL
Males	16	12	14	30	16	88
Females	14	28	30	11	27	110
Total	30	40	44	41	43	198

Values in the total row and total column (shaded) represent *marginal frequencies*. The frequencies for each category represent *joint frequencies*; these are the frequencies in the body of the table.

The marginal frequencies above show a range of 14 for total preferences among the various subjects. The marginal frequencies show the preference for history is quite a bit greater than the preference for math. In addition, the joint frequencies reveal quite a bit of information related to differences in preference between males and females. Females show a much greater preference for science, history, and art than males. Males show a much greater preference for literature than females.

Two-Way Relative Frequency Tables

As with a one-way relative frequency table, a two-way relative frequency table represents the ratios, or proportions, of frequencies of each category to the total frequencies. In the frequency table shown in the previous section, the frequency for each category must be divided by the total of 198. For example, the relative frequency of males who prefer math is equal to $\frac{16}{198}$, or approximately 0.08.

relative
= $\frac{\text{category you want}}{\text{total}}$

The following is a relative frequency table for the two-way table shown in the previous section:

	MATH	SCIENCE	HISTORY	LITERATURE	ART	TOTAL
Males	0.08	0.06	0.07	0.15	0.08	0.44
Females	0.07	0.14	0.15	0.06	0.14	0.56
Total	0.15	0.20	0.22	0.21	0.22	1

The frequencies for each category (shaded) represent *conditional relative frequencies*.

The following are a few statements that may be made using the information in the table:

a) The proportion of males preferring math represents 0.08, or 8%, of the sample.

b) The proportion of males preferring literature is much higher than the proportion of males preferring math.

c) The proportion of females preferring history represents 0.15, or 15%, of the sample and is higher than any other proportion of female preference for a subject.

Notice the total row and column each add up to 1, indicating 100% of the sample.

Calculation of conditional probabilities is covered in Chapter 9.

Review Questions

1. Create a bar graph of nominal data and identify the modal category.

2. Create a one-way frequency table representing categorical data. Then, create a one-way relative frequency table of the same data.

3. Compare marginal and joint frequencies.

4. Create a two-way frequency table. Then, create a two-way relative frequency table of the same data.

5. List the conditional relative frequencies for the information in the following table.

	CAT	DOG	BIRD	FISH	HAMSTER	TOTAL
Males	0.04	0.08	0.20	0.05	0.12	0.49
Females	0.06	0.07	0.19	0.14	0.06	0.51
Total	0.10	0.15	0.39	0.19	0.18	1

Answer Explanations

1. A sample bar graph may appear as follows:

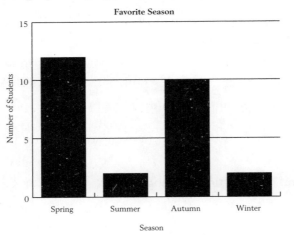

The modal category is "Spring."

2. A one-way frequency table may appear as follows:

CUP COLOR	FREQUENCY
Blue	3
Green	6
Yellow	4
Red	2
Orange	1

A relative frequency table for this data would appear as follows:

CUP COLOR	FREQUENCY
Blue	0.19
Green	0.38
Yellow	0.25
Red	0.13
Orange	0.06

3. In a two-way table, marginal frequencies are the frequencies in the total row and total column. Joint frequencies are the frequencies represented in the body of the table.

4. A two-way frequency table may appear as follows:

	HIKING	SKIING	SWIMMING	BIKING	WALKING	TOTAL
Juniors	8	7	4	14	15	48
Seniors	15	16	11	6	11	59
Total	23	23	15	20	26	107

A relative frequency table for this data would appear as follows:

	HIKING	SKIING	SWIMMING	BIKING	WALKING	TOTAL
Juniors	0.07	0.07	0.04	0.13	0.14	0.45
Seniors	0.14	0.15	0.10	0.06	0.10	0.55
Total	0.21	0.21	0.14	0.19	0.24	1

5. The conditional relative frequencies are 0.04, 0.08, 0.20, 0.05, 0.12, 0.06, 0.07, 0.19, 0.14, and 0.06.

Review Chapter 6:
Data Collection Methods

An *experiment* involves treatments given to one or more groups of participants. A specific intervention(s) is used with specific groups and compared to a *control group*, which is identical in all factors except that it does not receive the intervention. *Non-experimental research* does not involve treatments. There are various types of nonexperimental research. An *observational study* is a type of nonexperimental research in which a group or groups of participants are studied without interference from the researcher. Instead, participants are observed in an effort to describe various aspects, some of which may be predetermined.

Experiments and nonexperiments may involve an entire population—that is, a *census*—or a *sample*. A *survey* is a type of instrument given to either a census or a sample. A survey is typically used with nonexperimental research. However, surveys are sometimes given to participants prior to and/or following an intervention.

Types of Experimental Research

Experiments may be *true* or *quasi-experimental*. In a true experiment, participants are randomly selected for placement in a group. With quasi-experimental research, no random sampling is used. Quasi-experimental research is used when *convenient samples* are the only choice available. For example, when studying groups of students in a school, a researcher may have no choice but to study the classes as they are. It may not be feasible for students to be moved between groups.

Types of Nonexperimental Research

Nonexperimental research involves observation of participants. An observational study is the most commonly used type of nonexperimental research. Other nonexperimental research types include, but are not limited to, *ex post facto studies, surveys, case studies, longitudinal research,* and *historical research.*

Ex post facto studies observe participants but look to past occurrences for possible causes. This type of study is also called a *causal-comparative study.*

Surveys are used to determine the ideas and beliefs of a certain population or sample pertaining to certain topics. Surveys are qualitative in nature, but results from surveys can also be coded quantitatively and examined.

Case studies may involve one or more participants and are commonly less formal than surveys in that the participant may freely discuss his or her ideas without being constrained to a particular set of questions.

Longitudinal research involves the examination and comparison of a group of participants over a long period. For example, a researcher may track the success rate of a group of students throughout middle and high school.

Historical research is descriptive and involves examination of historical documents including interviews, transcriptions, books, articles, and other media.

Census vs. Sample

Data collection may involve an entire population or a sample. Typically, it is more realistic to sample a population. Then the random sample is used to make inferences regarding the population from which it is derived. For a survey, such an approach is called a *sample survey*. If an entire population is used, the survey is called a *census survey*.

Examples of Experimental and Nonexperimental Research

The examples in the following table reveal how research topics may be converted between experimental and nonexperimental research methodologies.

EXPERIMENTAL RESEARCH	NONEXPERIMENTAL RESEARCH
Examine the impact of constructivist teaching approaches on a group of students.	Examine the differences in final exam averages of two different classes.
Introduce a new curriculum to a group of students during the first semester of the final year of high school. Compare how closely the high-school GPAs and SAT scores correlate for the treatment group and a control group.	Examine the correlation between high-school GPAs and SAT scores.
Introduce usage of iPhones into a math classroom. Interview the treatment and control groups of students, regarding their beliefs about the impact of technology in the mathematics classroom.	Simply survey a random group of students, regarding their beliefs about the impact of technology in the mathematics classroom.

Examples of Censuses and Samples

The examples in the following table reveal how research studies may be converted between censuses and samples.

CENSUS	SAMPLE
Survey every member of the House of Representatives.	Survey a random sample of the members of the House of Representatives.
Give a pretest to every student in a classroom.	Give a pretest to a random sample of students in a classroom.
Compare the exam grades of every student in a college statistics course.	Compare the exam grades of every fifth student on a class roster for a college statistics course.
Survey every citizen within a two-mile radius of a voting center.	Survey a random sample of citizens within a two-mile radius of a voting center.

Review Questions

1.   Provide an example of an experimental study.

2.   Provide an example of a nonexperimental study.

3.   Provide an example of using a census and of using a sample in either an experimental or a nonexperimental research study.

4.   Describe a possible *ex post facto* study.

5.   Describe a possible longitudinal research study.

Answer Explanations

1. An example of an experimental study might involve examining the impact of implementing geometry software in the middle school mathematics classroom. Achievement of the group or groups using the

software will be compared to the achievement of a group or groups not using the software.

2. An example of a nonexperimental study might involve a case study in which a citizen of Haiti is interviewed regarding his or her accounts of a recent earthquake.

3. An example of a census would be a pretest given to every doctoral candidate in the teaching department at a university. Conversely, a sample would be a pretest given to a random sample of doctoral candidates in the teaching department at the university.

4. A possible *ex post facto* study might involve studying posttraumatic stress symptoms of a random group of formerly oppressed individuals.

5. A possible longitudinal research study might involve tracking the career successes of a random group of veterans over the course of 10 years.

Review Chapter 7:
Creating Samples and Surveys

Parameters vs. Statistics

A *parameter* is used to describe population values, whereas a *statistic* is used to describe sample values. In other words, data values gathered from an entire population are deemed parameters, and data values gathered from a sample (or samples) are considered statistics. Such values have an impact on the use of hypothesis testing—that is, z-scores are used when the population standard deviation is known, but t-scores are used when only the sample standard deviation is known.

After designing a survey, the researcher must decide whether to send the instrument to an entire population or to a sample. In reality, most surveys are sent to random samples, not entire populations, because of the time and cost involved for a full census.

Types of Random Sampling

Types of random sampling include, but are not limited to, *simple random sampling, stratified random sampling, cluster sampling,* and *systematic sampling.*

Simple random sampling is a technique that allows every member of a population an equal chance of being chosen as a participant. For example, a random number generator may be used to determine inclusion as a participant. Each population member would be assigned a number and chosen if his or her number is selected by the random number generator.

Stratified random sampling is a bit more involved in that a population is first stratified into groups. Then, a random sample is drawn from each stratum. For example, the House of Representatives may be divided into Republicans and Democrats. Next, a random sampling technique may be used to determine, from each group, the participants of the random sample.

Cluster sampling involves random selection of groups of participants, not individuals. For example, clusters of an organization such as Phi Kappa Delta, represented by chapters at various universities throughout the East Coast, may be randomly selected to receive surveys.

Systematic sampling is quite similar to simple random sampling. The difference lies in the fact that every nth person on a list is chosen for participation. For example, a researcher may decide to include every fifteenth citizen on a voting roster for participation in a random sample.

Sampling Bias

Samples may be biased due to a variety of factors. Sampling bias occurs when every member of a population does not have an equal chance of being selected for the sample. *Convenience sampling, nonresponse*, and *volunteerism* are sources of sampling bias. Convenience samples often involve intact groups such as classes of students. Such groups do not represent random samples and may be influenced by external variables. Intact classes of students may be influenced by the particular setting, level of teacher experience, instructional style, and so on. Nonresponse bias occurs when individuals or groups of individuals will not or cannot respond to a given survey. When individuals do not respond, the sample is not entirely representative of the population due to undercoverage of certain groups, demographics, and so on. Volunteerism is a source of sampling bias because individuals may have a certain agenda in responding. The results may be heavily skewed in a certain direction due to the characteristics and beliefs of the participants who come forward. In the case of health study volunteers, the group may have a different overall condition than nonvolunteers. Therefore, the results are not representative of the population as a whole. For example, a particular medicine may show different results for a healthier individual than for a sicker individual, but only healthy individuals may volunteer for the survey.

Survey Bias

A survey itself may also promote bias. Surveys may be designed in such a way that questions prompt participants to respond in a particular manner. In addition, the questions may be ordered so that a trend in answers will result—namely, questions may be probing for a certain response. With such a design, participants are not given the opportunity to respond openly and spontaneously regarding their true feelings or beliefs.

Survey bias also may result when an instrument uses language that is not equally understood by all participants from different demographic backgrounds. In addition, surveys may include questions that are not explicitly clear to the reader. Some surveys may be too long, not allowing adequate time for completing questions at the end.

Each of these survey design facets promotes survey bias.

Design of Effective Surveys

Effective surveys include appropriately ordered questions that are clear and concise. They are composed of questions that do not lead participants or include several components within one question. The language should be simple and direct, and questions should be written such that all individuals from various demographic backgrounds may understand the meaning. In addition, the researcher must decide on an appropriate length of time for completion of the instrument and include a number of questions that may be adequately answered in the estimated time.

In addition, effective surveys should be valid and reliable.

Validity and Reliability

When a survey measures what it purports to measure, it is said to be *valid*. For example, suppose a survey claims to measure politicians' beliefs regarding the current economy. If the survey includes a few questions related to foreign affairs, the degree of validity is decreased. Considering another instrument, suppose a mathematics exam is supposed to cover conditional probability but includes a few questions on surface area. In this case, the exam is less valid because it includes content questions that do not relate to conditional probability.

When survey results are consistent over a specified period, the survey is said to be *reliable*. In other words, if the same survey is given to the same group(s) of participants at different times and the results are consistent (or relatively consistent), the survey is said to be reliable. This type of reliability is known as test-retest. Different methods may be used to determine the degree of reliability.

Reliability is a necessary but insufficient condition for validity. This means that if a measure is valid, then it is reliable; however, it is possible for a measure to be reliable but not valid.

Coding by different researchers may be used to determine *inter-rater reliability*. This type of reliability indicates the degree of agreement between two or more raters. For example, two researchers may each view a number of video segments and assign a code for level of engagement during each segment. The inter-rater reliability would represent the ratio of the same codes used by the second rater to the total number of video segments viewed, or the percentage of agreement between the two researchers.

Reliability coefficients range from 0 to 1, with 0 indicating no reliability and 1 indicating perfect reliability.

The validity of a survey is the prominent concern when designing the survey.

Review Questions

1. Provide examples of two different random sampling techniques.

2. Provide examples of two forms of sampling bias. Explain why the samples will be biased.

3. Briefly describe the context of a survey and give a broad overview of how the survey may be created in the most effective manner. Provide a concrete example of an appropriate question and an inappropriate question.

4. Describe and compare validity and reliability of a survey.

5. A survey reveals inter-rater reliability of 0.9. Explain how this fact may be interpreted by the researcher and/or reader.

Answer Explanations

1. When employing simple random sampling, a researcher may place numbers in a bag, assign each unique number to an individual in the population, and create a sample based on numbers pulled from the bag. With stratified random sampling, a researcher may divide a population into groups—for example, juniors and seniors—and then use a simple random sampling or systematic sampling technique. For example, after dividing the population into the strata of juniors and seniors, the researcher may choose every tenth person on the roster in each group for participation in the sample.

2. Two forms of sampling bias include convenience samples and non-response. Suppose an instructor uses students in his two educational statistics classes to compose two samples for examination of student achievement. The samples represent convenience samples and are biased due to factors directly related to the instructor, his teaching style, the setting, the level of difficulty on exams, and so on. If the same instructor

surveys his students to determine their comfort level with hierarchical linear models and only one-fourth of the students respond, the sample is biased because the students responding may be overly comfortable (or uncomfortable) with the statistical method.

3. Suppose a researcher wants to survey students regarding their feelings about integrating laptop usage in the mathematics classroom. The survey should include direct and concise questions that are not leading in any way. In other words, a survey question should not read, "Don't you believe integration of laptops into the mathematics classroom is beneficial to achievement?" Instead, the question may read, "Do you think integration of laptops into the mathematics classroom is beneficial to achievement? Why or why not?" The questions should use language that is transferrable to all demographics. The questions should be specific and directly related to the overall theme of the survey. In addition, questions should be designed in a way that allows for distinct answers to each question. The survey length should correlate to the intended completion time.

4. Validity of a survey relates to the degree to which the survey measures what it is intended to measure. Reliability of a survey relates to the degree to which a survey yields consistent results. The validity of a survey is the primary concern when designing the instrument. If a survey is valid, it will be reliable. However, if a survey is reliable, it may not be valid.

5. An inter-rater reliability of 0.9 indicates that the rater codings on the whole survey agree 90% of the time. This reliability coefficient indicates a high correlation between ratings, showing reliable codings. In other words, if a researcher provides codes for survey responses according to some interval scale, and another rater reveals agreement 90% of the time, the codes may be deemed reliable.

Review Chapter 8: Planning an Effective Experiment

Types of Randomized Designs

The following sections introduce a few types of randomized designs used in experiments. Among these are completely randomized design and randomized block design. Types of randomized block design include matched-pairs design and repeated-measures design.

Completely Randomized Design

A completely randomized design creates random samples of size n, whereby each treatment is randomly assigned to a sample.

Randomized Block Design

With randomized block designs, the samples are created based on the similarity of the participants. In other words, randomized block designs create homogeneous samples prior to randomly assigning treatment. Randomized block designs include *matched pairs* and *repeated-measures designs*.

A matched-pairs design is one in which participants are grouped by pairs according to some *a priori* factor or factors. As with other randomized block designs, the treatment is then randomly assigned to the groups.

Repeated-measures design uses the same subjects for all aspects of the experiment via inclusion in the control and treatment groups. When the same subjects are examined over a long period, the study is deemed a *longitudinal study*.

Control Group and Treatment Group(s)

A *control group* is the group that does not receive a treatment or intervention or that receives a placebo. A *treatment group* is a group that receives some treatment or intervention. The effects, or outcomes, on the treatment group are then compared to the effects, or outcomes, on the control group.

Data Collection Methods and Analyses

An effective experiment must include proper data collection methods and analyses, whether they are quantitative, qualitative, or mixed.

Decisions regarding data collection methods include randomization approaches and instrument design. A researcher must also decide how to handle nonresponse bias issues.

The design of the instrument should correlate to the type of analyses that will be conducted. For example, if an experiment will be completely qualitative in nature, a survey may consist of mostly open-ended questions. Responses may also be coded and analyzed quantitatively. However, if an experiment will be quantitative, a survey may be designed to consist of only *Likert scale*–type questions, with response options ranging from "strongly disagree" to "strongly agree." A mixed-methods experiment would allow for a combination of open-ended and closed-ended questions.

Qualitative analyses include, but are not limited to, constant comparison, content analysis, and grounded theory. Such analyses focus on trends and patterns evidenced by written or spoken words. In many cases, a researcher will not limit the study with a set of *a priori* research questions. Instead, the researcher will simply look for resulting trends, patterns, and ideas within the discourse. Therefore, qualitative research is more *inductive* in nature.

Quantitative analyses include, but are not limited to, descriptive statistics, *t*-tests, analyses of variance, and linear or multiple regressions. Analyses are conducted on data used to answer a set of predesigned research questions. These questions are often derived after a thorough review of relevant literature. Quantitative research is *deductive* in design.

Descriptive statistics is separate from inferential statistics and includes calculations of measures of center, measures of spread, and measures of position. Inferential statistics includes hypothesis testing using analyses such as *t*-tests, analyses of variance, and regressions. These topics are covered in more detail in Chapters 12 and 14.

Bias

Bias due to sampling methods, nonrandomization, or nonresponse in random sampling may produce biases in data. Recall that sampling bias may stem from convenience sampling, nonresponse, or volunteerism. Also, recall that a survey (or other instrument) may be biased due to its design, lack of reliability, or lack of validity.

Confounding variables are also sources of bias. A *confounding variable* is a variable that is not accounted for in the study. In other words, confounding variables may impact the outcomes of the study but not be included as actual variables in the study. For example, when comparing student achievement in two different classrooms, a researcher may compare only the instructional strategies used. The instructors' years of teaching experience, however, may be a factor in student achievement. Years of teaching experience would be considered a confounding variable, or *covariate*, since the variable covaries with other variables in the study.

In some studies, the researcher may wish to use a technique known as blinding. *Blinding* is a technique used to hide the identity of individuals and/or products, methods, and the like included in a study. Participants' identities may be hidden from the researcher, which reduces the potential for bias in the data. In other studies, only the intervention is hidden from the participants. These techniques help prevent bias.

When blinding techniques are not used, the *placebo effect* may occur. The placebo effect happens when an individual (or individuals) feels that a difference has occurred regardless of whether it actually did. To prevent the placebo effect, a researcher may blind the groups, not allowing participants to know which treatment they have received.

Replications

Sometimes researchers want to replicate another study to compare results from a different sample to results from the original sample. In other cases, a researcher may want to compare results revealed with a somewhat different setting or methodology change. Furthermore, some studies are replicated simply to support the reliability and validity of the study.

Replications may be *strict* or *modified*. In a strict replication, all aspects of the study are replicated to the extent possible. In other words, the same conditions, research questions, and methodology are used. In some cases, however, a researcher wants to make slight or major modifications to an existing study to compare outcomes of the original study to those resulting from the modified study.

Generalizing Results

The ability to generalize results from a sample to the population as a whole is dependent on several factors. The researcher must consider the appropriateness of the sample size, the sampling technique used, the instrument design method used, and the methodology used. For example, if a quasi-experimental approach is used, this may be a limitation to the study, which impacts the ability to generalize the results for the sample to the population. With such an approach, the participants are not randomly assigned to different groups. In addition, the presence of unaccounted-for confounding variables may also impact generalizability.

Other limitations to studies include underrepresentation or overrepresentation, disproportionate sample sizes of groups, and lack of heterogeneity within the sample.

Review Questions

1. Provide an example of a completely randomized design and a randomized block design.

2. Briefly describe an experiment and identify the control and treatment group(s).

3. Briefly describe an experiment that may involve confounding variables. Identify the confounding variables and describe how they may affect the outcome of the study.

4. Describe a specific example of an occurrence of the placebo effect.

5. In general terms, describe the meaning of replication of a study.

Answer Explanations

1. An example of a completely randomized design may be one in which students are randomly selected to participate in three groups via systematic random sampling. In this case, students are not pregrouped according to any specific criteria. An example of a randomized block design might involve grouping students into categories according to textbooks used. Thus, more than one school may be involved. The treatment is then randomly assigned to students within the groups.

2. Suppose a mathematics professor wants to examine the effectiveness of a new software package on student achievement. He may implement the software with one randomly assigned group of students (the treatment group) and compare achievement results to another randomly assigned group that does not use the software (the control group).

3. Suppose a researcher examines the achievement of a group of students using some new technology. Some of the students have used this technology before, but others have not used the technology. The testing mechanism requires an understanding of the tool. The confounding variable is the experience with this tool. Students may have similar understandings of the material but have less experience with the testing mechanism. For example, "clickers" are often used in university classrooms, but some students have little experience with them.

4. Suppose a patient takes a placebo, believes he or she receives a certain helpful drug, and later claims an improvement. The placebo did not cause an improvement, but the patient's thinking did cause an improvement. The patient believed in the drug and, therefore, felt better.

5. When replicating a study, the researcher will either aim to replicate all aspects of the study, including the methodology, or he or she will make minor or major modifications to some or many aspects of the study. The goal is to compare the original results to those revealed with a new sample, setting, modifications, and so on. The goal also may be to verify the validity and reliability of the original study.

Review Chapter 9: Probability

Experimental and Theoretical Probability

Experimental probability is probability that is derived from an experiment and may be represented as the ratio of the number of times an event occurs to the total number of trials, or $P(A) = \dfrac{\text{number of times } A \text{ occurs}}{\text{total number of trials}}$.

Theoretical probability is probability based on theory. Theoretical probability may be represented as the ratio of the number of possible outcomes for an event to the sample space for the event, or $P(A) = \dfrac{\text{number of possible outcomes for } A}{\text{sample space}}$. The size of the sample space is the total number of outcomes.

Law of Large Numbers

The *Law of Large Numbers* states that as the number of trials of an experiment increases, the relative frequency of the experimental probabilities of an event will begin to approximate the theoretical probability of the event. For example, if a student rolls a die 1,000 times, the experimental probability of rolling a three will approximate $\frac{1}{6}$, the theoretical probability of rolling a three. Furthermore, the average of the results from trials will approximate the expected value, which is covered in the next section.

Expected Value

The *expected value* is the average of all possible values that may result from a trial. In other words, it is equal to the sum of the products of each value and the probability of obtaining that value. In the example of the roll of a die, the values rolled may be 1, 2, 3, 4, 5, or 6. The average is written as follows:

$$\frac{1+2+3+4+5+6}{6}$$

The result is 3.5. The expected value may also be written as follows:

$$\left(1 \cdot \frac{1}{6}\right) + \left(2 \cdot \frac{1}{6}\right) + \left(3 \cdot \frac{1}{6}\right) + \left(4 \cdot \frac{1}{6}\right) + \left(5 \cdot \frac{1}{6}\right) + \left(6 \cdot \frac{1}{6}\right)$$

This simplifies to the same expected value of 3.5. The value of 3.5 is the expected value of rolling a die, and it represents the average of the outcomes.

The expected value of spinning a spinner with sections labeled 1 to 8 is 4.5:

$$\left(\frac{1+2+3+4+5+6+7+8}{8}\right)$$

Consider this problem:

On a game show, Samantha will win $100 if she chooses Door #1, $200 if she chooses Door #2, and $300 if she chooses Door #3. What is the average amount of money she can expect to win?

The problem may be solved by writing the following expression:

$$\left(100 \cdot \frac{1}{3}\right) + \left(200 \cdot \frac{1}{3}\right) + \left(300 \cdot \frac{1}{3}\right)$$

The expression simplifies to $\left(\frac{100}{3}\right) + \left(\frac{200}{3}\right) + \left(\frac{300}{3}\right)$ or 200. Therefore, Samantha can expect to win $200.

Suppose, however, that the probabilities are not all the same. Consider the following problem:

The probabilities that Ashley will choose Texas A&M University, Texas Tech University, and Baylor University are 0.23, 0.46, and 0.31, respectively. Suppose the total tuitions for the same four-year program are approximately $54,000, $49,000, and $53,000, respectively. What is the average total tuition Ashley can expect to pay for a four-year program?

The problem can be solved as follows:

$$(54,000 \cdot 0.23) + (49,000 \cdot 0.46) + (53,000 \cdot 0.31) = 51,390$$

Therefore, Ashley can expect to pay $51,390 for a four-year program.

When more than one trial is completed, the expected value is interpreted as the average of the averages. Recall that a sampling distribution mean is the overall mean that results from plotting means of x random samples. As the number of random samples increases to infinity, the sampling distribution mean approaches the population mean. The same idea may be applied here: The expected value is parallel to the population mean.

The expected value for getting a certain outcome after x trials may be calculated using the binomial probability formula. Consider the following problem:

Suppose Adam may pull two cards from a bag containing 21 cards, replacing each card after it is drawn. There are five blue cards, 10 yellow cards, and six green cards. What is the expected value for pulling a yellow card?

In this problem, Adam may pull zero, one, or two cards; these are the number of trials. Thus, he may pull zero yellow cards, one yellow card, or two yellow cards.

The expected value is equal to the sum of the product of the x and $P(x)$-values calculated below. Each x-value represents the possible number of times a yellow card may be drawn: 0, 1, or 2.

The binomial formula (discussed again later) can be used to compute the following probabilities:

$$P(0) = \binom{2}{0}\left(\frac{10}{21}\right)^0\left(\frac{11}{21}\right)^2$$

$$P(1) = \binom{2}{1}\left(\frac{10}{21}\right)^1\left(\frac{11}{21}\right)^1$$

$$P(2) = \binom{2}{2}\left(\frac{10}{21}\right)^2\left(\frac{11}{21}\right)^0$$

The expected value may now be written as follows:

$$\left(0 \cdot \frac{121}{441}\right) + \left(1 \cdot \frac{220}{441}\right) + \left(2 \cdot \frac{100}{441}\right)$$

The result is approximately 0.95.

Simple Probability

A simple probability involves one event. The following are examples of simple probability questions:

1. What is the probability that Enrique rolls a four on a die?

2. What is the probability that Kevin draws a blue marble from a bag containing four red marbles, three blue marbles, and five yellow marbles?

3. What is the probability that Hannah gets heads on a coin flip?

4. What is the probability that Li draws a spade from a deck of cards?

    Each probability is theoretical in nature and may be written as follows:

$$P(A) = \frac{\text{number of possible outcomes for } A}{\text{sample space}}$$

The solutions (and explanations) for the four preceding questions are as follows:

1. $\frac{1}{6}$

There is only one way Enrique can get a four, but there are six outcomes in the sample space.

2. $\frac{1}{4}$

There are three blue marbles (or possible outcomes for A), but there are 12 outcomes in the sample space: $\frac{3}{12}$ reduces to $\frac{1}{4}$.

3. $\frac{1}{2}$

There is only one head on a coin, but there are two outcomes in the sample space.

4. $\dfrac{1}{4}$

There are 13 spades in a deck of 52 cards: $\dfrac{13}{52}$ reduces to $\dfrac{1}{4}$.

Compound Probability

A compound probability is the probability of two or more events.

Probability of A or B

When considering the *union* of events A and B, written as $P(A$ or $B)$ or $P(A \cup B)$, one must decide whether the events are *overlapping* or *disjoint* (*mutually exclusive*).

If events A and B are overlapping, then $P(A$ or $B) = P(A) + P(B) - P(A$ and $B)$.

If events A and B are disjoint (not overlapping), then $P(A$ or $B) = P(A) + P(B)$.

The following are some specific examples:

Aaron rolls a die and flips a coin. What is the probability that he rolls a 3 or gets heads?

Notice that the events are disjoint. The problem may be solved as follows:

$$P(3 \text{ or heads}) = \frac{1}{6} + \frac{1}{2} = \frac{2}{3}$$

Now, consider this problem:

Marcus rolls a die. What is the probability he rolls a number less than 3 or an odd number?

These events are overlapping. The problem may be solved as follows:

$$P(\text{less than 3 or odd}) = \frac{2}{6} + \frac{3}{6} - \frac{1}{6} = \frac{4}{6} = \frac{2}{3}$$

Notice that the probability of the intersection of the two events was *subtracted* from the sum of the individual probabilities.

Probability of A and B

When discussing the *intersection* of events A and B, written as $P(A$ and $B)$ or $P(A \cap B)$, one must consider whether the events are *independent* or *dependent*.

If events A and B are independent, then $P(A$ and $B) = P(A) \cdot P(B)$.

If events A and B are dependent, then $P(A$ and $B) = P(A) \cdot P(B|A)$.

The following are some specific examples:

Jackson rolls a die and flips a coin. What is the probability that he rolls a two and gets tails?

The events are independent, so the following equation may be written:

$$P(2 \text{ and tails}) = \frac{1}{6} \cdot \frac{1}{2} = \frac{1}{12}$$

Now, consider this problem:

A bag contains 12 red marbles, three blue marbles, and five green marbles. What is the probability that Arlene draws a blue marble, replaces it, and draws another blue marble?

Since the first marble is replaced, the events are independent. The problem may be solved as follows:

$$P(\text{blue and blue}) = \frac{3}{20} \cdot \frac{3}{20} = \frac{9}{400}$$

Now, suppose the problem is altered to read as follows:

A bag contains 12 red marbles, three blue marbles, and five green marbles. What is the probability that Arlene draws a blue marble, replaces it, and draws a green marble?

The events are still independent, and the problem may be solved as follows:

$$P(\text{blue and green}) = \frac{3}{20} \cdot \frac{5}{20} = \frac{3}{80}$$

Now, suppose the problem is altered once more to read as follows:

A bag contains 12 red marbles, three blue marbles, and five green marbles. What is the probability that Arlene draws a blue marble, does not replace it, and draws another blue marble?

Since the first marble is not replaced, the events are dependent. The problem may be solved as follows:

$$P(\text{blue and blue}) = \frac{3}{20} \cdot \frac{2}{19} = \frac{3}{190}$$

Notice that the possible number of blue marbles for the second draw has decreased by one. Also, notice that size of the sample space for the second draw has decreased by one.

Finally, suppose the second draw involves the probability of another colored marble. The problem may be rewritten as follows:

A bag contains 12 red marbles, three blue marbles, and five green marbles. What is the probability that Arlene draws a blue marble, does not replace it, and draws a green marble?

In this case, the sample space of the second draw will decrease by one. However, the total number of possible outcomes for the second event will not decrease. The problem may be written as follows:

$$P(\text{blue and green}) = \frac{3}{20} \cdot \frac{5}{19} = \frac{15}{380}$$

x	f(x)
0	$\dfrac{\binom{10}{0}\binom{11}{2}}{\binom{21}{2}} = \dfrac{55}{210}$
1	$\dfrac{\binom{10}{1}\binom{11}{1}}{\binom{21}{2}} = \dfrac{110}{210}$
2	$\dfrac{\binom{10}{2}\binom{11}{0}}{\binom{21}{2}} = \dfrac{45}{210}$

Conditional Probability

Conditional probability is the probability that one event will occur given that the other event has occurred. This may be written as $P(A|B)$ or $P(B|A)$, either of which is read as "the probability of A, given B" and "the probability of B, given A," respectively.

Conditional probability is often examined using two-way frequency tables. Consider the two-way table that follows:

	FRESHMAN	SOPHOMORE	JUNIOR	SENIOR	TOTAL
Male	57	50	50	57	218
Female	53	32	60	41	186
Total	110	82	114	98	404

What is the probability that a student is a male or a sophomore?

The formula to solve this probability may be written as follows:

$$P(M \text{ or } S) = P(M) + P(S) - P(M \text{ and } S)$$

Substituting the probabilities yields the following result:

$$P(M \text{ or } S) = \frac{218}{404} + \frac{82}{404} - \frac{50}{404} = \frac{250}{404}$$

The probability that a student is a male and a sophomore may be solved as follows:

$$P(M \text{ and } S) = P(M) \cdot P(S|M)$$

$$P(M \text{ and } S) = \frac{218}{404} \cdot \frac{50}{218}$$

$$P(M \text{ and } S) = \frac{50}{404}$$

This is an important connection to make. Refer back to the section titled "Probability of A and B" for a review of this formula used with dependent events.

Now, suppose we are given the following conditional probability problem:

The probability of event A is 0.28, the probability of event B is 0.56, and the probability of event B, given A is 0.18. What is the probability of A or B?

This may be written as follows:

$$P(A \text{ or } B) = P(A) + P(B) - P(A \text{ and } B),$$
$$\text{where } P(A \text{ and } B) = P(A) \cdot P(B|A)$$

Therefore, the problem may be solved as follows:

$$P(A \text{ or } B) = 0.28 + 0.56 - (0.28 \cdot 0.18)$$
$$P(A \text{ or } B) = 0.7896$$

Using the Binomial Distribution

As we briefly discussed in the earlier section on expected value, the binomial distribution can be used to calculate probabilities.

The formula for the probability of x successes using a binomial distribution is $P(x) = \binom{n}{x}\pi^x(1 - \pi)^{n-x}$, where x represents the number of successes, n represents the number of trials, and ϖ represents the probability of each success.

Consider the following problem:

Ben rolls a die eight times. What is the probability that he gets exactly two sixes?

In this problem, eight represents the number of trials, two represents the number of successes, and $\frac{1}{6}$ represents the probability of success.

Substituting these values into the formula results in the following:

$$P(x) = \binom{8}{2}\left(\frac{1}{6}\right)^2\left(1 - \frac{1}{6}\right)^{8-2}$$
$$P(x) \approx 0.26$$

The binomial probability distribution function of a graphing calculator may also be used to find the probability. Choose 2VARS and then BINOMPDF. Then, enter the values of n, ϖ, and x after the open parenthesis. For this case, enter 8, $\frac{1}{6}$, 2, after the open parenthesis. The result is approximately 0.26.

The following should be entered: $\text{BINOMPDF}\left(8,\left(\frac{1}{6}\right),2\right)$.

To calculate probabilities of "at least" x successes, compute the sums of the probabilities.

For example, suppose you want to know the probability that Ben rolls *at least* five sixes. In this case, you are not looking for an exact number of rolls. You would write the following:

$$P(\text{at least 5 sixes}) = P(x = 5) + P(x = 6) + P(x = 7) + P(x = 8)$$

Each probability may be calculated manually, as previously shown, or you may use the BINOMPDF function of a graphing calculator.

Using a calculator, enter the following:

$\text{BINOMPDF}\left(8,\left(\frac{1}{6}\right),5\right)$ + $\text{BINOMPDF}\left(8,\left(\frac{1}{6}\right),6\right)$ + $\text{BINOMPDF}\left(8,\left(\frac{1}{6}\right),7\right)$ + $\text{BINOMPDF}\left(8,\left(\frac{1}{6}\right),8\right)$

Therefore, $P(\text{at least 5 sixes}) \approx 0.005$.

When calculating the probability of an x that is less than, less than or equal to, greater than, or greater than or equal to a certain value, use a cumulative distribution function. Likewise, if determining the probability of an interval of values, use a cumulative distribution function.

For example, suppose you want to know the probability that Ben will get a number that is less than four when rolling a die eight times. To calculate $P(x < 4) = P(0) + P(1) + P(2) + P(3)$, we can either use the binomial formula for each term or speed up the calculation using a calculator's binomial cumulative distribution function.

The problem may be entered as $\text{BINOMCDF}\left(8,\left(\frac{1}{6}\right),3\right)$, which is approximately 0.97.

Probability distribution functions, including the binomial and normal distributions, and cumulative distribution functions are used in many more contexts. This chapter has not presented all of them. There are different cumulative distribution functional equations for different intervals of data.

Review Questions

1. Provide an example of an experimental and a theoretical probability.

2. Suppose Cara may win any dollar amount from \$1 to \$10, with each amount equally likely. What is the average dollar amount she can expect to win?

3. Jacob rolls a die and flips a coin. What is the probability that he rolls a number less than three or gets tails?

4. What is the probability that Ron draws a spade from a deck of 52 cards, does not replace the card, and then draws another spade?

5. There is a 2% probability that a software CD will be defective. What is the probability that at least two of five randomly selected CDs will be defective?

Answer Explanations

1. For an example of experimental probability, suppose you get three heads after 10 tosses of a coin. This experimental probability is $\frac{3}{10}$. The theoretical probability of drawing a winning card out of a bag of 100 cards is $\frac{1}{100}$.

2. The expected value may be calculated as follows:

$$\left(1 \cdot \frac{1}{10}\right) + \left(2 \cdot \frac{1}{10}\right) + \left(3 \cdot \frac{1}{10}\right) + \left(4 \cdot \frac{1}{10}\right) + \left(5 \cdot \frac{1}{10}\right) +$$
$$\left(6 \cdot \frac{1}{10}\right) + \left(7 \cdot \frac{1}{10}\right) + \left(8 \cdot \frac{1}{10}\right) + \left(9 \cdot \frac{1}{10}\right) + \left(10 \cdot \frac{1}{10}\right)$$

Therefore, the expected value is 5.5. She can expect to win \$5.50.

3. These are independent events; therefore, the probability may be written as follows:

$$P(\text{less than 3 or tails}) = \frac{2}{6} + \frac{1}{2} = \frac{5}{6}$$

4. In this case, the events are not independent, so we use the conditional probability formula $P(A \text{ and } B) = P(A) \cdot P(B|A)$. Thus, the probability may be written as follows:

$$P(\text{spade and spade}) = \frac{13}{52} \cdot \frac{12}{51} = \frac{1}{17}$$

5. The probability may be calculated as follows:

BINOMPDF(5, 0.02, 2) + BINOMPDF(5, 0.02, 3) + BINOMPDF(5, 0.02, 4) + BINOMPDF(5, 0.02, 5) ≈ 0.004. The probability may also be calculated by writing $1 -$ BINOMCDF(5, 0.02, 1).

Review Chapter 10: Independent Events and Random Variables

C hapter 9 introduced the topic of independent events. In this chapter, we will cover independence in more depth.

Independence of Events

Consider the following conditions for independence (and dependence):

Events A and B are *independent* if the following statements are true:

$$P(A|B) = P(A)$$
$$P(B|A) = P(B)$$

It follows that events A and B are *dependent* if the statements that follow are true:

$$P(A|B) \neq P(A)$$
$$P(B|A) \neq P(B)$$

The probability of two independent events, A and B, both occurring may be written as follows:

$$P(A \text{ and } B) = P(A) \cdot P(B)$$

The probability of two dependent events, A and B, both occurring may be written as follows:

$$P(A \text{ and } B) = P(A) \cdot P(B|A) \text{ and } P(A \text{ and } B) = P(B) \cdot P(A|B)$$

Examples of Independence

The following are independent events:

- drawing a spade from a standard deck of cards, replacing it, and drawing another spade
- drawing a spade, replacing it, and drawing an ace
- drawing a blue marble from a bag of marbles, replacing it, and drawing a green marble

Consider the following problem:

What is the probability that Tyler draws a club from a standard deck of cards, replaces it, and then draws another club?

In this problem, the first draw represents event A, and the second draw represents event B.

The compound probability may be written as:

$$P(A \text{ and } B) = P(A) \cdot P(B)$$
$$P(A \text{ and } B) = \frac{13}{52} \cdot \frac{13}{52}$$

Notice that the number of possible clubs does *not* decrease for the second draw. Also, the sample space does *not* decrease for the second draw. In other words, the probability of the second draw (event B) given that the first draw (event A) has occurred is equal to the probability of the second draw: $\left(\frac{13}{52} = \frac{13}{52}\right)$.

Examples of Dependence

The following are dependent events:

- drawing a spade from a deck of cards, not replacing it, and drawing another spade
- drawing a spade, not replacing it, and drawing an ace
- drawing a blue marble from a bag, not replacing it, and drawing a green marble

Consider the following problem:

What is the probability that Tyler draws a club, does not replace it, and then draws another club?

The first draw represents event A, and the second draw represents event B.

The compound probability may be written as:

$$P(A \text{ and } B) = P(A) \cdot P(B|A)$$
$$P(A \text{ and } B) = \frac{13}{52} \cdot \frac{12}{51}$$

Notice that the number of possible clubs decreased for the second draw. Also, the sample space decreased for the second draw. In other words, the probability of the second draw (event B) given that the first draw (event A) has occurred is *not* equal to the probability of the second draw $\left(\frac{12}{51} \neq \frac{13}{52} \right)$.

Means of Sums and Differences of Independent Random Variables

A *random variable* is a numerical measure of a random phenomenon. For example, random variable A might be the height of a randomly selected person, and random variable B might be the number of times George selects a yellow card after selecting two cards from a bag.

Given random variables A and B, the population mean sum may be written as $\mu_{a+b} = \mu_a + \mu_b$. In other words, the two means can be added to reveal the mean of the sum.

Given random variables A and B, the population mean difference may be written as $\mu_{a-b} = \mu_a - \mu_b$. The mean of the difference is equal to the value given by one population mean subtracted from the other population mean.

As the number of sample means increases to infinity, the expected value approaches the population mean. Therefore, the expected value may be used to represent the means of random variables. The following formulas, in which E represents the expected value of the random variables, may be stated:

$$E(A + B) = E(A) + E(B)$$
$$E(A - B) = E(A) - E(B)$$

Examples

On a game show, Mara will win $20 if she opens Door #1 but lose $10 if she opens Door #2. The sum of her winnings is $10.

The expected value of rolling a die is 3.5. The expected value of spinning a spinner with eight sections labeled 1 to 8 is 4.5. The expected value of the sum of the two random variables is equal to the sum of the expected value of rolling a die and the expected value of spinning a spinner. Therefore, the expected value of the sum of the two events is 3.5 + 4.5 = 8.

The table below may be used to calculate expected values of the variables x and y, both of which can take on the values 1 or 2. We can also calculate the sum and differences of the expected values (means):

	1	2
1	0.3	0.25
2	0.2	0.25

The expected values may be calculated as follows:

$$E(x) = 1 \cdot (0.3 + 0.25) + 2 \cdot (0.2 + 0.25)$$
$$E(x) = 0.55 + 0.9$$
$$E(x) = 1.45$$

$$E(y) = 1 \cdot (0.3 + 0.2) + 2 \cdot (0.25 + 0.25)$$
$$E(y) = 0.5 + 1$$
$$E(y) = 1.5$$

The sum may be written as follows:

$$E(x + y) = E(x) + E(y)$$
$$E(x + y) = 1.45 + 1.5$$
$$E(x + y) = 2.95$$

The differences may be written as follows:

$$E(x - y) = E(x) - E(y)$$
$$E(x - y) = 1.45 - 1.5$$
$$E(x - y) = -0.05$$

and

$$E(y - x) = E(y) - E(x)$$
$$E(y - x) = 1.5 - 1.45$$
$$E(y - x) = 0.05$$

Variance of Sums and Differences of Independent Random Variables

The independence of two random variables is established the same way it is for events: random variables A and B are independent if $P(A$ and $B) = P(A) \cdot P(B)$.

For independent random variables A and B, it is possible to equate the variance of the sum and the variance of the difference as follows:

$$\text{Variance}(A + B) = \text{Variance}(A - B) =$$
$$\text{Variance}(A) + \text{Variance}(B)$$

In other words, for independent random variables A and B, the variance of the sum of A and B is equal to the variance of the difference between A and B, both of which are equal to the sum of the variances of A and B.

Examples

Consider the problem below:

The variance of the sum of A and B equals 0.82. What is the variance of the difference?

Solution: 0.82000

Now, consider this problem:

The variance of A equals 0.63. The variance of B equals 0.28. What is the variance of the sum of A and B? What is the variance of the difference between A and B?

Solution: 0.91; 0.91

Finally, consider this problem:

The variance of the difference between A and B equals 0.21. What is the variance of the sum of A and B?

Solution: 0.21

Review Questions

1. Provide an example of independent events and of dependent events.

2. Provide a problem that includes independent events. Show the calculation used to find the probability of A and B. Explain why the events are independent.

3. Provide a problem that includes dependent events. Show the calculation used to find the probability of A and B. Explain why the events are dependent.

4. Consider the following table, which gives the probabilities that the variables x and y take on the values 5 or 6:

	5	6
5	.3	.4
6	.1	.2

Based on the table, what is $E(x + y)$?

5. The variance of A is 0.30. The variance of B is 0.15. If A and B are independent random variables, what is the variance of the difference between A and B?

Answer Explanations

1. An example of independent events involves drawing a card marked 5 from a bag, replacing it, and drawing another card. An example of dependent events involves drawing the same card, not replacing it, and drawing another card.

2. What is the probability that Estelle draws an ace from a full deck of cards, replaces it, and then draws a heart? The probability may be written as follows:

$$P(A \text{ and } B) = P(A) \cdot P(B)$$
$$P(A \text{ and } B) = \frac{4}{52} \cdot \frac{13}{52}$$

The events are independent because the probability of the second draw (event B) given that the first draw (event A) has occurred is equal to the probability of the second draw. The probability of the second draw is unchanged by the first draw.

3. What is the probability that Sharon draws an ace from a full deck of cards, does not replace it, and then draws another ace? The probability may be written as:

$$P(A \text{ and } B) = P(A) \cdot P(B|A)$$
$$P(A \text{ and } B) = \frac{4}{52} \cdot \frac{3}{51}$$

The events are dependent because the sample space decreases in the second draw. In other words, the first draw impacts the second draw. The probability of the second draw (event B) given that the first draw (event A) has occurred is not equal to the probability of the second draw: $\left(\frac{3}{51} \neq \frac{4}{52}\right)$.

4. The expected value sum may be calculated as follows:

$$E(x) = 5 \cdot (0.3 + 0.4) + 6 \cdot (0.1 + 0.2)$$
$$E(x) = 3.5 + 1.8$$
$$E(x) = 5.3$$

$$E(y) = 5 \cdot (0.3 + 0.1) + 6 \cdot (0.4 + 0.2)$$
$$E(y) = 2 + 3.6$$
$$E(y) = 5.6$$

Therefore,

$$E(x + y) = E(x) + E(y)$$
$$E(x + y) = 5.3 + 5.6$$
$$E(x + y) = 10.9.$$

5. The variance of the difference is equal to the sum of the two variances, or 0.45.

Review Chapter 11:
The Normal Distribution

Underlying Concepts

A *normal distribution* of data is one in which the frequencies of values increase and decrease at the same rate. The following histogram represents a normal distribution. Notice the normal distribution is bell-shaped and symmetric.

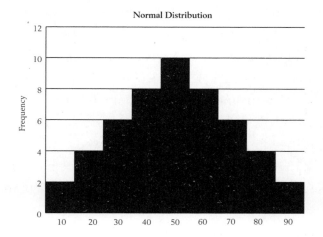

In general, a normal distribution does *not* have a certain mean or standard deviation. A *standard* normal distribution (covered further in the last section of this chapter) does have a particular mean and standard deviation.

In the previous histogram, the data has a mean of 50 and a standard deviation of 10. Recall that standard deviation represents the deviation of the scores from the mean.

With normally distributed data, 68% of the values fall within ±1 standard deviation of the mean; 95% of the values fall within ±2 standard deviations of the mean; and 99.7% of values fall within ±3 standard deviations of the mean.

Therefore, in the preceding histogram, 68% of the values fall between 40 and 60; 95% of the values fall between 30 and 70; and 99.7% of the values fall between 20 and 80.

Notice that normally distributed data does *not* include extreme values, or *outliers*, which may skew the data. Also, notice that 0.15% of the values fall below 20 and 0.15% of the values fall above 80.

Measures of Central Tendency

With normally distributed data, the mean, median, and mode all occur at the same value.

Consider the histogram shown earlier. The mode is represented by the highest bar and, therefore, is 50. The mean is also 50. The median is the middle value of the data set, which is shown to be in ascending order. This value is again 50. These values may be checked by entering the values into a list in a graphing calculator according to their frequencies and computing the measures of central tendency.

With nonnormally distributed data, the measures of central tendency do not fall at the same point. Recall that skewed data results in a mean that is pulled toward the extreme values. Thus, the mean may be more than or less than the median, depending on the direction of the skewness.

Sampling Distribution

A *sampling distribution* of means and proportions may be created by drawing n samples and plotting their means and proportions. In other words, a sampling distribution of a mean is the distribution of the means of n random samples. For example, if 100 random samples are drawn from a population, and each mean determined and plotted, the resulting distribution is known as the sampling distribution of the mean. The mean of the sampling distribution may be used to approximate the mean of the parent population, μ. The *Central Limit Theorem* states that for any distribution with mean μ and standard deviation σ, the sampling distribution approaches a normal distribution with mean μ and standard deviation $\frac{\sigma}{\sqrt{n}}$. With an increase in the sample size, n, the sampling distribution will more closely approximate a normal distribution. The usefulness of this theorem is that the sampling distribution approaches a normal distribution even if the original population distribution is not normal.

A sampling distribution of proportions involves the plotting of certain proportions from each sample. For example, a researcher may examine the proportion of participants who are Democrats. Within each random sample, the proportion of participants who are Democrats may be determined and plotted. As the number of random samples increases, the distribution of the proportions in the sampling distribution will approach a normal distribution with a mean proportion that approximates the population proportion.

Standard Normal Distribution

A *standard normal distribution* is composed of standardized scores with a mean of 0 and a standard deviation of 1. A standard normal distribution is a distribution of standardized scores (z-scores), as opposed to raw scores. Such a distribution allows one to find the area under a normal distribution curve using a normal distribution, or z-table.

A z-score is the standardized score that compares the ratio of the difference of the observed value from the mean to the population standard deviation. A z-score also represents the number of standard deviations a value is above or below the mean. This score can be used to determine the area under the normal distribution curve that is a certain number of standard deviations above or below the mean.

A z-score is represented as $z = \dfrac{X - \mu}{\sigma}$.

Suppose we want to compare a value of 82 to a population with a mean of 88 and a standard deviation of 2. A z-score can be calculated by writing $\dfrac{82 - 88}{2}$, which equals −3. The z-score reveals that a value of 82 is 3 standard deviations below the mean of 88.

This z-score may also be used to determine the area under the curve that is 3 standard deviations below the mean. Using the normal distribution, or z-table, locate the z-value of 3 (the absolute value of all z-scores is used). The column titled "Mean to z" represents the area under the curve from the mean to the z-score. Thus, 0.4987, or 49.87% of the area under the curve, is 3 standard deviations below the mean. Stated another way, 49.87% of the scores fall between 82 and 88.

In this case, the column titled "Larger Portion" represents the area above the z-score of −3. This area is 0.9987, or 99.87%. The column titled "Smaller Portion" represents the area below the z-score of −3. This area is 0.0013, or 0.13%.

Thus, we can state the following:

- The area under the curve between the mean and the value that is 3 standard deviations below the mean is 49.87%.

- The area under the curve above the value that marks 3 standard deviations below the mean is 99.87% (larger portion).

- The area under the curve that is less than the value that marks 3 standard deviations below the mean is 0.13% (smaller portion)

- The area under the curve above the mean is 50%.

In summary, 49.87% of scores fall between 82 and 88, 0.13% of scores fall below 82, and 99.87% of scores fall above 82. Note: Sometimes it is helpful to draw a normal curve and label the standard deviation and mean.

The "Smaller Portion" column will be helpful when completing hypothesis testing, which will be covered in Chapter 12.

Review Questions

1. In a general sense, describe how a normal distribution compares to a nonnormal distribution.

2. Provide the values for the mean, median, and mode of a sample data set that is normally distributed.

3. Explain how the mean of a sampling distribution relates to the mean of a population.

4. Compare and contrast a normal distribution and a standard normal distribution.

5. Fred scores 92 on his physics exam. The class average is 80, with a standard deviation of 6. What percentage of the class scored below Fred's score? What percentage of the class scored between 80 and 92?

Answer Explanations

1. A normal distribution represents data that increase and decrease in frequency at the same rate. The distribution is bell-shaped and symmetric. A nonnormal distribution does not include the same rate of increase/decrease with regards to frequency. Likewise, the distribution is skewed to some degree.

2. A normally distributed data set may have mean, median, and mode values of 75 each.

3. The mean of a sampling distribution is used to represent the population mean. As the size of the random sample increases, the mean of the sampling distribution more closely approximates the population mean, μ.

4. A normal distribution and a standard normal distribution both show the same rate of increase and decrease in frequency while adhering to a bell-shaped curve and symmetric properties. However, a normal distribution may take on various values for the mean and standard deviation, while a standard normal distribution has a set mean of 0 and a standard deviation of 1.

5. The z-score is $\dfrac{(92 - 80)}{6} = 2$. From the z-table, 97.72% of test scores fall below $z = 2$; therefore, 47.72% (that is, 0.9772 − 0.5) scored between 80 and 92.

Review Chapter 12: Hypothesis Testing

Basic Concepts

The following is a list of basic concepts that must be understood to complete hypothesis testing:

- *p*-values
- level of significance
- critical value
- degrees of freedom
- null and alternative hypotheses
- directional and nondirectional hypotheses
- margin of error
- Type I and II errors

This chapter presents a brief overview of each of these important topics. Let's begin with a look at null and alternative hypotheses.

A *null hypothesis*, or the hypothesis of no difference, states that no difference exists between the score and the population mean or between two means. The null hypothesis may be represented as H_0. The *alternative hypothesis* (H_A) is the hypothesis that states that there is a difference. This difference may be *directional*, with the direction either above or below the mean.

The following is an example of a null hypothesis and an example of an alternative hypothesis:

[handwritten: P low / reject null / high = fail to reject / P]

H_0 = no difference exists between the group taught by constructivist methods and the group taught by traditional methods

H_A = there is a difference between the two groups

When the direction of the hypothesis is declared, a one-tailed test is used. When the researcher does not have a prediction as to the direction of the outcome, a two-tailed test should be used. In most instances, a two-tailed test is used.

Consider the following: If a company claims a certain number of ounces of a product per bottle and the researcher assumes the ounces in a random sample will not be more than the claimed amount, he or she may decide to use a one-directional test.

A *p-value* is the probability of rejecting the null hypothesis. This value is compared to the *level of significance*, denoted by α, determined by the researcher. Often, the value of $\alpha = 0.05$ is used as the level of significance. The *p*-value must be less than or equal to the level of significance to reject the null hypothesis. For example, if the researcher determines the level of significance to be 0.05 and the resulting *p*-value is 0.07, then the researcher must fail to reject the null hypothesis.

Type I and II errors are often confused; however, the concepts are fairly straightforward. A *Type I error* is an error resulting from the rejection of a null hypothesis when it should not be rejected. In other words, a researcher may declare a statistically significant difference when, in fact, there isn't one. Conversely, a *Type II error* is an error resulting from the failure to reject a null hypothesis. In other words, a researcher may fail to declare a statistically significant difference when, in fact, there is a statistically significant difference.

REALITY ABOUT H_0	DECISION	
	DO NOT REJECT H_0	REJECT H_0
H_0 True	Correct Decision	Type I Error
H_0 False	Type II Error	Correct Decision

Type I and II errors may result from the level of significance determined by the researcher. For example, if the level of significance is
decided to be 0.01, a Type II error may occur. The level of significance
may be too small and may not capture the values falling between probabilities of 0.05 and 0.01. If the level of significance is decided to be 0.1,
a Type I error may occur. Often, a researcher has a very good reason for
setting a level of significance this low or high. He or she needs to make
a case to support the decision, since it may result in one of these errors.
Thus, 0.05 is often used as a preferred level of significance.

The *degrees of freedom* are equal to the sample size minus 1. Degrees
of freedom will be used when locating critical t-values on a t-table.

The *margin of error* represents the estimated difference between the
sample mean and the population mean. The margin of error may also be
used to calculate confidence intervals. This topic will be covered in the
next chapter.

The margin of error may be calculated using the following formula:

$$E = z_{\frac{\alpha}{2}} \cdot \frac{\sigma}{\sqrt{n}}$$

In this formula, E represents the margin of error, σ represents the
population standard deviation, and n represents the sample size. The
critical value $z_{\frac{\alpha}{2}}$ is the z-value that corresponds to a tail proportion of $\frac{\alpha}{2}$
in the standard normal distribution, where α is the level of significance
and $1 - \alpha$ is the level of confidence.

Consider the following:

A sample of size 50 has a mean of 145 and a standard deviation of 15.
Using a 95% level of confidence, we can compute the margin of error.
Since the sample size is fairly large, the sample standard deviation can be
used in place of the population standard deviation.

$$E = 1.96 \cdot \frac{15}{\sqrt{50}}$$

The margin of error is approximately 4.16.

The critical z-value of 1.96 is determined by subtracting the area of
0.025 from 0.5. (With a 95% level of confidence, 5% of the scores are
divided equally between the two tails: $0.05 \div 2 = 0.025$.) The z-score

corresponding to an area of 0.025 in the left tail may be located in a standard z-table. The corresponding z represents the critical z-value. This value is 1.96. (Find where the row labeled –1.9 and the column labeled .06 meet.)

Other common critical values are $z = 1.645$ for a 90% level of confidence, and $z = 2.575$ for a 99% level of confidence.

T-Distribution or Z-Distribution

A t-distribution is used when the population standard deviation is not known. A z-distribution is used when the population standard deviation is known.

Comparing Individual Scores to Population Mean

Consider the following problem:

> Mara scores a 75 on her statistics exam. The class average is 80, with a standard deviation of 2. Considering a level of significance of 0.05, is there a statistically significant difference between her score and the class average? Explain.

In this case, since the class represents the population, a z-test may be used. The following formula may be used to compare the individual score to the population mean:

$$z = \frac{X - \mu}{\sigma}$$

Here, X represents the individual score, μ represents the population mean, and σ represents the population standard deviation.

Substituting 75 for X, 80 for μ, and 2 for σ results in the following:

$$z = \frac{75 - 80}{2}$$
$$z = 2.5$$

Therefore, Mara's score is 2.5 standard deviations below the mean of

80. The absolute value of this z-score can be located in a z-table to determine the area between the mean and the score. This value should be subtracted from 0.5 to determine the area to the left of the z-score. This probability is equal to $0.5 - 0.4938$, which is 0.0062. In a z-table that includes the "Smaller Portion," the value located in the "Smaller Portion" column will also represent the probability. When using a table that gives the area to the left of z, $z = -2.5$ yields a value of 0.0062 directly.

Since the p-value of 0.0062 is less than 0.05, there is a statistically significant difference between her score and the class average. The null hypothesis of no difference may then be rejected.

Comparing Sample Mean to Population Mean (One-Sample Test)

Now, suppose we want to compare a sample mean to a population mean when we know only the sample standard deviation. In this case, we will use a one-sample t-test.

Consider the following problem:

A random sample of 30 branches of a company reveals an average of 55 products sold per day, with a standard deviation of four products. The company's headquarters reports an average of 60 products sold per day. Considering a 0.05 level of significance, is the average number of products sold by one branch significantly different from the average number of products reported by the headquarters? Explain.

The following formula may be used:

$$t = \frac{\overline{X} - \mu}{\left(\frac{s}{\sqrt{n}}\right)}$$

Therefore, the t-value may be calculated by writing the following:

$$t = \frac{55 - 60}{\left(\frac{4}{\sqrt{30}}\right)}$$

$$t \approx -6.8$$

The number of degrees of freedom is equal to 29. The critical t-value for a one-tailed test, with a level of significance (α) of 0.05, is 1.699. Since the calculated t-value has an absolute value that is more than the critical t-value, there is a statistically significant difference between the averages. The null hypothesis should be rejected.

Now, suppose we tweak the problem to set the sample standard deviation as the population standard deviation. Doing so will allow us to use a z-distribution with the following formula:

$$z = \frac{\overline{X} - \mu}{\left(\frac{\sigma}{\sqrt{n}}\right)}$$

The z-value will be the same value of -6.8. However, we may locate this value using a standard z-table. Anything lower than $z = -3.49$ is reported as having an area below the z-score as 0.0001. Thus, we can again declare statistical significance between the averages.

You could calculate these tests using a graphing calculator. For both tests, choose STAT and then CALC. For the one-sample t-test, choose T-TEST and enter the population mean, sample mean, sample standard deviation, and sample size. For the one-sample z-test, choose Z-TEST and enter the population mean, population standard deviation, sample mean, and sample size. A hypothesis that is nondirectional will work, since you will not know beforehand whether the sample will or will not report a mean higher or lower than the mean for the headquarters.

Comparing Two Sample Means

As with one-sample tests, when the population standard deviation is not known, a t-distribution should be used. When the population standard deviation is known, a z-distribution should be used.

When comparing two sample means, you need the pooled variance. Such a calculation is quite complex. In this book, we will examine how to do a two-sample test using the graphing calculator.

Consider the following problem:

One sample of 30 physical therapist assistants reports an annual salary of $45,000, with a standard deviation of $2,000. Another sample of 45 physical therapist assistants reports an annual salary of $43,000, with a standard deviation of $1,500. Is there a statistically significant difference between the means? Explain.

Choose a 2-SAMPLE T-TEST after choosing STAT and TESTS. Enter the following:

$$\overline{X}_1 = 45,000$$
$$s_{x_1} = 2,000$$
$$n_1 = 30$$
$$\overline{X}_2 = 43,000$$
$$s_{x_2} = 1,500$$
$$n_2 = 45$$

Choose POOLED VARIANCE and then CALCULATE.

The p-value is less than 0.001 with a large t-value. Thus, there is a statistically significant difference between the means.

To compare two population means with two population standard deviations, use a two-sample z-test. Use the same procedure on the calculator; however, choose 2-SAMPLE Z-TEST instead, and enter the population standard deviations.

Review Questions

1. Explain how p-values relate to level of significance.

2. Given a sample of size 40 with a mean of 80 and a standard deviation of 10, calculate the margin of error.

3. Elisha scores a 23 on the ACT. If the average is 21, with a standard deviation of 2 points, determine if her score is significantly higher than the average. Explain.

4.　A random sample of 50 bottles of a drink shows an average of 19.9 ounces per bottle, with a standard deviation of 0.1 ounces. If the reported average is 20 ounces per bottle, determine whether the average of the random sample is significantly different from the population average. Explain.

5.　A class of 25 members shows an average of 80 on a statistics exam, with a standard deviation of 3 points. A class of 30 members shows an average of 85 on a statistics exam, with a standard deviation of 8 points. Determine whether there is a statistically significant difference between the averages of the samples. Explain.

Answer Explanations

1.　*P*-values reveal the probability for rejection, or area under the curve in the tail either above or below the critical value. The level of significance is the value chosen by the researcher that is used to determine significance. For a result to be statistically significant, the *p*-value must be less than or equal to the level of significance.

2.　Margin of error ≈ 3.1

3.　No, there is not a statistically significant difference, as evidenced by a *p*-value of 0.1587.

4.　Yes, there is a statistically significant difference, as evidenced by a *t*-value of approximately -7 and a *p*-value of almost 0.

5.　Yes, there is a statistically significant difference, as evidenced by a *t*-value of approximately -3 and a *p*-value of less than 0.01.

Review Chapter 13: Confidence Intervals

A *confidence interval* is an interval that likely contains the population mean or proportion. A population mean or proportion is known as a *parameter*. A confidence interval is also known as an *interval estimate*. It is created by subtracting the margin of error from the sample mean (or proportion) and then adding the margin of error to the sample mean (or proportion).

Confidence Interval for a Population Mean

Recall that the margin of error for a mean may be calculated using the formula $E = z_{\frac{\alpha}{2}} \cdot \frac{\sigma}{\sqrt{n}}$, where z represents the critical value for a particular level of confidence for a two-tailed test, σ represents the population standard deviation, and n represents the sample size. When the population standard deviation is not known and the sample size is greater than 30, the sample standard deviation may be substituted for σ.

Therefore, a confidence interval for a mean may be represented as $\overline{X} \pm z_{\frac{\alpha}{2}} \cdot \frac{\sigma}{\sqrt{n}}$.

Recall that the critical value for a 95% level of confidence is 1.96. The critical value of 1.96 is determined by subtracting the area of 0.025 from 0.5. The area between the 2.5% cutoff on one end and half of the area under the curve is 0.475. This area corresponds to a critical z-value of 1.96.

The critical value for a 90% level of confidence is 1.645. This value is determined by subtracting the area of 0.05 from 0.5. The area between the 5% cutoff on one end and half of the area under the curve is 0.45. This area corresponds to a critical z-value of 1.645.

Confidence Interval for a Population Proportion

When discussing the confidence interval for a population proportion, the idea of a *point estimate* must be introduced. A point estimate is the value used to approximate the population value. When you are discussing a population mean, $\overline{X}$ is the best point estimate. When discussing a population proportion, however, $\hat{p}$ is the best point estimate.

The point estimate $\hat{p}$ may be calculated using the formula $\hat{p} = \frac{x}{n}$, where x represents the number of successes and n represents the number sampled.

The margin of error for a population proportion may be determined using the following formula:

$$E = z_{\frac{\alpha}{2}} \cdot \sqrt{\frac{\hat{p}\hat{q}}{n}}$$

In this formula, $\hat{p} = \frac{x}{n}$, $\hat{q} = 1 - \hat{p}$, and n represents the number sampled. A confidence interval for a proportion may be represented as

$$\hat{p} \pm z_{\frac{\alpha}{2}} \cdot \sqrt{\frac{\hat{p}\hat{q}}{n}}.$$

Comparing Sample Mean to Population Mean

Let's look at some examples. Consider the following problem:

> A company producing moisturizing cream claims to include 5 ounces in each tube of cream. It also claims a standard deviation of 0.2 ounces. From a sample of 40 tubes of cream, the sample mean is found to be 4.8 ounces per tube. What is the 95% confidence interval?

The problem may be solved by first calculating the margin of error using the formula $E = z_{\frac{\alpha}{2}} \cdot \frac{\sigma}{\sqrt{n}}$. Substituting 1.96 for z, 0.2 for σ, and 40 for n gives $E = 1.96 \cdot \frac{0.2}{\sqrt{40}}$, which is approximately 0.06.

Therefore, the confidence interval may be written as 4.8 ± 0.06, or (4.74, 4.86).

The confidence interval may be interpreted as follows: For 95% of all samples of tubes, the true population mean will likely fall between 4.74 and 4.86.

The problem can also be solved using a graphing calculator. Choose STAT, TESTS, and ZINTERVAL. Enter 0.2 for the population standard deviation, 4.8 for the sample mean, and 40 for the sample size.

The calculator results reveal decimals to the thousandths place, but when rounded, these decimals equal the confidence interval shown earlier.

Now, determine whether the difference between the sample mean and the population mean is significant. Since the company's claim of 5 ounces per tube does not fall within the confidence interval, we may declare a statistically significant difference between the number of ounces found in the sample mean and that of the population mean. We may also use a one-sample z-test to verify the findings. The results show a p-value less than 0.001, thus providing evidence to reject the null hypothesis and declare statistical significance.

The preceding problem included a population standard deviation and population mean. Let's consider a problem that contains only a sample standard deviation and sample mean.

Consider the problem:

> From a random sample of 35 voters, the mean annual salary is determined to be $38,000, with a sample standard deviation of $500. For a 95% confidence level, what is the interval that likely contains the population mean?

Since the sample size is larger than 30, we can compute a confidence interval as shown previously. We may also use a t-interval to obtain a more exact interval.

Let's look at both methods:

The problem may be solved by first calculating the margin of error using the formula $E = z_{\frac{\alpha}{2}} \cdot \frac{\sigma}{\sqrt{n}}$. Substituting 1.96 for z, 500 for σ, and 35 for n gives $E = 1.96 \cdot \frac{500}{\sqrt{35}}$, which is approximately 165.65.

Therefore, the confidence interval may be written as $38,000 \pm 165.65$, or (37,834.35, 38,165.65).

The population mean is likely to fall between $37,834.35 and $38,165.65.

If computing a t-interval, a graphing calculator may be used. Choose STAT, TESTS, and then TINTERVAL. Enter the sample mean of 38,000, the sample standard deviation of 500, and the sample size of 35. Choose 0.95 c-level and click CALCULATE.

The results show a confidence interval of (37,828, 38,172), which is very close to the interval we found using the formula for a population mean and population standard deviation.

Therefore, any population mean outside the confidence interval above could be declared as significantly different.

Comparing Sample Proportion to Population Proportion

Now, let's look at a problem that compares a sample proportion to a population proportion.

Consider the following problem:

In a random sample of 100 college students, 42 stated that they have a smartphone. What is the 90% confidence interval for the true population proportion having a smartphone?

The problem may be solved by first calculating the margin of error for the proportion. To do so, the point estimate $\hat{p}$ must first be determined. Recall that $\hat{p} = \frac{x}{n}$. Thus, the point estimate may be written as

$\hat{p} = \frac{42}{100}$, or 0.42. Now, $\hat{q}$ must be calculated (recall that $\hat{q} = 1 - \hat{p}$). Therefore, $\hat{q} = 0.58$.

Now, the margin of error may be calculated using the formula $E = z_{\frac{\alpha}{2}} \cdot \sqrt{\frac{\hat{p}\hat{q}}{n}}$. The margin of error may be written as $E = 1.645 \cdot \sqrt{\frac{(0.42)(0.58)}{100}}$, which is approximately 0.08.

The confidence interval may be written as 0.42 ± 0.08, or (0.34, 0.5). Thus, the population proportion of students having a smartphone is likely between 0.34 and 0.5, considering a 90% level of confidence.

A given population proportion outside this interval is unlikely to be the true population proportion.

Comparing Two Sample Means

Sometimes you may need to compare two sample means using a confidence interval.

Consider the following problem:

> The mean number of ounces found in a random sample of 50 boxes of Cereal A brand's cereal boxes is 12.25 ounces. The reported standard deviation is 0.5 ounces. The mean number of ounces found in a random sample of 45 boxes of Cereal B brand's cereal boxes is 12 ounces, with a reported standard deviation of 0.3 ounces. Compute a 95% confidence interval for the difference between the means.

To calculate the confidence interval, choose STAT, TESTS, and then 2-SAMPLEZINT. Enter 0.5 ounces for the first standard deviation, 0.3 for the second standard deviation, 12.25 for the first sample mean, 12 for the second sample mean, 50 for the first sample size, and 45 for the second sample size. The confidence interval is approximately (0.086, 0.414). This confidence interval contains the possible values of the differences between the two sample means. The null hypothesis is the hypothesis of no difference, or 0. Since 0 is not included in the confidence interval we calculated, we can declare a statistically significant difference between the two samples.

The z-interval may also be calculated using the formula $\left(\overline{X_1} - \overline{X_2}\right) \pm z_{\frac{\alpha}{2}}\sqrt{\left(\frac{\sigma_1}{n_1}\right)^2 + \left(\frac{\sigma_2}{n_2}\right)^2}$.

The conclusion that the means are statistically different may be verified by using a two-sample z-test.

Using a graphing calculator, choose STAT, TESTS, and then 2-SAMPLEZTEST. A z-test is used because the population standard deviation is known. Enter the same information used previously. To determine whether the difference between the means is significant, you must interpret the p-value.

The results show a p-value of approximately 0.003. Thus, considering a significance level of 0.05, the null hypothesis may be rejected and a significant difference between the two sample means may be declared.

Comparing Two Sample Proportions

In other situations, you may need to compare two sample proportions using a confidence interval.

Consider the problem that follows:

> In a random sample of 70 students at Texas A&M University, 40 are taking a philosophy class. In a random sample of 80 students at UT-Austin, 30 are taking a philosophy class. The sample of students at Texas A&M reveals a standard deviation of three students, while the sample of students at UT-Austin reveals a standard deviation of four students. Compute a 95% confidence interval for the difference between the proportions.

To calculate the confidence interval, choose STAT, TESTS, and then 2-PROPZINT. A z-interval may be used since the sample sizes are larger than 30. Enter 20 for the first x-value, 65 for the first n, 30 for the second x-value, and 80 for the second n. Choose 95% confidence level and click CALCULATE. The confidence interval is approximately (0.039, 0.354). This confidence interval contains the possible values of the differences between the two sample proportions. The null hypothesis is the hypothesis of no difference, or 0. Since 0 is not included in the confidence interval shown here, we can declare a statistically significant difference between the two proportions.

The $\hat{p}$ interval also may be calculated using the following formula:

$$\hat{p}_1 - \hat{p}_2 \pm z_{\frac{\alpha}{2}} \cdot \sqrt{\frac{\hat{p}_1 \hat{q}_1}{n_1} + \frac{\hat{p}_2 \hat{q}_2}{n_2}}$$

The conclusion that the proportions are significantly different may also be verified by using a two-sample z-test.

Using a graphing calculator, choose STAT, TESTS, and then 2-PROPZTEST. Enter the same information used previously for the confidence interval. To determine whether the difference between the means is significant, you must interpret the p-value.

The results show a p-value of approximately 0.016. Thus, considering a significance level of 0.05, the null hypothesis may be rejected and a statistically significant difference between the two sample proportions may be declared.

Review Questions

1. Suppose Caroline's company claims to sell $3,600 worth of candles each month, with a reported standard deviation of $150. From a random sample of 36 months' worth of sales, the sample mean amount of sales is found to be $3,400. Find the 95% confidence interval and interpret.

2. In a random sample of 120 citizens, the mean monthly mortgage is $813, with a standard deviation of $25. Find the 95% confidence interval and interpret.

3. In a random sample of 30 Democrats, 10 buy one specialty coffee drink per day. Find the 90% confidence interval for the population proportion of Democrats buying one specialty coffee drink per day.

4. The mean score on Mr. Ericson's final statistics exam for a group of 35 students is 82. The reported standard deviation for his exam is 2 points. The mean score on Ms. Lee's final statistics exam for a group of 40 students is 80. The reported standard deviation for her exam is 3 points. Find the 95% confidence interval for the difference between the two means and interpret.

5. In a random sample of 130 Texas A&M University students, 20 plan to go to Disney World this summer. In a random sample of 80 Texas Tech University students, four plan to go to Disney World this summer. Compute a 90% confidence interval for the difference between the two proportions and interpret.

Answer Explanations

1. The confidence interval is $(3,351, 3,449)$. Since her monthly claim is not found in the interval, it is unlikely that her claim is correct. In other words, the true population sales likely fall between $3,351 and $3,449. The difference between the sample mean and claimed population mean is significant.

2. The confidence interval is approximately $(808.53, 817.47)$. Thus, the population mean monthly mortgage will likely fall between $808.53 and $817.47. A population monthly mortgage falling outside this interval would be considered statistically significant.

3. The confidence interval for the population proportion is approximately $(0.1917, 0.4749)$, or 19% to 47%.

4. The confidence interval is approximately $(0.858, 3.142)$. Thus, the difference between the means fall within this interval. Since 0 does not

fall within this interval, it can be declared that there is a statistically significant difference between the sample means.

5. The confidence interval is approximately (0.04, 0.17). Thus, the differences between the proportions fall within this interval. Since 0 is not found within this interval, it can be declared that there is a statistically significant difference between the proportions.

Review Chapter 14: Regression, Chi-Square Tests, and Power

Regression

A *regression* is a test that determines the correlation between one or more independent variables and a dependent variable. A linear regression includes one independent and one dependent variable, whereas a multiple regression includes more than one independent variable.

The degree of linearity, or the correlation coefficient (r), is used to determine the strength of the correlation. The least-squares regression line may be used to make predictions about one variable given the value of another variable.

Recall that a correlation coefficient is a value that depicts the strength of a linear relationship and ranges from -1 to 1, with numbers closest to either integer indicating strong relationships, either negative or positive. Values close to 0 correspond to weak linear relationships.

Return to Chapter 4 to review estimation and calculation of least-squares regression lines, correlation coefficients, and Pearson's correlation coefficient (r).

The coefficient ρ, or Spearman's rho, is another correlation coefficient that may be used to reveal the strength between variables. Spearman's rho is less biased than Pearson's correlation, r. In addition, it is not impacted as much by extreme outliers and may be used for data that are not normally distributed. Furthermore, ρ may be preferred when using small sample sizes. A formula or statistical software package may be used to calculate ρ.

When manually calculating ρ, use the formula $\rho = 1 - \dfrac{6\sum d^2}{n(n^2-1)}$, where ρ represents rho, d represents the difference between the paired x- and y-values, and n represents the number of paired values.

Consider the small data set that follows:

x	8	8	3	8	7	6	9	2	8	7
y	9	6	3	3	4	3	3	3	10	3

The differences between the paired x- and y-values may be written as follows:

$$-1, 2, 0, 5, 3, 3, 6, -1, -2, 4$$

The squared differences are as follows:

$$1, 4, 0, 25, 9, 9, 36, 1, 4, 16$$

The sum of the squared differences equals 105.
The number of paired values is 10.
Substituting the known values into the formula gives the following:

$$\rho = 1 - \frac{6(105)}{10(10^2 - 1)}$$

Therefore, ρ is approximately 0.36.

This correlation coefficient may be compared to Pearson's correlation coefficient using the graphing calculator. Note that Spearman's is preferred with such a small sample size. However, Pearson's correlation coefficient should be comparable.

Enter the x- and y-values into two separate lists. Choose STAT, CALCULATE, and then LINREG($ax + b$). Press Enter. The r-value is the Pearson's correlation coefficient. In this case, that value is approximately 0.4, which is somewhat larger than the Spearman's rho coefficient. Pearson's shows a stronger correlation because it is more biased with small sample sizes.

Conducting a Linear Regression

You can conduct a linear regression using either Excel or a graphing calculator. Both correlation coefficients will represent Pearson's correlation coefficient, r.

When using Excel, simply enter values into two separate columns. Each column will represent either the independent or the dependent variable values.

Consider these x-values:

$$8, 6, 8, 10, 1, 1, 5, 5, 2, 8, 2, 10, 7, 2, 10,$$
$$5, 4, 6, 2, 7, 6, 1, 2, 5, 3, 5, 10, 4, 4, 1$$

Consider these y-values:

$$26, 32, 45, 22, 40, 39, 21, 49, 46, 49, 38, 42, 22, 34, 44,$$
$$39, 45, 28, 23, 29, 39, 49, 25, 50, 42, 48, 40, 24, 44, 21$$

After entering the values into two separate columns in Excel, choose Data Analysis and then Regression. Input the y-values and then the x-values by highlighting the values in each column. The summary output will include a "Multiple R"; this is the correlation coefficient.

In this case, $r \approx 0.012$, which shows approximately 0, or no correlation, between the two variables.

A graphing calculator also can be used to find Pearson's r, as previously discussed. Enter the x- and y-values into two separate lists. Choose STAT, CALCULATE, and then LINREG$(ax + b)$. Press Enter. The r-value is the Pearson's correlation coefficient. The value is approximately 0.012.

Significance with a Regression

Excel or a graphing calculator also may be used to determine significance of a linear regression. In other words, we may determine whether the correlation is significant by interpreting the p-value provided by each tool.

With Excel, you need to find the p-value given for the X Variable 1. This p-value represents the significance of the correlation. In the case of the data set given on page 228, the p-value is approximately 0.95. Given a level of significance of 0.05, we will declare nonsignificance with this correlation.

With a graphing calculator, choose STAT, TESTS, and then LINREGTTEST. Represent the x- and y-values, according to their list names, and choose CALCULATE. The resulting p is the p-value.

Notice the relationship between a low correlation coefficient and a high p-value. A low correlation coefficient indicates a nonsignificant relationship (and high p-value), whereas a high correlation coefficient is linked to a significant relationship (and low p-value).

Chi-Square Tests

A *chi-square test* examines the significance between frequencies of *categories* of variables. In other words, the test examines significance between differences in observed and expected frequencies. Specifically, such a test examines the goodness of fit of the model or normality of the distribution.

Frequencies of categorical variables should be mutually exclusive. Also, counts should be greater than or equal to 1.

The only parameter included in a chi-square distribution is degrees of freedom. When the degrees of freedom increase, the chi-square distribution approaches a more normal, or symmetric, distribution. Also, the mean approaches the number of degrees of freedom, and the variance approaches the product of 2 and the number of degrees of freedom.

With a chi-square test, the number of degrees of freedom is equal to the number of categories, n, minus 1.

Conducting a Chi-Square Test

The formula for calculating chi-square is $\chi^2 = \sum \frac{(O - E)^2}{E}$, where O represents each observed value and E represents each expected value.

Consider this example.

The number of miles driven by categories of sales professionals over the course of last year is shown in the following table:

RANK	NUMBER OF MILES DRIVEN
Intern	2,100
Associate	2,350
Senior	2,025

Over the course of this year, interns drove an average of 2,085 miles, associates drove an average of 2,300 miles, and seniors drove an average of 2,050 miles. Is there a significant difference between the number of miles driven this year and the number driven last year?

A chi-square test can be used to compare the observed (present-year) miles and the expected (past-year) miles.

Using the formula $\chi^2 = \sum \frac{(O - E)^2}{E}$, we can record the following:

$$\chi^2 = \frac{(15)^2}{2,085} + \frac{(50)^2}{2,300} + \frac{(-25)^2}{2,050} \approx 1.5$$

For degrees of freedom of 2, a chi-square statistic of 1.5 lies between 0.5 and 0.25, closer to 0.5. Since 0.25 is larger than a level of significance of 0.05, we will fail to reject the null hypothesis and, therefore, declare no significant difference between the observed and expected frequencies.

Take a look at another problem.

Suppose a journal typically publishes 25% mixed-methods articles, 50% quantitative articles, and 25% qualitative articles. The journal publishes 32 articles per year.

This year, the journal publishes seven mixed-methods articles, 18 quantitative articles, and 7 qualitative articles.

Is there a statistically significant difference between the numbers of each type of article published this year and the norm for the journal?

The chi-square statistic can be calculated as follows:

$$\chi^2 = \frac{(-1)^2}{8} + \frac{(2)^2}{16} + \frac{(-1)^2}{8} = 0.5$$

For degrees of freedom of 2, a chi-square statistic of 0.5 lies between 0.9 and 0.75, while closer to 0.75. Since 0.75 is larger than a level of significance of 0.05, we will fail to reject the null hypothesis and, therefore, declare no significant difference between the numbers of each article published this year and the numbers of each type that is normally published.

Power

The concept of power has many facets. *Power* is the probability of accurately rejecting a null hypothesis. In other words, it is the probability of being able to find statistical significance. Technically, power is written as $power = 1 - \beta$, where β is the probability of failing to reject a null hypothesis.

Power ranges from 0 to 1, with 0.80 considered a strong power.

Consider the following problem:

A population reports an average annual salary of $50,000, with a standard deviation of $20,000. Elena plans to randomly sample 30 citizens and wishes to determine the power of detecting a statistically significant difference of $10,000 between the sample annual average salary and the population annual salary.

Delta (δ) may be represented by the formula $\delta = d\sqrt{n}$, where d is equal to the ratio of the difference between the sample mean and population mean to the population standard deviation.

Therefore, in Elena's study, $d = \dfrac{10,000}{20,000}$ and $\delta = 0.5\sqrt{30}$, or approximately 2.7. For a level of significance of 0.05, a delta of 2.7 shows a power of 0.77. The power may be determined by locating the row in the power table that represents the δ value of 2.7, finding the column that represents the level of significance of 0.05, and then identifying the value that shows the intersection of the row and column.

The sample size needed to obtain a particular power may also be calculated.

Suppose Elena wants to determine the size of the sample needed to obtain a power of at least 0.80. She may use the formula $n = \left(\dfrac{\delta}{d}\right)^2$. For a level of significance of 0.05, $\delta = 2.80$ is needed for a power of 0.80.

Using the d of 0.5 determined earlier results in the following: $n = \left(\dfrac{2.80}{0.5}\right)^2$, or approximately 31.36. Thus, a sample size of 32 is needed to obtain a power of 0.80.

Review Questions

1. Calculate Pearson's correlation coefficient using the following data set.

    x-values:

    $$8, 2, 2, 9, 5, 4, 4, 9, 4, 3, 4, 1, 3, 7, 5, 6, 1, 7, 1, 4$$

    y-values:

    $$17, 19, 17, 18, 16, 18, 28, 27, 22, 30,$$
    $$19, 16, 27, 21, 30, 26, 29, 23, 29, 19$$

2. Using the data set from the previous question, find the approximate p-value and state whether a significant relationship does or does not exist.

3. In the past, Deborah has written 20 grant proposals each year, and she sent 15% to the Heritage Foundation, 60% to the Carnegie Foundation, and 25% to the Arizona Community Foundation. This year, Deborah sent two to the Heritage Foundation, 10 to the Carnegie Foundation, and eight to the Arizona Community Foundation. Is there a significant difference between the number of proposals sent to each foundation this year and the number of proposals sent to each group in the past? Explain.

4. For five categories of data, what is the p-value range for $\chi^2 = 1.5$?

5. Peter hopes to detect a significant difference of 50 between a sample mean and population mean for a population with a standard deviation of 75. If he wants the power to be 0.85 and uses 0.01 for the level of significance, what sample size does he need?

Answer Explanations

1. $r \approx 0.12$

2. The p-value is approximately 0.6. There is not a statistically significant relationship between the variables.

3. The chi-square statistic is approximately 2.47. For degrees of freedom of 2, the approximate p-value is 0.3. Since 0.3 is greater than 0.05, we will fail to reject the null hypothesis and declare no significant difference.

4. $0.75 < p < 0.9$

5. $n = 29$

THE BIG PICTURE: HOW TO PREPARE YEAR-ROUND

No matter how far in the future you plan to take the AP Statistics Exam, the time to start preparing is now. And this part of your book is here to help. Here you'll learn how to register for the exam, how to make the most of your preparation time both in the classroom and outside of it, and how to manage the stress an exam of this magnitude may bring. As you get closer to your exam date, make sure you use all the materials provided in this book. That way, when the day of the exam arrives, you'll be ready to maximize your score!

Strategies for Long-Term Preparation

Step 1: Get Registered

The AP Statistics Exam is offered once a year, generally in May (to coincide with the end of the school year). If you're enrolled in an AP Statistics course at your high school, you'll probably take the exam there or at another local school. Even if the exam is offered at another school in your district, your teacher or the AP coordinator in your district usually handles testing arrangements and supervises the registration process. So, you just need to make sure you're talking to the right people and getting the right information. It's never too early to ask when you'll be registering and when you'll be testing!

If unusual circumstances make it impossible for you to test on the official testing date, you may be able to test during a late-testing period offered late in the month. However, don't wait until the last minute to determine if you'll be able to do so. If you know the scheduled exam date is going to be problematic, be proactive! Contact your guidance counselor or AP coordinator for assistance.

What if you're not enrolled in an AP Statistics course at school? Can you still take this examination? The answer to that question is a resounding yes! Each year hundreds of home-schooled and independent-study students take this examination. To learn where you can take the exam, when it is offered, and how to register, contact the administrators of the exam, the College Board (www.collegeboard.com). The College Board can direct you to local institutions offering the examination. You can then contact that school to make arrangements. (Tip: When you call, ask to speak to the AP coordinator. If no one in the school is so designated, ask to speak to the guidance counselor, who can usually direct you.)

Here are some important points to keep in mind as you get started.

- **Do you know what you need to know?** We can't emphasize enough how important it is to make sure you have accurate information about this exam. Refer to the College Board's official website (www.collegeboard.com) for current information about the exam, including eligibility, late testing, special accommodations for students with disabilities, and reduced testing fees for low-income students. This site also provides information on how your score is reported to the colleges and universities you're interested in attending. Don't depend on getting this information from anyone else! Since you purchased this book, obviously you're interested in doing well on the examination. Don't risk losing points by not knowing what you need to know. Time spent on early research can pay off for you down the road.

- **It's never too early to get started.** The tricky thing about an examination like the AP Statistics Exam is that you really get only one opportunity each year to take this exam. If you're enrolled in an AP course, ask your teacher no later than January or February how to register for the exam (if that hasn't already been explained and discussed in class, of course). If you're not enrolled in an AP class in a school, take the initiative! Contact the College Board before March 1. Determine where the exam will be administered locally. Then contact that school's AP coordinator to register.

- **Make sure you register for the correct exam.** As silly as it may sound, some testers have found out the hard way that it's entirely possible to go through the whole preparation process only to discover they've registered for the wrong AP exam. During the registration process, check and double-check that you're registering for AP Statistics, not AP Calculus AB or AP Calculus BC (or anything else!).

- **Remember, it's worth it!** You might be worried about your anxiety level for this exam. You might be thinking that in the overall scheme of senior year and college prep, this exam is less important than others you need to worry about. You may be concerned about not doing well. If your thought process is running in this direction, slow down for a minute! Consider how little you have to lose if you score poorly on the exam and how much you have to gain if you do well. Plus, you may do better than you expect if you make the best use of study time and material at your disposal. (Consider especially the resources in this book.) Even if, after all is said and done, you don't do well, remember, a low score only means you won't get college credit for the course. It usually doesn't affect your ability to get into the college of your choice. Plus, if you're concerned, you can cancel your score so that it won't appear on the report the College Board sends to colleges. Finally, many colleges value the fact that students chose to challenge themselves with AP coursework, even if those students don't ultimately get college credit for the class. The only thing you'll really have lost is your time and the testing fee.

Step 2: Become an Expert Student

To do well on the exam, you must retain a ton of information, both in and out of the classroom. You'll have to work hard and study. Did you know that studying is a discipline in and of itself that many people just don't know how to do well? It's true. Even the smartest people need to learn how to study to maximize their ability to learn.

One of the most critical study skills involves notes. More specifically, it involves taking effective notes rather than just writing down everything your teacher says. Don't underestimate how important good note-taking is both during class and while you're studying alone or with a partner. Good note-taking serves several purposes. First (and most obviously), note-taking is important for making sure you have recorded the key points being made by your instructor (or your study partner). Since this person is very familiar with the material and the exam, he or she knows where you should focus your time, so you should glean as much knowledge from him or her as possible. Second, effective note-taking is important because the process of working on notes can actually help you in your retention of the material. For example, the deceptively simple act of writing and rewriting your notes reinforces your memory. Additionally, writing in conjunction with listening or reading forces your brain to fire up additional cognition skills, making it a lot more likely that you'll remember what you're recording.

Here are some tips for taking great notes.

- **Listen actively.** The first key to taking good notes is to practice active listening—that is, listening in a structured way to understand and evaluate what's being said. Active listeners are not distracted, thinking about other things, or considering what they will say next. (In the classroom, this means opening up your mind rather than thinking about some question you might ask your teacher.) Active listening also does not involve writing down every single thing the teacher says. Rather, it means listening in a structured way so that you hear the main ideas, pay attention to cues that impart meaning, and keep your eyes on the speaker (not on your notebook).

  ○ Listen for main ideas. Before you even begin the note-taking process, consider the topic under discussion and be ready to organize your notes around that topic. Do some prethinking about the topic and work from that angle. Also listen for transitions into new topics as the teacher works his or her way through the material.

  ○ Pay attention to cues. If you're taking notes in class, certain words and phrases tend to reflect the way the discussion is organized. For example, the teacher usually starts with an introduction, and this introduction generally provides the framework around how the topic will be treated. Also listen for transition words such as "next," "the following," and numbered/bulleted lists.

○ Don't just stare at your notebook. Information is conveyed by speakers in a number of ways, many of them nonverbal. Keep an eye on the instructor's body language and expressions. These are the nonverbal cues that will help you determine what's important and what's not.

- **What do good notes look like?** Good notes are not just a jumbled mass of everything. It's unrealistic and ineffective to try to write down everything there is to say about a topic. Instead, learn to focus on key words and main points. Here are some tips on how to proceed.

  ○ Start with a clean sheet. Indicate today's date and the main topic. This will jog your memory later, when you study these notes.

  ○ If the instructor is using slides, don't just copy word for word or number for number what's on the slide. Instead, jot down the title of the slide and the key idea, concept, or overall topic under discussion (this should be apparent from the title of the slide deck, the title of the slide itself, or the instructor's introduction).

  ○ Listen actively to your instructor's treatment of the material and his or her points of emphasis. Try to really listen to what is being said. Then, as your teacher makes important points, write them down in bullet-point or summarized fashion. Don't worry too much about organization in the moment. Just do your best to capture the discussion in a way that makes sense to you.

  ○ If you're confused about something, ask for clarification. Many students make the mistake of not asking for help when the teacher makes a statement that is confusing or unclear. Sometimes even the best teachers go too fast or fail to transition you through the material plainly. It's much better to ask for help than to write down a bunch of information that makes no sense to you later.

  ○ This is an important and often-overlooked point: once class is over, rewrite or retype your notes, using the opportunity to also fold in information from your textbook or other resources. This is your opportunity to bring real organization, clarity, and understanding to the material. You should rewrite or retype your notes regularly (preferably daily, but if that's not possible, at least weekly). You'll be amazed at how much more sense the material makes if you take the time to look at it critically and rework it in a way that makes sense to you on a regular basis.

- ○ Take notes from your books and other resources as well as your class notes. AP Statistics covers a lot of material. Paying attention to what gets attention in resources can help you focus.

- ○ Review your notes before class every day. Doing so serves as a reminder of where you left off and also helps you to transition from concept to concept. Work mindfully to make connections among the material that you're learning. Those connections will serve you well later.

- **How do you read to understand?** Material such as this book and your class textbook can make the difference between a passing and failing grade or between a so-so and an excellent score. However, you need to understand what you're reading so that you can supplement your class notes.

  - ○ Do a complete read-through. Start with the objectives of the chapter. Review the questions at the end.

  - ○ Map out important points. Once you've read through the material and have an overall understanding, write down the important points and leave space to fill in details or practice problems. Wherever possible, find your own words. Avoid copying text exactly from the book. Paraphrasing the material in your own words helps you engage with the material and facilitates your learning.

  - ○ Reread the material. Once you have the main points mapped out, reread the material with an eye toward filling in details or completing practice problems under each of the main ideas.

- Fill in the details. Now that you've reread, write details under each main point—again, do not copy the words exactly from the book, but use your own words so that you retain the information. Use details from the book or other resource and from your class notes.

- Put the book aside, and read through your notes. Do you understand what you've written? Have you accurately represented the main ideas? Did you fill in the appropriate level of detail? Did you try to solve some practice problems?

- Review, review, review. Read your notes over and over again. That's how you get the information to stick.

Step 3: Create a Realistic Study Plan

If you're like many students with challenging classes, extracurricular activities, and other priorities, you may have a limited amount of time to review for this exam. This section will help you get the most out of your limited test-preparation time and make it really count. You need a plan specifically for you—one that addresses your needs and considers the time you have available. No two people will have exactly the same plan or use this book in exactly the same way. To develop a personalized test-prep plan, you'll need to identify your weak points and then allocate time to address them efficiently and effectively.

Here are the three basic steps to creating a personalized test-prep plan.

1. **Identify your weak points.** Start by taking the **Diagnostic Exam** in this book (see pages 45 to 88). This will show you what you're up against. It will also help you get a feel for the exam and identify the subject areas where you need to focus. Based on your performance, you can prioritize the topics to review, starting with the areas in which you are weakest. If your time is limited or if you feel you're not ready to take a complete practice exam, focus your review by skimming the diagnostic exam and

identifying those areas where you have the most difficulty with understanding.

2. **Develop a review plan and a schedule.** Figure out how much time you can devote each week to exam preparation and reserve specific blocks of time for this purpose. Create a written schedule that includes specific time slots and activities or content areas for review. This will help you pace yourself to get through all the material you want to review. You'll likely find there are content areas or question types you want to focus on more than others. Also, make sure your plan includes time to master test-taking strategies and actually take the practice exams.

3. **Practice, practice, practice.** If there's one thing more important than reviewing the concepts of statistics, it's putting them into practice. While your homework is likely to give you a good amount of practice, be sure not to stop practicing until you get the concepts down. If you find that you struggle with a particular topic, try solving more problems until you feel comfortable with the topic. As you complete practice problems, try to use a consistent way of organizing your work. This will help you save time and avoid mistakes. It will also help keep your work in order and maximize your score in the free-response portion of the AP exam. In addition, write out your work just as you would when solving a free-response problem on the exam. You'll find that having an imaginary audience in mind sharpens your mind and helps you avoid skipping key steps and avoiding sloppy errors.

Step 4: Use All the Resources at Your Disposal

This book is an excellent way to prepare for this exam. It includes not only the diagnostic exam but two full practice exams. Each exam has unique questions, so you get the opportunity to address different areas of the content in many different ways.

Additionally, another practice exam is available to you free of charge at mymaxscore.com. Detailed answers and explanations are provided for both the multiple-choice and free-response sections.

Check out the website for the College Board (www.collegeboard .com). At this site, you can find actual released exams that are no longer in circulation, along with general information about the exam and testing advice. You can also download the AP Statistics course description, so you'll know what you're up against. The course description is a good way to identify topics that your AP class may or may not cover prior to the AP exam. For topics that are unfamiliar, plan to ask your teacher or study partner to review those concepts with you, or take time to study them on your own so that you're 100% prepared for the exam.

You'll also find many other exam resources in your library, at the local bookstore, or online. Look around to see what's available and figure out ways to work that material into your study time if you can.

Good luck! Happy studying!

Taking the Practice Exams

This part of your book includes two complete practice exams. A third practice exam is available for you on our website. Taking the exam multiple times allows you to confirm your knowledge of the material and increase your comfort with the format and design of the examination itself. To get the most out of your practice material, try to mimic the testing environment as closely as possible. That means you should have only the examination and answer sheet open as you work. It also means you should carefully time yourself to make sure you stay within the parameters of the examination. Ask a friend to time you, or use a timer to make sure you do not spend more time than allowed on each section of the exam. As you complete each section, remember to apply all the strategies you learned about in this book.

Just like the real AP examination, each practice exam includes two sections. Section I includes 40 multiple-choice questions, each of which is followed by five answer options. Read the question and the answer options carefully before selecting your response. Remember, you are looking for the *best* response to each question. It may be best to plan to use your practice exams more than one time, so you may want to write your answers on a separate sheet of paper.

You will have 90 minutes to complete all 40 questions in Section I.

Take a five-minute break before moving to Section II, the free-response portion of the AP Statistics exam. In Section II, you'll find four to six free-response questions and one investigative task. There are several ways to approach the material in this section. Some people review all the free-response questions and then begin with the ones they know they can answer quickly and accurately. Others work on the investigative task first, as it requires more thought and creativity than some of the other questions. By taking the practice exams a few times, you can find the approach that works best for you.

You will have 90 minutes to complete all the questions in Section II. Plan to spend about 60 minutes on the shorter free-response questions and 30 minutes on the longer investigative task.

After you have completed the practice exam, use the key provided to check your answers. Suggested responses for the free-response questions are given.

Good luck!

This book contains two practice exams. Visit mymaxscore.com to download your free third practice exam with answers and explanations.

AP Statistics Practice Exam 1

Statistics

SECTION I

Time—90 minutes

40 questions

Directions: Solve each of the following problems. After examining the answer choices, select the best solution to the problem. No credit will be given for anything written in the exam book. Do not spend too much time on any one problem.

1. The following boxplot represents a data set.

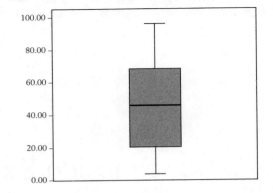

Which of the following data sets is represented by the boxplot above?

A. 87, 21, 97, 67, 98, 21, 55, 66, 55, 83, 89, 65,
    59, 39, 7, 60, 11, 6, 84, 5, 97, 31, 28, 43, 75

B. 34, 64, 33, 92, 64, 39, 35, 12, 53, 18, 8, 85, 21,
    5, 70, 90, 57, 44, 47, 64, 11, 46, 13, 50, 76

C. 9, 94, 79, 18, 53, 64, 99, 12, 61, 27, 82, 34,
    80, 7, 65, 9, 96, 84, 25, 55, 74, 3, 7, 89, 60

D. 93, 84, 83, 78, 97, 10, 58, 8, 93, 40, 72, 58, 55,
    21, 55, 85, 88, 28, 42, 80, 31, 33, 37, 73, 18

E. 47, 70, 93, 47, 25, 82, 65, 80, 83, 43, 50, 51, 81,
    92, 73, 99, 94, 4, 28, 29, 42, 33, 55, 82, 41

2. The following data represent a range of costs to fill a gas tank.

$75, $67, $99, $74, $58, $52, $81, $73, $87, $61,
$88, $56, $96, $83, $70, $79, $91, $86, $83, $75

Which of the following graphs represents a frequency plot of the gas costs?

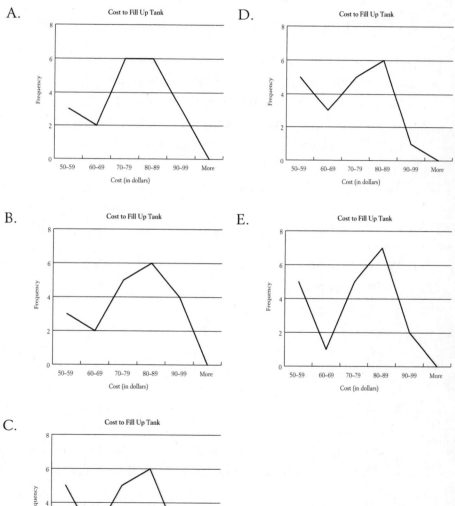

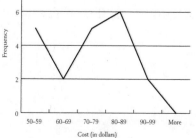

3. The following is a random sample of house prices in a local community.

    $279,500, $172,000, $94,750, $98,500, $253,250,
    $268,000, $101,250, $120,000, $257,000, $125,000,
    $259,000, $228,500, $291,000, $274,000, $91,250,
    $263,000, $229,000, $133,950, $120,000, $270,000

    Which of the following statements is true?

    A. The mean is greater than the median and mode.
    B. The mean is greater than the median only.
    C. The median is greater than the mean only.
    D. The median is greater than the mean and mode.
    E. The mode is greater than mean only.

4. The following is a set of scores for a statistics exam.

    97, 78, 78, 63, 90, 75, 88, 84, 60, 75,
    98, 87, 90, 98, 66, 62, 69, 68, 66, 91

    Which of the following best represents the standard deviation of the statistics scores?

    A. 10.8
    B. 11.2
    C. 12.8
    D. 13.2
    E. 14.8

5. Suppose a population has a mean of 125 and a standard deviation of 10. How many standard deviations below the mean is a value of 75?

    A. 3
    B. 4.5
    C. 5
    D. 5.5
    E. 6

6. A data point is 2.5 standard deviations above the population mean.
    Which of the following represents the z-score of the data point?

    A. 2
    B. 2.5
    C. 5
    D. 7.5
    E. 10

7. What is the median of the following bar graph?

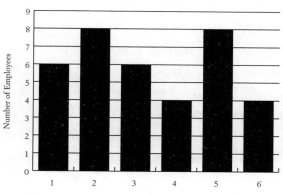

Number of Grants Written

    A. 2.5
    B. 3
    C. 3.5
    D. 4
    E. 4.5

8. Which of the following statements best compares the data in the back-to-back stemplot that follows?

DATA SET A	STEM	DATA SET B
3, 5, 6, 9	0	2, 3, 6, 7, 8, 9
4	1	1, 4, 5, 9
0, 1, 1, 6	2	2, 7
1, 2, 7, 9	3	0, 2, 4, 8
1, 6, 6, 7	4	0
3, 8, 8	5	0, 4, 9

A. Data set A has a larger center and more variability.
B. Data set A has a smaller center, while the variability for the two data sets is comparable.
C. Data set A has a smaller center and more variability.
D. Data set A has a smaller center and less variability.
E. Data set A has a larger center, while the variability for the two data sets is comparable.

9. Which of the following best represents the correlation coefficient, r, for the data that follows?

x	3	6	8	9	11	13	15	18	20	24
y	10	26	30	45	55	60	70	95	100	110

A. 0.68
B. 0.77
C. 0.85
D. 0.92
E. 0.99

10. Which of the following equations best represents the least-squares regression line for the points shown in the scatterplot that follows?

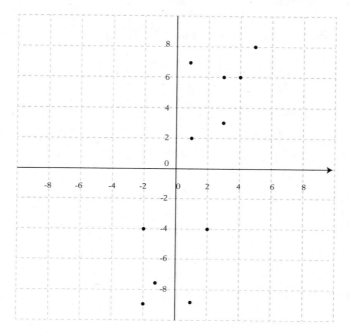

A. $y = 2x + 2$

B. $y = 2x - 3$

C. $y = 4x - 4$

D. $y = 4x + 6$

E. $y = x - 8$

11. Given a correlation coefficient of 0.4, which of the following best represents the strength of the relationship between the variables?

A. There is no correlation between the variables.

B. There is a very weak correlation between the variables.

C. There is some correlation between the variables.

D. There is a strong correlation between the variables.

E. There is a very strong correlation between the variables.

12. Given the points (3, 12), (3, 19), (20, 11), (20, 10), (13, 12), (13, 4), (11, 13), (6, 6), (9, 6), (14, 17), (19, 14), (18, 20), (12, 13), (6, 19), and (2, 3), which of the following best represents four of the points found on the residual plot of this data?

   A. (3, 1.18), (9, −5.66), (12, 0.92), (19, 0.94)
   B. (2, 1.08), (6, −4.32), (18, 2.14), (20, 1.62)
   C. (13, 0.98), (14, 1.22), (18, 2.28), (20, 2.04)
   D. (2, 0.88), (3, 12.44), (9, −10.08), (12, 1.48)
   E. (12, 13.68), (14, 17.08), (18, 18.22), (20, 16.42)

13. To achieve linearity, the following data set has been transformed.

x	1	2	3	4	5	6	7	8	9	10
y	2	12	28	85	250	730	2,100	6,500	19,720	59,100

   The transformed data set is represented by the scatterplot that follows.

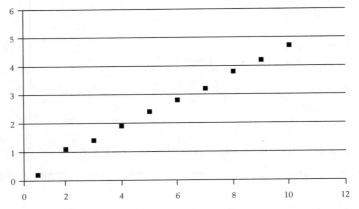

   Which of the following transformations occurred?

   A. The logarithm of each y-value was used.
   B. The square root of each y-value was used.
   C. The reciprocal of each y-value was used.
   D. The logarithm of each x- and y-value was used.
   E. The reciprocal of each x-value was used.

14. Which of the following transformation approaches results in the highest level of linearity as evidenced by the correlation coefficient, r, for the data that follows?

x	1	2	3	4	5	6	7	8	9	10
y	2	10	20	30	54	70	100	134	170	202

    A.   Take the logarithm of the y-values only.
    B.   Take the logarithm of the x- and y-values.
    C.   Take the square root of the y-values.
    D.   Square the y-values.
    E.   Find the reciprocals of the y-values.

15. Given the statements below, which of the following is true?

I.   A statistic includes s or σ.
II.   A parameter includes μ or $\overline{X}$.
III. A statistic includes s or $\overline{X}$.
IV. A parameter includes μ and σ.

    A.   I only
    B.   II only
    C.   I and III
    D.   III and IV
    E.   IV only

16. Which of the following does not represent an experimental study?

    A. A group of randomly selected participants is surveyed to determine beliefs regarding reasons for oppression.
    B. The achievement of students in two classes, each of which uses a different geometry software package, is examined.
    C. The reading skills of children who receive only hardback books to read and those who receive software reading systems are compared.
    D. The level of agreement for a random group of citizens regarding a politician's beliefs is examined both before and after a personal memoir is read.
    E. The effects of a new drug are compared for random groups of younger and older patients.

17. A professor randomly surveys groups of researchers who regularly present at research laboratory conferences across the country. Which type of sampling technique does the professor use?

    A. Simple random sampling
    B. Systematic random sampling
    C. Cluster sampling
    D. Stratified random sampling
    E. Snowball sampling

18. Which of the following does not describe a randomized block design?

    A. Interviewing husbands and wives to determine and compare beliefs related to politics
    B. Comparing the achievement of a group of students over the course of six years
    C. Comparing student performance on a pretest and posttest
    D. Surveying sales knowledge of interns prior to and following training sessions
    E. Comparing the achievements of students in two math classes taught by different instructional methods

19. Martin draws a card from a deck of cards, replaces the card, and repeats the process a total of 100 times. How many times may he expect to get a face card?

   A.   10
   B.   20
   C.   23
   D.   25
   E.   52

20. Jean-Philippe draws a marble out of a bag containing five blue marbles, three yellow marbles, and two green marbles. What is the probability that he draws a yellow marble or a green marble?

   A. $\frac{1}{2}$

   B. $\frac{1}{5}$

   C. $\frac{2}{3}$

   D. $\frac{4}{5}$

   E. $\frac{3}{4}$

21. Tony spins a spinner with eight equally spaced sections labeled 1 to 8. What is the probability that the spinner lands on an even number or a number greater than 4?

   A. $\frac{7}{8}$

   B. $\frac{3}{8}$

   C. $\frac{3}{4}$

   D. $\frac{1}{2}$

   E. $\frac{5}{6}$

22. Anita flips a coin and draws a card from a full deck of cards. What is the probability that she gets tails and draws an ace card?

   A. $\frac{15}{26}$

   B. $\frac{1}{4}$

   C. $\frac{1}{52}$

   D. $\frac{2}{3}$

   E. $\frac{1}{26}$

23. What is the probability that Douglas draws a club from a full deck of cards, does not replace it, and draws another club?

   A. $\frac{3}{52}$

   B. $\frac{1}{26}$

   C. $\frac{1}{17}$

   D. $\frac{1}{52}$

   E. $\frac{2}{51}$

24. What is the probability that Sheila draws a heart from a full deck of cards, replaces it, and then draws a jack?

   A. $\frac{13}{663}$

   B. $\frac{1}{26}$

   C. $\frac{1}{52}$

   D. $\frac{3}{52}$

   E. $\frac{169}{2,704}$

25. Given the two-way frequency table that follows, which of the following best represents the probability that a student is a sophomore or studies philosophy?

	COLLEGE ALGEBRA	PHILOSOPHY	AMERICAN HISTORY	TOTAL
Freshman	11	14	16	41
Sophomore	13	17	19	49
Total	24	31	35	90

A. $\frac{7}{10}$

B. $\frac{3}{5}$

C. $\frac{4}{5}$

D. $\frac{3}{4}$

E. $\frac{7}{8}$

26. Robin rolls a die two times. What is the expected value for the number of twos she will roll?

A. $\frac{1}{6}$

B. $\frac{1}{4}$

C. $\frac{1}{8}$

D. $\frac{1}{3}$

E. $\frac{1}{5}$

27. Kevin has one $5 bill, two $10 bills, and three $1 bills. Which of the following best represents the expected value for the amount of money he will get if he draws one bill from his pocket?

   A. $3.89
   B. $4.21
   C. $4.67
   D. $4.99
   E. $5.23

28. Aidan draws two cards from a deck of cards. Which of the following best represents the expected value for the number of hearts he draws?

   A. 0.3
   B. 0.4
   C. 0.5
   D. 0.6
   E. 0.7

29. Adam spins a spinner with eight equally spaced sections labeled 1 to 8. If he spins the spinner 100 times, which of the following best represents the probability the spinner will land on exactly 20 eights?

   A. 0.01
   B. 0.05
   C. 0.09
   D. 0.12
   E. 0.15

30. Kendra rolls a die. If she rolls the die 50 times, which of the following best represents the probability she will roll at least 10 fours?

   A.   0.18
   B.   0.22
   C.   0.28
   D.   0.34
   E.   0.38

31. Given a normal distribution, which of the following best represents the area under the normal curve that is more than three standard deviations below the mean?

   A.   0.001
   B.   0.005
   C.   0.01
   D.   0.05
   E.   0.1

32. Given a normal distribution, which of the following best represents the area under the normal curve that is to the left of a z-score of -1.48?

   A.   5%
   B.   6%
   C.   7%
   D.   8%
   E.   9%

33. Given a normal distribution, which of the following best represents the area under the normal curve that is to the left of a z-score of 2.63?

   A. 0.996
   B. 0.496
   C. 0.896
   D. 0.446
   E. 0.786

34. Given a normal distribution, which of the following best represents the area under the normal curve between the mean and a z-score of −0.35?

   A. 0.08
   B. 0.14
   C. 0.22
   D. 0.32
   E. 0.36

35. A sample of 65 subjects has a mean of 180 and a standard deviation of 20. Given a 90% level of confidence, which of the following best represents the margin of error?

   A. 3.64
   B. 3.78
   C. 4.08
   D. 4.34
   E. 4.66

36. A professor randomly selects 80 students who have taken his Introductory Statistics final exam. The random sample shows a mean of 78. The standard deviation for this exam is 6 points. Which of the following best represents the confidence interval for a 95% level of confidence?

    A. (72.37, 75.29)
    B. (76.69, 79.31)
    C. (78.32, 81.44)
    D. (79.89, 82.55)
    E. (81.45, 84.39)

37. Robin scores an 1850 on her SAT exam. Suppose the average SAT score is 1500, with a standard deviation of 300. Which of the following best represents the p-value?

    A. 0.08
    B. 0.12
    C. 0.03
    D. 0.24
    E. 0.33

38. A company producing a type of lotion claims to include 6.5 ounces per tube. A random sample of 50 tubes of lotion shows a mean of 6.4 ounces and a standard deviation of 0.2 ounces. Which of the following best represents the t-value?

    A. −2.8
    B. −3.2
    C. −3.5
    D. −4.2
    E. −6.4

39. A random sample of 30 students from Dr. Wilson's statistics class shows a mean score of 77 on a final exam, with a standard deviation of 3 points. A random sample of 35 students from Dr. Thompson's statistics class shows a mean score of 79 on a final exam, with a standard deviation of 2 points. Which of the following statements is true?

A. There is a significant difference between the class means, as evidenced by a p-value less than 0.001.

B. There is a significant difference between the class means, as evidenced by a p-value less than 0.01.

C. There is not a significant difference between the class means, as evidenced by a t-value of approximately −0.68.

D. There is not a significant difference between the class means, as evidenced by a p-value greater than 0.05.

E. There is not a significant difference between the class means, as evidenced by a p-value greater than 0.10.

40. Recently, 1,000 articles were submitted to each of three peer-reviewed journals. The number of articles accepted for publication is recorded in the following table.

JOURNAL	NUMBER OF ARTICLES ACCEPTED FOR PUBLICATION
Journal A	92
Journal B	144
Journal C	75

In the past, Journal A typically accepted 10% of submitted articles for publication. Journal B typically accepted 15% of submitted articles for publication. Journal C typically accepted 8% of submitted articles for publication. Which of the following statements is true?

I. The p-value is less than 0.05.
II. The chi-square statistic is approximately 1.2.
III. There is a significant difference between the most recent number of articles accepted for publication and the typical number accepted for publication.
IV. There is not a significant difference between the most recent number of articles accepted for publication and the typical number accepted for publication.

   A. I and III
   B. II and III
   C. II and IV
   D. III only
   E. IV only

END OF SECTION I

Statistics

SECTION II

Time—90 minutes

6 questions

Part A

Time—About 60 minutes

Questions 1–5

Directions: Show all your work. Indicate clearly the methods you use, because you will be scored on the correctness of your methods as well as on the accuracy and completeness of your results and explanations.

1. The following data represents the ages of patrons at a local fair.

    48, 5, 9, 29, 93, 88, 44, 67, 84, 8, 61, 68, 33, 16, 35, 4,
    26, 80, 11, 18, 47, 17, 88, 66, 52, 55, 65, 70, 92, 38

    Describe a graphical representation that would appropriately represent the ages of the patrons. Justify your choice in representation.

2. A random sample of home prices in a neighborhood outside Washington, D.C., is as follows:

    $140,000, $179,000, $264,000, $251,000, $280,000,
    $161,000, $374,000, $382,000, $203,000, $358,000,
    $248,000, $227,000, $241,000, $263,000, $367,000,
    $269,000, $338,000, $204,000, $370,000, $292,000

    (a) Which measure of center will best represent the center of the data? Justify your choice.

    (b) What is the standard deviation of the home prices, to the nearest whole dollar?

    (c) If the population mean price is $225,000 with a standard deviation of $75,000, approximately how many standard deviations below the population mean is a house priced at $179,000? Show the process used to arrive at your answer.

3.   A correlation between SAT scores and high-school GPAs for a random group of college students is represented in the following scatterplot.

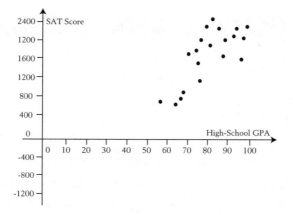

(a) Estimate the least-squares regression line. Describe the estimation procedure used.

(b) Describe the correlation of the data, including an estimation of the correlation coefficient.

(c) Given a high-school GPA of 80, what SAT score may be predicted?

4. The numbers of freshmen, sophomores, juniors, and seniors participating in a local, off-campus volunteer organization are shown in the frequency table that follows:

CLASSIFICATION	NUMBER OF STUDENTS
Freshman	12
Sophomore	18
Junior	14
Senior	20

(a) Create a relative-frequency table of the data.
(b) What measure of center(s) may be determined from the data?
(c) Create a new two-way frequency table that incorporates the data shown in the table. Discuss the marginal and joint frequencies. Discuss at least two deductions that may be made using the marginal frequencies shown in the two-way frequency table.

5. A student scores an 86 on a final statistics exam. The class average is 80, with a standard deviation of 2 points.

(a) How many standard deviations above the mean is the student's score?
(b) What is the area under the normal curve above the student's score?
(c) What is the area under the normal curve between the student's score and the class average?

END OF PART A

Statistics
SECTION II
Part B
Time—About 30 minutes
Question 6

Directions: Show all your work. Indicate clearly the methods you use, because you will be scored on the correctness of your methods as well as on the accuracy and completeness of your results and explanations.

6. A random sample of 45 citizens in county A shows an average annual donation of $1,000, with a standard deviation of $100. A random sample of 55 citizens in county B shows an average annual donation of $1,200, with a standard deviation of $200.

    (a) Do citizens in county B make a significantly larger annual donation, on average? Justify your answer.
    (b) Determine the average annual donation for the population of each sample, using a 95% confidence interval.
    (c) Determine the average annual donation for the population of each sample, using a 90% confidence interval. Discuss whether the 90% confidence interval results in differences in significance and population means.
    (d) Discuss the type of distribution used for analyzing the data. Discuss whether using another distribution would change the probability level. Explain why it would or would not change the p-value.
    (e) Discuss the directional test used in the analysis, as well as why the particular directional test was chosen. How would the result from the other directional test compare to the result given for the directional test used? Explain.

END OF PRACTICE EXAM 1

Practice Exam 1 Answers and Explanations

Section I: Multiple-Choice Questions

ANSWER KEY

1. B	21. C
2. A	22. E
3. D	23. C
4. C	24. C
5. C	25. A
6. B	26. D
7. B	27. C
8. E	28. C
9. E	29. A
10. B	30. D
11. C	31. A
12. A	32. C
13. A	33. A
14. C	34. B
15. D	35. C
16. A	36. B
17. C	37. B
18. E	38. C
19. C	39. B
20. A	40. C

ANSWER EXPLANATIONS

1. **B.** The minimum value is 5, the maximum value is 92, the median is 46, the first quartile is 19.5, and the third quartile is 64. The boxplot represents each of these five values.

    Difficulty level: Easy

2. **A.** The frequency of costs ranging from $50 to $59 is 3. The frequency of costs ranging from $60 to $69 is 2. The frequency of costs ranging from $70 to $79 is 6. The frequency of costs ranging from $80 to $89 is 6. The frequency of costs ranging from $90 to $99 is 3. The frequency plot for Choice A correctly represents these frequencies.

    Difficulty level: Easy

3. **D.** The mean is $196,447.50, the median is $228,750, and the mode is $120,000. Thus, the median is greater than the mean and mode.

    Difficulty level: Easy

4. **C.** The formula for finding the standard deviation is $s_x = \sqrt{\dfrac{\sum (X - \overline{X})^2}{N-1}}$. The standard deviation is equal to the square root of the ratio of the sum of the squared differences to one less than the sample size. Entering the list into a graphing calculator and choosing STDDEV from the list will provide the standard deviation. The standard deviation is approximately 12.8.

    Difficulty level: Medium

5. **C.** A z-score represents the number of standard deviations a score is above or below the mean. A z-score is calculated using the formula $z = \dfrac{X - \mu}{\sigma}$, where X represents the score, μ represents the population mean, and σ represents the population standard deviation. Substituting 75 for X, 125 for μ, and 10 for σ gives $z = \dfrac{75 - 125}{10}$, or $z = -5$. Thus, a value of 75 is 5 standard deviations below the mean of 125.

    Difficulty level: Easy

6. **B.** The number of standard deviations a score is above the mean is

represented by the z-score. Thus, a data point that is 2.5 standard deviations above the mean has a z-score of the same value.

Difficulty level: Medium

7.　**B.** Given the frequencies represented by the bar graph, the data may be listed as follows: 1, 1, 1, 1, 1, 1, 2, 2, 2, 2, 2, 2, 2, 2, 3, 3, 3, 3, 3, 3, 4, 4, 4, 4, 5, 5, 5, 5, 5, 5, 5, 5, 6, 6, 6, 6. Since the data set has an even number of values, the median is the average of the two middle values of this data set when it is arranged in ascending order. The median is the average of 3 and 3, or 3.

Difficulty level: Easy

8.　**E.** Data set A has a larger center, since it shows a larger number of bigger scores. The median for data set A is 31.5, while the median for data set B is 20.5. The standard deviation may be calculated for both data sets, which will show an approximate standard deviation of 17.8 for data set A and 17.6 for data set B. Notice the number of values close to each mean is comparable.

Difficulty level: Medium

9.　**E.** The x- and y-values may be entered into a graphing calculator. Calculating the least-squares regression line gives the r-value of approximately 0.99. Note: On a graphing calculator, choose STAT, CALC, and then LINREG($ax + b$).

Difficulty level: Medium

10. **B.** From visual inspection, it appears that the y-intercept of the least-squares regression line is about −3. The slope can be estimated by choosing two points very close to the estimated line. Choosing the points $(-1, -7)$ and $(1, -1)$ gives a slope of 2.5. Thus, it may be estimated that the slope is closer to 2 than to 4. The line $y = 2x - 3$ is the best choice for the least-squares regression line. The line may also be calculated by entering the x- and y-values into a graphing calculator and choosing STAT, CALC, and then LINREG($ax + b$). Doing so gives an approximate line of $y = 2.15x - 3$.

Difficulty level: Hard

11. **C.** Pearson's correlation coefficient ranges from -1 to 1, with values closest to -1 and 1 indicating strong correlations. An r-value of 0.1 or 0.2 indicates a very weak correlation. Although an r-value of 0.4 is still considered weak, it is not *very* weak. In other words, we could say there is some degree of correlation.

Difficulty level: Easy

12. **A.** To determine the points found on the residual plot, the least-squares regression line must be calculated first. Enter the x- and y-values into a graphing calculator or Excel spreadsheet and calculate the regression line. Next, look at the x-values provided in each of the answer choices. Evaluate the least-squares regression line for these x-values and see if the amounts given by the predicted values subtracted from the actual values are the same as the y-values presented in each answer choice. In this case, the least-squares regression line is approximately $y = 0.14x + 10.4$. Evaluation of the line for the x-values of 3, 9, 12, and 19 gives approximately 10.82, 11.66, 12.08, and 13.06. Subtraction of these predicted values from the actual values gives 1.18, -5.66, 0.92, and 0.94, respectively. Thus, four of the points on the residual plot are $(3, 1.18)$, $(9, -5.66)$, $(12, 0.92)$, and $(19, 0.94)$.

Difficulty level: Hard

13. **A.** The logarithm of each y-value was used, giving approximate y-values of 0.3, 1.1, 1.4, 1.9, 2.4, 2.9, 3.3, 3.8, 4.3, and 4.8. With a model that appears to be exponential, taking the logarithm of the y-values will result in a more linear model.

Difficulty level: Hard

14. **C.** To obtain the highest r-value for a model that is quadratic in nature, the square root of all y-values may be calculated and used in the transformed model. Taking the logarithm of the x- and y-values also reveals a high level of correlation here (approximately 0.998). However, using the square root of all y-values gives an approximate r-value of 0.999, which is even higher.

Difficulty level: Hard

15. **D.** A statistic refers to a mean or standard deviation resulting from a given sample of a population. Thus, a statistic includes s or $\overline{X}$. A parameter refers to the actual population mean or population standard deviation. Thus, a parameter includes μ or σ.

Difficulty level: Easy

16. **A.** A nonexperimental study does not involve a treatment or intervention given to a group or groups of participants. Simply surveying a group of subjects regarding their beliefs does not constitute an experiment.

Difficulty level: Easy

17. **C.** The groups of researchers who present at the various research laboratories constitute clusters. From the clusters, the professor may survey all researchers in each cluster, or a random sample from each cluster.

Difficulty level: Easy

18. **E.** Choice E does not state that the classes were matched according to some *a priori* factor(s). Also, the classes weren't given a pre- or post-assessment. There is nothing that states the samples are similar.

Difficulty level: Medium

19. **C.** The theoretical probability of drawing a face card after one draw is $\frac{12}{52}$. Thus, after 100 draws, he can expect to get a total number of face cards equal to the product of 100 and $\frac{12}{52}$, or approximately 23.

Difficulty level: Medium

20. **A.** If A and B are mutually exclusive events, then the probability of A or B may be calculated using the formula $P(A \text{ or } B) = P(A) + P(B)$. Thus, the probability Jean-Philippe draws a yellow marble or a green marble may be written as $P(\text{yellow or green}) = \frac{3}{10} + \frac{2}{10} = \frac{5}{10} = \frac{1}{2}$.

Difficulty level: Medium

21. **C.** If A and B are dependent events, then the probability of A or B may be calculated using the formula $P(A \text{ or } B) = P(A) + P(B) - P(A \text{ and } B)$. The probability of the spinner's landing on an even number is $\frac{4}{8}$. The probability of the spinner's landing on a number greater than 4 is also $\frac{4}{8}$. The probability of the spinner's landing on an even number

and a number greater than 4 is $\frac{2}{8}$. Thus, the probability of the spinner's landing on an even number or a number greater than 4 may be written as $P(\text{even or greater than } 4) = \frac{4}{8} + \frac{4}{8} - \frac{2}{8}$, or $\frac{3}{4}$.

Difficulty level: Medium

22. **E.** If A and B are independent events, then the probability of A and B may be calculated using the formula $P(A \text{ and } B) = P(A) \cdot P(B)$. The probability of getting tails is $\frac{1}{2}$. The probability of drawing an ace card is $\frac{4}{52}$. The probability of getting tails and an ace card may be written as $P(A \text{ and } B) = \frac{1}{2} \cdot \frac{4}{52}$, or $\frac{1}{26}$.

Difficulty level: Medium

23. **C.** If A and B are dependent events, then the probability of A and B may be calculated using the formula $P(A \text{ and } B) = P(A) \cdot P(B|A)$. The sample space for the second draw, event B, is decreased by 1. The number of possibilities for event B is also decreased by 1. Thus, the probability may be written as $P(A \text{ and } B) = \frac{13}{52} \cdot \frac{12}{51}$, or $\frac{1}{17}$.

Difficulty level: Medium

24. **C.** If A and B are independent events, then the probability of A and B may be calculated using the formula $P(A \text{ and } B) = P(A) \cdot P(B)$. Thus, the probability may be written as $P(A \text{ and } B) = \frac{13}{52} \cdot \frac{4}{52} = \frac{1}{52}$.

Difficulty level: Medium

25. **A.** The probability of the dependent events, A or B, may be calculated using the formula $P(A \text{ or } B) = P(A) + P(B) - P(A \text{ and } B)$. The probability a student is a sophomore or studies philosophy may be written as $P(S \text{ and } P) = \frac{49}{90} + \frac{31}{90} - \frac{17}{90}$, or $\frac{7}{10}$.

Difficulty level: Medium

26. **D.** The theoretical probability of rolling a 2 is $\frac{1}{6}$. After two rolls, the expected value is equal to the product of 2 and $\frac{1}{6}$, or $\frac{1}{3}$. You can also calculate the probabilities of each x-value, or roll ($X = 0$, 1, or 2), and write the expected value as the sum of the products of each x-value and

the corresponding probability. In this case, the expected value may be written as $E(X) = \left(0 \cdot \frac{25}{36}\right) + \left(1 \cdot \frac{10}{36}\right) + \left(2 \cdot \frac{1}{36}\right) = \frac{12}{36} = \frac{1}{3}$.

Difficulty level: Medium

27. **C.** The expected value may be written as $E(X) = \left(5 \cdot \frac{1}{6}\right) + \left(10 \cdot \frac{2}{6}\right) + \left(1 \cdot \frac{3}{6}\right)$, or approximately 4.67. Thus, the expected value is approximately \$4.67.

Difficulty level: Medium

28. **C.** The *x*-values and probabilities are represented in the table below:

x	f(x)
0	$\dfrac{\binom{13}{0}\binom{39}{2}}{\binom{52}{2}}$
1	$\dfrac{\binom{13}{1}\binom{39}{1}}{\binom{52}{2}}$
2	$\dfrac{\binom{13}{2}\binom{39}{0}}{\binom{52}{2}}$

The approximate expected value may be written as $E(X) = (0 \cdot 0.56) + (1 \cdot 0.38) + (2 \cdot 0.06)$ or 0.5.

Difficulty level: Hard

29. **A.** The BINOMPDF function of a graphing calculator may be used to find the probability of a discrete number of successes. The function BINOMPDF (n, ϖ, x), may be used, where *n* represents the number of trials, ϖ represents the probability of success of one trial, and *x* represents the number of total successes. In this case, the probability may be written as BINOMPDF $(100, 0.125, 20)$, which is approximately 0.01, or 1%. The answer may also be found using the binomial probability formula:

$$P(20) = \frac{100!}{20! \cdot 80!}\left(\frac{1}{8}\right)^{20}\left(\frac{7}{8}\right)^{80}$$

Difficulty level: Hard

30. **D.** When you look at a range of successes, as in this case, use the BINOMCDF function. For a cumulative distribution function, where the successes are equal to "at least" some value, the following function should be used: $1 - \text{BINOMCDF}(n, \varpi, x - 1)$, where n represents the number of trials, ϖ represents the probability of success for one trial, and x represents the minimum number of successes. In this case, the minimum number of successes is 10, since she is looking for the probability of getting at least 10 fours. The following function may be entered into the calculator: $1 - \text{BINOMCDF}(50, 0.17, 9)$, which is approximately 0.34.

Difficulty level: Hard

31. **A.** A distance of 3 standard deviations below the mean is represented by a z-score of -3. Using the absolute value of -3, the z-value of 3 shows a smaller portion area of 0.0013. Thus, the area under the curve more than 3 standard deviations below the mean is 0.0013, or approximately 0.001. The area may also be determined by subtracting the mean-to-z area of 0.4987 from an area of 0.5. The total area under the curve is 1, with 0.5 between the mean and the upper tail and 0.5 between the mean and the lower tail. Thus, the area below 3 standard deviations from the mean is equal to the difference of 0.5 and the area from the mean to 3 standard deviations below the mean, or 0.4987, which equals 0.0013.

Difficulty level: Medium

32. **C.** A z-score of -1.48 shows a mean-to-z area of 0.4306 and a smaller-portion area of 0.0694. Thus, the area under the curve *to the left* of the z-score is approximately 0.07, or 7%.

Difficulty level: Medium

33. **A.** A z-score of 2.63 shows a mean-to-z area of 0.4957. Thus, the area to the left of this positive z-score is 0.9957 (the sum of 0.5 and 0.4957). The area is also equal to the larger portion area, shown in a z-table.

Difficulty level: Medium

34. B. A z-score of -0.35 shows a mean-to-z area of 0.1368, or approximately 0.14.

Difficulty level: Medium

35. C. The formula for calculating margin of error is $E = z_{\frac{\alpha}{2}} \cdot \frac{\sigma}{\sqrt{n}}$. Since the sample size is fairly large, the sample standard deviation may be substituted for the population standard deviation in the formula. The critical z-value for a 90% level of confidence is 1.645. Substituting the known values gives $E = 1.645 \cdot \frac{20}{\sqrt{65}}$, or approximately 4.08.

Difficulty level: Hard

36. B. The confidence interval may be determined using the formula-confidence interval $= \overline{X} \pm z_{\frac{\alpha}{2}} \cdot \frac{\sigma}{\sqrt{n}}$. The critical z-value for a 95% level of confidence is 1.96. Substituting the known values gives confidence interval $= 78 \pm 1.96 \cdot \frac{6}{\sqrt{80}}$. Thus, the confidence interval may be approximately represented as $(76.69, 79.31)$. The ZINTERVAL function of a graphing calculator may also be used to calculate the approximate confidence interval. Enter the population standard deviation, sample mean, sample size, and confidence level of 0.95.

Difficulty level: Hard

37. B. The p-value may be determined by first calculating the z-score. Note: Since the population standard deviation is given, a z-score may be used. The z-score may be written as $z = \dfrac{1{,}850 - 1{,}500}{300}$, or $z \approx 1.17$. The p-value for a z-score of 1.17 is 0.12.

Difficulty level: Medium

38. C. The t-value for this one-sample t-test may be calculated using the formula $t = \dfrac{\overline{X} - \mu}{\left(\frac{s}{\sqrt{n}}\right)}$. Substituting the given sample mean, population mean, sample standard deviation, and sample size gives $t = \dfrac{6.4 - 6.5}{\left(\frac{0.2}{\sqrt{50}}\right)}$, or approximately -3.5. A graphing calculator may also be used to find the t-value. Choose STAT, TESTS, and T-TEST.

Difficulty level: Medium

39. B. To compare the two sample means, with sample standard deviations reported, a two-sample t-test should be used. Choose STAT, TESTS, and 2-SAMPT-TEST. Enter the sample mean, sample standard deviation, and sample size for the first sample. Then, do the same for the second sample. In this case, you can choose a nondirectional test. Pooling or not pooling the variance will result in similar p-values, both less than 0.01. Given a level of significance of 0.05, there is a statistically significant difference between the two sample means.

Difficulty level: Hard

40. C. The chi-square statistic may be calculated as $\chi^2 = \dfrac{(92 - 100)^2}{100} + \dfrac{(144 - 150)^2}{150} + \dfrac{(75 - 80)^2}{80}$, which is approximately 1.2. For 2 degrees of freedom, a chi-square statistic of 1.2 lies between probabilities of 0.5 and 0.75 but closer to 0.5. Since 0.5 is greater than the level of significance of 0.05, it can be declared that no significant difference exists between the numbers of articles accepted recently and in the past.

Difficulty level: Hard

Section II, Part A: Free-Response Questions

1. Since the data show a large range (range of 89), a histogram would be a good representation to show the frequencies of intervals of ages of patrons attending the fair. The heights of the bars of the histogram would represent the frequencies of patrons of different ages represented by each interval. The histogram may include the following intervals: 1–10, 11–20, 21–30, 31–40, 41–50, 51–60, 61–70, 71–80, 81–90, and 91–100. Frequencies for these intervals would be 4, 4, 2, 3, 3, 2, 5, 1, 4, and 2.

Difficulty level: Medium

2.

(a) The best measure of center would be the median, due to the large range (range of $242,000). The distribution is also skewed to the left.

The median is not impacted by extreme outliers or skewed data and will give a more accurate value for the center of the home prices.

(b) $74,425

(c) A house priced at $179,000 is approximately 0.61 standard deviations below the population mean of $225,000. The z-score will show the number of standard deviations the home price is below the population mean. The z-score may be written as $z = \dfrac{179{,}000 - 225{,}000}{75{,}000}$, which is approximately -0.61.

   Difficulty level: Hard

3.

(a) A line of best fit would seem to cross the y-axis at approximately $-1{,}200$. The slope of the line is difficult to estimate visually due to the scale. However, two points very close to the line appear to be approximately (90, 1,900) and (95, 2,150), which give a slope of 50. Since the points are not right on the line, a slope of 35 might be a better estimate. Thus, the equation $y = 35x - 1{,}200$ is a good estimate for the least-squares regression line.

(b) The data seem to show a fairly strong linear relationship. The GPA scores and SAT scores seem to show a correlation of at least 0.7. The correlation is positive; as the GPA scores increase, the SAT scores also increase.

(c) Based on the estimated least-squares regression line (found in part (a) of the solution), the predicted SAT score may be determined by evaluating the line for a GPA (or x-value) of 80. Doing so gives $y = 35(80) - 1200$, or 1600. From the scatterplot, it is easy to see that an SAT score of 1600 may certainly correlate to a GPA of 80.

   Difficulty level: Hard

4.

(a) The following is a relative frequency table of the data:

CLASSIFICATION	RELATIVE FREQUENCY OF NUMBER OF STUDENTS
Freshman	0.19
Sophomore	0.28
Junior	0.22
Senior	0.31

(b) Since the data represents categories of data, the mode is the only measure of center that may be discerned from the data in the table.

(c) The following is a two-way frequency table:

	FRESHMAN	SOPHOMORE	JUNIOR	SENIOR	TOTAL
High School A	12	18	14	20	64
High School B	10	16	14	22	62
Total	22	34	28	42	126

The marginal frequencies are the totals in the margins while the joint frequencies are the frequencies in the body of the table. The marginal frequencies reveal that the number of seniors is almost twice that of the number of freshmen. The marginal frequencies also reveal that the numbers of students from each high school are comparable.

Difficulty level: Hard

5.

(a) The student's score is 3 standard deviations above the mean. The number of standard deviations above the mean is determined by the z-score: $z = \dfrac{86 - 80}{2}$, or $z = 3$.

(b) The area under the normal curve above the student's score is equal to the difference of 0.5 and the mean-to-z area of 0.4987, for an upper tail area of 0.0013.

(c) The area under the normal curve between the student's score and the class average is equal to the mean-to-z area, or 0.4987.

Difficulty level: Hard

Section II, Part B: The Investigative Task

6.

(a) Yes, a two-sample *t*-test reveals a *p*-value less than 0.001. Thus, the null hypothesis of no difference should be rejected, and a significant difference between the counties' average annual donations should be declared.

(b) Using a 95% confidence level, the population average annual donation for county A is likely to fall between $970.80 and $1,029.20. The same confidence level, applied to county B, shows a likely population donation between $1,147.10 and $1,252.90.

(c) Using a 90% confidence level, the population average annual donation for county A is likely to fall between $975.48 and $1,024.52. The same confidence level, applied to county B, shows a likely population donation between $1,155.63 and $1,244.37. Neither the 95% nor the 90% confidence intervals for the two means overlap, so the same conclusion of a significant difference could be drawn either way.

(d) A *t*-distribution was used because the population standard deviations were not given. However, had a two-sample *z*-test been used, the *p*-value would still be less than 0.001, resulting in the same conclusion as described in (a). Since both sample sizes are larger than 30, the *p*-value calculated from either distribution will be comparable. The *z*- and *t*-values are almost identical, both with a value of approximately −6.5.

(e) A two-directional, or two-tailed test, was used, because it would not be known which county has a higher average annual donation amount. A two-directional test gives a *t*-value of approximately −6.5. The critical *t*-value for a two-tailed test with 40 degrees of freedom and a *p*-value of 0.001 is 3.551. Had the analysis been altered to use a one-directional, or one-tailed test, the *t*-value would still be less than this critical value of 3.551, again corresponding to a p-value less than 0.001. The results would still cause a rejection of the null hypothesis and a declaration of difference between the average annual donations.

Difficulty level: Hard

AP Statistics Practice Exam 2

Statistics

SECTION I

Time—90 minutes

40 questions

Directions: Solve each of the following problems. After examining the answer choices, select the best solution to the problem. No credit will be given for anything written in the exam book. Do not spend too much time on any one problem.

1. The human resources department at a company gathers data from a survey, which inquires about the number of miles driven per day by a random sample of the company's employees. The numbers of miles driven per day are as follows:

    8, 88, 39, 84, 67, 70, 88, 89, 60, 46, 58, 70, 56, 6, 81, 37, 83, 60, 31, 35, 35, 71, 55, 26, 21, 61, 48, 40, 76, 13

Which of the following histograms accurately represents the data?

A.

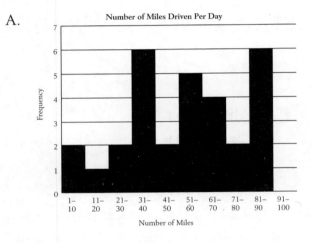

B.

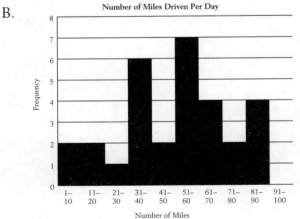

C.

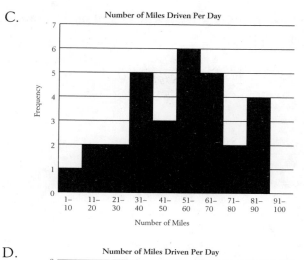

Number of Miles Driven Per Day

D.

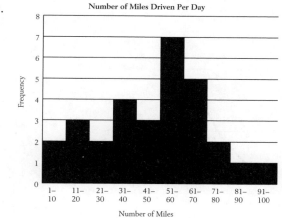

Number of Miles Driven Per Day

E.

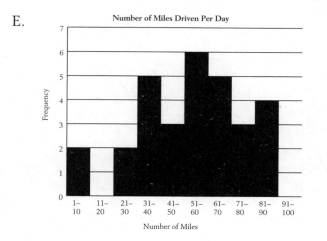

Number of Miles Driven Per Day

2. Which of the following cumulative frequency plots accurately represents the data that follow?

12, 43, 32, 46, 1, 29, 50, 63, 33, 19,
74, 59, 70, 60, 70, 63, 51, 1, 98, 12

A.

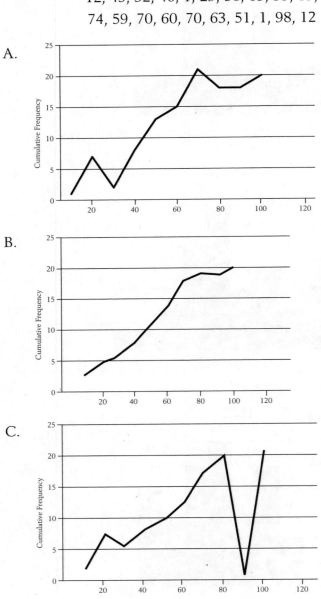

B.

C.

D.

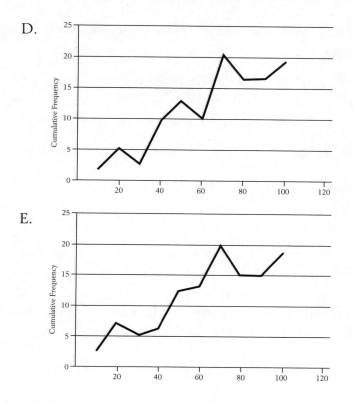

E.

3. Elisha needs to create a boxplot to represent the data that follow:

1, 1, 1, 2, 4, 4, 5, 6, 8, 14, 15, 17, 17, 18, 19, 20,
23, 26, 27, 27, 30, 30, 32, 33, 34, 37, 37, 40, 45, 49

Which of the following correctly represents the first and third quartiles?

A. 5 and 30
B. 5.5 and 31
C. 6 and 32
D. 6.5 and 32.5
E. 8 and 33

4. Tony records his freelance writing income per month for the past 2 years as follows:

    $2,300, $2,800, $4,200, $3,300, $3,800, $3,500, $4,200, $2,600, $2,200, $3,100, $2,700, $4,000, $4,100, $2,700, $2,600, $2,800, $4,200, $4,600, $3,700, $2,200, $4,400, $3,200, $3,800, $4,500

    Which of the following best represents the standard deviation?

    A. $722.40
    B. $746.80
    C. $781.60
    D. $802.40
    E. $824.60

5. Which of the following best represents the variance of the data set that follows?

    10, 9, 50, 32, 23, 15, 36, 11, 38, 21, 22, 30

    A. 118
    B. 125
    C. 139
    D. 148
    E. 163

6. Data sets A and B are represented in the back-to-back stemplot that follows:

DATA SET A	STEM	DATA SET B
2, 7, 9	0	2, 2, 9
2, 7, 7, 9	1	0, 1, 1, 3, 7, 9
0, 0, 3, 4, 4, 4, 8	2	8
0, 6, 6	3	4, 4, 5, 7
1, 9	4	3, 3, 8
2	5	3, 5, 9

Which of the following statements is true?

A. Data set A has a smaller center and larger variability than data set B.

B. Data set A has a smaller center and smaller variability than data set B.

C. Data set A has a larger center and a larger variability than data set B.

D. Data set A has a larger center and smaller variability than data set B.

E. The center and variability for the two data sets are very similar.

7. A data set value has a z-score of 2. How many standard deviations above the mean is the value?

A. 1
B. 1.5
C. 2
D. 2.5
E. 3

8. The frequencies of ages of focus group participants in two focus groups are shown in the double-bar graph that follows:

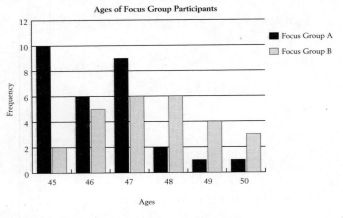

Which of the following statements is true?

A. Focus group A has a larger median age and smaller mean age.
B. Focus group A has a larger median age and larger mean age.
C. Focus group A has a smaller median age and smaller mean age.
D. Focus group A has a smaller median age and larger mean age.
E. The exact values of the mean and median ages for the two groups cannot be determined from the bar graph.

9. Which of the following best describes the correlation shown in the scatterplot that follows?

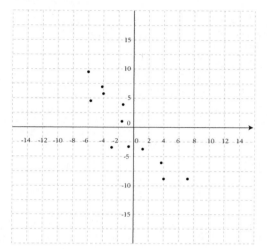

A. Strong, positive correlation
B. Strong, negative correlation
C. Weak, positive correlation
D. Weak, negative correlation
E. No correlation

10. Which of the following best represents the correlation coefficient, r, for the x-y table that follows?

x	1	3	3	5	5	7	7	8	9	9
y	14	10	16	17	19	11	19	13	12	18

A. 0.08
B. 0.15
C. 0.22
D. 0.29
E. 0.34

11. Which of the following best represents the least-squares regression line for the scatterplot that follows?

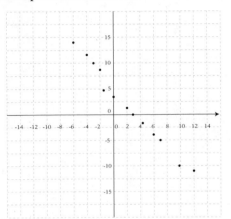

A. $y = -8.6x + 10.4$
B. $y = -4.2x + 8.6$
C. $y = 3.6x + 7.2$
D. $y = -1.4x + 5.2$
E. $y = -6.8x + 4.8$

12. Which of the following represents points on the residual plot of the data for the data set that follows?

x	y
0	3
1	−1
2	−6
3	−8

A. (0, 0.3), (1, 0.1), (2, −1.1), (3, 0.7)
B. (0, 0.8), (1, 0.6), (2, 1.4), (3, 1.2)
C. (0, 0.2), (1, −0.4), (2, −1.8), (3, −1.1)
D. (0, 1.7), (2, 2.2), (3, 2.8), (4, 3.2)
E. (0, 1.2), (2, 0.8), (2, −3.1), (3, 4.2)

13. A random sample of high school students is surveyed to determine university preferences. The frequencies are represented in the table that follows:

UNIVERSITY	FREQUENCY
Texas A&M University	20
University of Arizona	32
New Mexico State University	40
University of Texas at Austin	42
Arizona State University	16

Which of the following tables best represents the relative frequencies?

A.

UNIVERSITY	FREQUENCY
Texas A&M University	0.18
University of Arizona	0.08
New Mexico State University	0.32
University of Texas at Austin	0.34
Arizona State University	0.08

B.

UNIVERSITY	FREQUENCY
Texas A&M University	0.13
University of Arizona	0.18
New Mexico State University	0.32
University of Texas at Austin	0.25
Arizona State University	0.12

C.

UNIVERSITY	FREQUENCY
Texas A&M University	0.16
University of Arizona	0.24
New Mexico State University	0.28
University of Texas at Austin	0.28
Arizona State University	0.04

D.

UNIVERSITY	FREQUENCY
Texas A&M University	0.11
University of Arizona	0.23
New Mexico State University	0.26
University of Texas at Austin	0.31
Arizona State University	0.09

E.

UNIVERSITY	FREQUENCY
Texas A&M University	0.13
University of Arizona	0.21
New Mexico State University	0.27
University of Texas at Austin	0.28
Arizona State University	0.11

14. Given the two-way frequency table that follows, which of the following best represents the relative frequency for college freshmen who are Democrats?

	DEMOCRAT	REPUBLICAN	INDEPENDENT	TOTAL
Freshman	15	18	10	43
Sophomores	15	16	14	45
Total	30	34	24	88

  A. 11%
  B. 13%
  C. 15%
  D. 17%
  E. 19%

15. Which of the following best describes a study that examines the past for causes of current situations?

  A. *Ex post facto* study
  B. Survey
  C. Case study
  D. Longitudinal study
  E. Quasi-experimental study

16. If a random number generator is used to determine assignment of participants into groups, which random sampling technique is used?

  A. Snowball sampling
  B. Systematic random sampling
  C. Cluster sampling
  D. Stratified random sampling
  E. Simple random sampling

17. Which of the following statements are true?

I.   A *t*-distribution should be used when the population standard deviation is known.

II. A *t*-distribution should be used when the population standard deviation is not known.

III. A *z*-distribution compares standardized scores.

IV. A *t*-distribution compares raw scores.

    A. I and III
    B. I, III, and IV
    C. II and III
    D. II and IV
    E. II, III, and IV

18. Which of the following analyses are deductive?

I.   *t*-tests
II. Content analysis
III. Constant comparison
IV. Linear regression

    A. I only
    B. I and III
    C. I and IV
    D. II and III
    E. II and IV

19. Which of the following is NOT a reasonable limitation to a study?

    A. Employing a quasi-experimental design
    B. Using a randomized block design
    C. Using a sample size less than 30
    D. Unaccounted confounding variables
    E. Disproportionate sample sizes

20. If Aidan draws a card from a deck of cards a total of 100 times, which of the following best represents the experimental probability of drawing an ace?

    A. $\frac{1}{4}$

    B. $\frac{4}{13}$

    C. $\frac{1}{13}$

    D. $\frac{2}{9}$

    E. $\frac{4}{9}$

21. A bag contains 10 cards labeled 1 to 10. What is the expected value of drawing a card from the bag?

    A. 3.5

    B. 4

    C. 4.5

    D. 5

    E. 5.5

22. What is the expected value of tossing a coin?

    A. 0.25

    B. 0.5

    C. 1

    D. 1.25

    E. 1.5

23. Brian rolls a die two times. What is the expected value of rolling an even number?

    A.   0.25
    B.   0.5
    C.   0.75
    D.   1
    E.   1.25

24. What is the probability of drawing a spade from a deck of cards?

    A. $\frac{1}{13}$
    B. $\frac{13}{51}$
    C. $\frac{1}{6}$
    D. $\frac{1}{4}$
    E. $\frac{4}{9}$

25. Monique rolls a die and tosses a coin. What is the probability that she rolls a three or gets heads?

    A. $\frac{7}{12}$
    B. $\frac{1}{6}$
    C. $\frac{5}{6}$
    D. $\frac{2}{3}$
    E. $\frac{1}{2}$

26. Gitta spins a spinner with eight equally spaced sections labeled 1–8 and rolls a die. What is the probability that the spinner lands on a number greater than three or the die lands on a four?

    A. $\frac{11}{16}$

    B. $\frac{5}{48}$

    C. $\frac{3}{4}$

    D. $\frac{2}{3}$

    E. $\frac{5}{6}$

27. Hannah rolls a die and draws a card from a standard deck of cards. What is the probability that she rolls a number greater than four and draws an ace?

    A. $\frac{16}{39}$

    B. $\frac{1}{13}$

    C. $\frac{4}{13}$

    D. $\frac{1}{39}$

    E. $\frac{4}{9}$

28. Michael tosses a coin and rolls a die. What is the probability that he gets tails and rolls a number less than three?

    A. $\frac{1}{6}$

    B. $\frac{1}{18}$

    C. $\frac{5}{6}$

    D. $\frac{1}{4}$

    E. $\frac{2}{3}$

29. What is the probability that Robin rolls a number less than three or an odd number with a die?

   A. $\frac{2}{5}$

   B. $\frac{5}{6}$

   C. $\frac{2}{3}$

   D. $\frac{1}{6}$

   E. $\frac{1}{3}$

30. What is the probability that Aaron draws a heart from a deck of cards, replaces the card, and then draws a queen?

   A. $\frac{17}{52}$

   B. $\frac{1}{52}$

   C. $\frac{1}{4}$

   D. $\frac{4}{13}$

   E. $\frac{1}{51}$

31. What is the probability that Michelle draws a spade from a deck of cards, does not replace the card, and draws another spade?

   A. $\frac{39}{2,704}$

   B. $\frac{4}{13}$

   C. $\frac{273}{884}$

   D. $\frac{1}{68}$

   E. $\frac{3}{51}$

32. What is the probability that Amos draws a king from a deck of cards, does not replace the card, and then draws another king?

    A. $\dfrac{1}{221}$

    B. $\dfrac{4}{663}$

    C. $\dfrac{7}{52}$

    D. $\dfrac{30}{221}$

    E. $\dfrac{3}{676}$

33. Given the two-way table that follows, which of the following best represents the probability that an employee prefers espressos or takes the bus to work?

	LATTE	ESPRESSO	CAPPUCCINO	BLENDED BEVERAGE	TOTAL
Bus	2	7	15	15	39
Vehicle	2	2	3	15	22
Total	4	9	18	30	61

    A. 61%
    B. 63%
    C. 65%
    D. 67%
    E. 69%

34. What is the mean of a standard normal distribution?

    A. 0
    B. 1
    C. 10
    D. 25
    E. 50

35. A cereal company claims to include 19 ounces of cereal in each bag of cereal, with a standard deviation of 0.1 ounces. A sample bag is found to contain 18.9 ounces. How many standard deviations below the mean is the number of ounces contained in the sample bag?

   A.   0.5
   B.   1
   C.   1.5
   D.   2
   E.   2.5

36. Which of the following best represents the area under a normal curve between a z-score of 1.92 and the mean?

   A.   35%
   B.   38%
   C.   41%
   D.   44%
   E.   47%

37. Which of the following best represents the area under a normal curve to the right of a z-score of 2.93?

   A.   0.002
   B.   0.005
   C.   0.008
   D.   0.012
   E.   0.016

38. Which of the following best represents the area under a normal curve that is above 2.85 standard deviations below the mean?

    A. 98.64%

    B. 98.82%

    C. 98.96%

    D. 99.36%

    E. 99.78%

39. A coffee manufacturer claims to include 12 ounces in each container of cappuccino mix. A random sample of 50 containers shows a mean of 11.9 ounces per container, with a standard deviation of 0.1 ounces. Considering a 0.05 level of significance, which of the following statements is true?

    A.   There is a significant difference between the number of ounces per container in the sample and the number of ounces claimed by the coffee manufacturer, as evidenced by a t-value of approximately -1.6.

    B.   There is a significant difference between the number of ounces per container in the sample and the number of ounces claimed by the coffee manufacturer, as evidenced by a t-value of approximately -7.1.

    C.   There is not a significant difference between the number of ounces per container in the sample and the number of ounces claimed by the coffee manufacturer, as evidenced by a t-value of approximately -1.2.

    D.   There is not a significant difference between the number of ounces per container in the sample and the number of ounces claimed by the coffee manufacturer, as evidenced by a t-value of approximately -7.1.

    E.   There is a significant difference between the number of ounces per container in the sample and the number of ounces claimed by the coffee manufacturer, as evidenced by a t-value of approximately -1.2.

40. At University A, a random sample of 30 graduate assistants shows a mean annual salary of $15,000, with a standard deviation of $500. At University B, a random sample of 35 graduate assistants shows a mean annual salary of $16,000, with a standard deviation of $1,000. Which of the following statements is true?

A. There is a significant difference between the annual mean salaries for the two samples, with a p-value less than 0.001.

B. There is a significant difference between the annual mean salaries for the two samples, with a p-value between 0.01 and 0.05.

C. There is not a significant difference between the annual mean salaries for the two samples, with a p-value greater than 0.10.

D. There is not a significant difference between the annual mean salaries for the two samples, with a p-value between 0.50 and 0.10.

E. There is not a significant difference between the annual mean salaries for the two samples, with a p-value less than 0.05.

END OF SECTION I

Statistics
SECTION II
Time—90 minutes

6 questions

Part A

Time—About 60 minutes

Questions 1–5

Directions: Show all your work. Indicate clearly the methods you use, because you will be scored on the correctness of your methods as well as on the accuracy and completeness of your results and explanations.

1. Jason scores a 1200 on his SAT exam. Suppose the mean SAT score is 1500, with a standard deviation of 100.

   (a) How many standard deviations below the mean SAT score is Jason's score?

   (b) What percentage of test-takers scored below Jason's score?

   (c) What percentage of test-takers scored somewhere between Jason's score and the mean SAT score?

2. A cereal manufacturer claims a standard deviation of 0.2 ounces of cereal for each box. A random sample of 36 boxes reveals a mean number of ounces equal to 22.5.

   (a) Compute the approximate margin of error for a 95% level of confidence.

   (b) Compute the approximate confidence interval for a 95% level of confidence.

   (c) Based on the confidence interval, provide a possible value for the true number of ounces of cereal per box. Explain the process used to arrive at the true value.

3. A candle-making company claims to include 3 ounces of wax in each jar, with a standard deviation of 0.1 ounces. A random sample of 45 jars shows a mean of 2.9 ounces of wax per jar. Using a 95% confidence level, is it likely the company's claim is true? Why or why not?

4. The average annual salary of 30 randomly selected employees at a large mathematics organization is $40,000, with a standard deviation of $1,000. The company claims an average annual salary of $41,000.

    (a) Is there a significant difference between the company's claim for average annual salary and the average annual salary shown by the sample? Explain.
    (b) Provide an approximate p-value.

5. Out of a random sample of 50 voters, 15 are Democrats.

    (a) Find the margin of error for the population proportion that is Democrat, using a 90% level of confidence.
    (b) What is the 90% confidence interval for the population proportion that is Democrat?
    (c) What is a possible true population proportion for Democrats? Justify your answer.

    END OF PART A

Statistics
SECTION II
Part B
Time—About 30 minutes
Question 6

Directions: Show all your work. Indicate clearly the methods you use, because you will be scored on the correctness of your methods as well as on the accuracy and completeness of your results and explanations.

6. The number of inches of rainfall per month in the city of Houston during the months of June through September is recorded in the table that follows. Notice that this year's numbers of inches of rainfall per month are compared to the recorded averages for numbers of inches of rainfall per month.

MONTH	# OF INCHES PER MONTH THIS YEAR	RECORDED AVERAGES FOR # OF INCHES PER MONTH
June	5.6	5.9
July	3.9	3.8
August	4.1	3.8
September	4.2	4.1

(a) What is the chi-square statistic?

(b) How many degrees of freedom were used in the analysis? Explain how the number of degrees of freedom was determined.

(c) Provide the approximate p-value. Explain how the p-value was estimated.

(d) Is there a significant difference between the numbers of inches of rainfall per month this year in the city of Houston and the recorded averages for the numbers of inches of rainfall received per month? Explain.

(e) If the month of September were not included in the analysis, would this change the declaration of significance? Support your decision with an approximate p-value.

END OF PRACTICE EXAM 2

Practice Exam 2 Answers and Explanations

Section 1: Multiple-Choice Questions

ANSWER KEY

1. A		21. E	
2. B		22. B	
3. C		23. D	
4. C		24. D	
5. E		25. A	
6. B		26. A	
7. C		27. D	
8. C		28. A	
9. B		29. C	
10. A		30. B	
11. D		31. E	
12. A		32. A	
13. E		33. D	
14. D		34. A	
15. A		35. B	
16. E		36. E	
17. C		37. A	
18. C		38. E	
19. B		39. B	
20. C		40. A	

ANSWER EXPLANATIONS

1. **A.** The frequencies for the number of miles driven per day in the given intervals, ranging from 1–10 through 90–100, are 2, 1, 2, 6, 2, 5, 4, 2, 6, and 0. Choice A shows a histogram with these frequencies.

    Difficulty level: Easy

2. **B.** Within the intervals, ranging from 1–10 to 91–100, the frequencies were 2, 3, 1, 2, 3, 3, 4, 1, 0, and 1. The cumulative frequencies were 2, 5, 6, 8, 11, 14, 18, 19, 19, and 20. Choice B correctly represents these cumulative frequencies.

    Difficulty level: Medium

3. **C.** The median of the lower half of the scores (first quartile) is 6. The bottom half has 15 scores. The median of the lower half of the scores is the middle value, with seven scores above and seven scores below the first quartile. The median of the upper half of the scores (third quartile) is 32, because there are seven scores below that value in the upper half and seven scores above that value.

    Difficulty level: Easy

4. **C.** The standard deviation may be calculated by entering the data into a list in the graphing calculator. Choose 2STAT, MATH, and then STDDEV. The standard deviation may also be computed manually by using the formula $s_x = \sqrt{\dfrac{\sum (X - \overline{X})^2}{N - 1}}$, where X represents each value, $\overline{X}$ represents the mean of the values, and N represents the number of values. The approximate differences between the values and the mean may be written as $-1{,}095.83$, -595.83, 804.17, -95.83, 404.17, 104.17, 804.17, -795.83, $-1{,}195.83$, -295.83, -695.83, 604.17, 704.17, -695.83, -795.83, -595.83, 804.17, $1{,}204.17$, 304.17, $-1{,}195.83$, $1{,}004.17$, -195.83, 404.17, and $1{,}104.17$. The sum of the approximate squared differences is $14{,}049{,}583$. Division of the squared differences by 23 (the number of values minus 1) gives approximately $610{,}851.43$. The square root of this number is approximately 781.60. Thus, the standard deviation for his monthly freelance writing income is approximately $781.60.

    Difficulty level: Medium

5. **E.** The variance may be calculated by entering the data into a list in the graphing calculator. Choose 2STAT, MATH, and then VARIANCE. The variance is approximately 163. The variance is also the square of the standard deviation, and may be computed manually using the formula $s_x^2 = \dfrac{\sum(X-\overline{X})^2}{N-1}$. The mean of the data is $\overline{X} = 24.75$. The differences between the values and the mean are $-14.75, -15.75, 25.25, 7.25, -1.75, -9.75, 11.25, -13.75, 13.25, -3.75, -2.75,$ and 5.25. The sum of the squared differences is 1,794.25. Dividing this by $n-1 = 11$ yields a variance of approximately 163.

Difficulty level: Medium

6. **B.** Data set A shows a center of approximately 24, and data set B shows a center around 32. Data set A shows more scores clustered around the mean, thus showing less variability. The actual median, mean, and standard deviation for data set A are 23.5, 24.5, and approximately 13.24; the actual median, mean, and standard deviation for data set B are 31, 28.15, and approximately 18.37.

Difficulty level: Medium

7. **C.** A z-score reports the number of standard deviations a value is above or below the mean. Thus, a value with a z-score of 2 is 2 standard deviations above the mean.

Difficulty level: Easy

8. **C.** Focus group A shows a smaller mean age and median age. The approximate mean of focus group A is 46.3; the approximate mean of focus group B is 47.5. The medians of focus groups A and B are 46 and 47.5, respectively. The comparisons between these measures of center may also be made by visually examining the double-bar graph. Notice that focus group A has a larger number of younger participants. Thus, the center is going to be smaller. Also, notice that focus group B has an equal number of participants, of ages 47 and 48. Thus, the median may easily be discerned as 47.5. Since focus group A has a larger number of younger participants, the median will be less than 47.5 years.

Difficulty level: Hard

9. **B.** The correlation is negative because the y-values decrease as the x-values increase. It is a strong correlation because the points show a strong linear association. In other words, if a best-fit line were drawn through the points, the margin of error between each point and the line would be small. For your own information, the approximate r-value for the correlation is −0.91.

Difficulty level: Easy

10. **A.** The x- and y-values may be entered into two separate lists in a graphing calculator. Next, choose STAT, CALC, and then LINREG$(ax + b)$. The r-value is approximately 0.08.

Difficulty level: Medium

11. **D.** The least-squares regression line can be estimated visually. The y-intercept of a line passing through the points, which have little variation about the line, appears to be approximately 5. The line $y = -x + 5$ seems to be an approximate fit. Notice the line seems to have a slope of approximately 1. A steeper slope would not seem to fit the data. The points may be entered into lists in a graphing calculator, with the least-squares regression line computed by choosing STAT, CALC, and then LINREG$(ax + b)$. The least-squares regression line is approximately $y = -1.4x + 5.2$.

Difficulty level: Hard

12. **A.** The least-squares regression line must be calculated first. After you enter the x- and y-values into two separate lists in a graphing calculator and then choose STAT, CALC, and LINREG$(ax + b)$, the least-squares regression line may be written. The least-squares regression line is $y = -3.8x + 2.7$. Evaluating the line for x-values of 0, 1, 2, and 3 gives predicted y-values. The predicted y-values are 2.7, −1.1, −4.9, and −8.7. Subtraction of these predicted y-values from the actual y-values of 3, −1, −6, and −8 gives 0.3, 0.1, −1.1, and 0.7. Therefore, the points on the residual plot are (0, 0.3), (1, 0.1), (2, −1.1), and (3, 0.7).

Difficulty level: Hard

13. **E.** The relative frequencies may be written as $\frac{20}{150}, \frac{32}{150}, \frac{40}{150}, \frac{42}{150},$ and $\frac{16}{150}$, which round to the following decimals: 0.13, 0.21, 0.27, 0.28, and 0.11.

Difficulty level: Easy

14. **D.** The relative frequency may be written as $\frac{15}{88}$, which represents the ratio of freshmen who are Democrats (15) to the total number of students surveyed (88); $\frac{15}{88} \approx 0.17$, or 17%.

Difficulty level: Medium

15. **A.** While the other nonexperimental studies and one experimental study provided may include components of past experiences, an *ex post facto* study, or causal-comparative study, is the only study that specifically looks to the past to determine causes of a current occurrence or situation.

Difficulty level: Easy

16. **E.** Simple random sampling provides every subject an equal chance of being chosen. Assigning subjects a number and then using a random number generator to obtain a list of numbers is an example of simple random sampling. Systematic random sampling includes a more specific plan, such as choosing every twentieth person from a list.

Difficulty level: Easy

17. **C.** A *t*-distribution is needed when the population standard deviation is not known and only the sample standard deviation is given. Z-distributions and *t*-distributions both compare standardized scores, not raw scores, hence the conversion to *z*-scores and *t*-values.

Difficulty level: Easy

18. **C.** *T*-tests and linear regressions, which are both quantitative analyses (and part of inferential statistics), are deductive in nature since the analyses seek answers to a set of *a priori* designed research questions. The researcher seeks to make deductions regarding some claimed hypotheses. With deductive analyses, the researcher is not seeking to build a theory, which is an inductive process. Constant comparison and content

analysis are qualitative methods that seek to identify patterns, which is part of inductive reasoning.

Difficulty level: Easy

19. **B.** A randomized block design is a type of randomized sampling and is thus not a limitation to a study. Randomized sampling is needed to reduce bias in the data. Randomized block designs include matched pairs and repeated measures.

Difficulty level: Medium

20. **C.** As the number of trials increases, the experimental probability begins to approximate the theoretical probability. In this case, the theoretical probability of drawing an ace is $\frac{4}{52}$, which reduces to $\frac{1}{13}$. Thus, the best approximation for the experimental probability is $\frac{1}{13}$.

Difficulty level: Medium

21. **E.** The expected value is equal to the sum of the products of the probability of drawing each card and the card's value. Thus, the expected value may be written as $\left(1 \cdot \frac{1}{10}\right) + \left(2 \cdot \frac{1}{10}\right) + \left(3 \cdot \frac{1}{10}\right) + \left(4 \cdot \frac{1}{10}\right) + \left(5 \cdot \frac{1}{10}\right) + \left(6 \cdot \frac{1}{10}\right) + \left(7 \cdot \frac{1}{10}\right) + \left(8 \cdot \frac{1}{10}\right) + \left(9 \cdot \frac{1}{10}\right) + \left(10 \cdot \frac{1}{10}\right),$ which simplifies to $\frac{1}{10} + \frac{2}{10} + \frac{3}{10} + \frac{4}{10} + \frac{5}{10} + \frac{6}{10} + \frac{7}{10} + \frac{8}{10} + \frac{9}{10} + \frac{10}{10},$ or 5.5.

Difficulty level: Medium

22. **B.** The probabilities of getting heads or tails are both $\frac{1}{2}$. Assigning a value of 0 to heads and 1 to tails allows you to write the following expected value: $\left(0 \cdot \frac{1}{2}\right) + \left(1 \cdot \frac{1}{2}\right)$, which equals $\frac{1}{2}$. Thus, the expected value of a coin toss is $\frac{1}{2}$, or 0.5. Also, note the theoretical probability of getting heads or tails is $\frac{1}{2}$.

Difficulty level: Medium

23. **D.** The expected value is equal to the sum of the products of each x-value and the corresponding probabilities. The following table can be

used to represent the x-values and probabilities of each. The x-values represent the possibilities of rolling an even number. Since there are 2 rolls, he may get 0, 1, or 2 even numbers: $\dfrac{\binom{3}{0}\binom{3}{2}}{\binom{6}{2}}$.

x	$f(x)$
0	$\dfrac{\binom{3}{0}\binom{3}{2}}{\binom{6}{2}} = \dfrac{3}{15}$
1	$\dfrac{\binom{3}{1}\binom{3}{1}}{\binom{6}{2}} = \dfrac{9}{15}$
2	$\dfrac{\binom{3}{2}\binom{3}{0}}{\binom{6}{2}} = \dfrac{3}{15}$

Thus, the expected value may be written as $E(X) = \left(0 \cdot \dfrac{3}{15}\right) + \left(1 \cdot \dfrac{9}{15}\right) + \left(2 \cdot \dfrac{3}{15}\right)$, or $E(X) = 1$. Notice that 1 is also equal to the product of the theoretical probability of rolling an even number and the number of rolls.

Difficulty level: Hard

24. **D.** There are 13 spades in a standard deck of cards, which contains 52 cards in all. Thus, the probability of getting a spade is $\dfrac{13}{52}$, which reduces to $\dfrac{1}{4}$.

Difficulty level: Medium

25. **A.** For independent events, the probability of A or B may be calculated using the formula $P(A \text{ or } B) = P(A) + P(B) - P(A \text{ and } B)$. Thus, the probability of rolling a three or getting heads may be written as $P(3 \text{ or heads}) = \dfrac{1}{6} + \dfrac{1}{2} - \dfrac{1}{12} = \dfrac{7}{12}$.

Difficulty level: Medium

26. **A.** For independent events, the probability of A or B may be calculated using the formula $P(A \text{ or } B) = P(A) + P(B) - P(A \text{ and } B)$. Thus, the probability the spinner lands on a number greater than three or the die lands on a four may be written as $P(>3 \text{ or } 4) = \frac{5}{8} + \frac{1}{6} - \frac{5}{8} \cdot \frac{1}{6} = \frac{33}{48} = \frac{11}{16}$.

Difficulty level: Medium

27. **D.** The probability of independent events A and B may be calculated using the formula $P(A \text{ and } B) = P(A) \cdot P(B)$. Thus, the probability the die lands on a number greater than four and she draws an ace may be written as $P(>4 \text{ and ace}) = \frac{2}{6} \cdot \frac{4}{52}$, which equals $\frac{1}{39}$.

Difficulty level: Medium

28. **A.** The probability of independent events A and B may be calculated using the formula $P(A \text{ and } B) = P(A) \cdot P(B)$. Thus, the probability he gets tails and the die lands on a number less than three may be written as $P(\text{tails and} < 3) = \frac{1}{2} \cdot \frac{2}{6}$, which equals $\frac{1}{6}$.

Difficulty level: Medium

29. **C.** For overlapping events, the probability of A or B may be calculated using the formula $P(A \text{ or } B) = P(A) + P(B) - P(A \text{ and } B)$. Thus, the probability she rolls a number less than three or an odd number may be written as $P(<3 \text{ or odd}) = \frac{2}{6} + \frac{3}{6} - \frac{1}{6}$, which equals $\frac{2}{3}$.

Difficulty level: Medium

30. **B.** The events are independent since he replaces the first card. The probability of independent events A and B may be calculated using the formula $P(A \text{ and } B) = P(A) \cdot P(B)$. Neither the sample space nor the number of possible outcomes for event B will decrease. Thus, the probability may be written as $P(\text{heart and queen}) = \frac{13}{52} \cdot \frac{4}{52}$, which equals $\frac{1}{52}$.

Difficulty level: Medium

31. **E.** The events are dependent since she does not replace the first card. The probability of dependent events A and B may be calculated using the formula $P(A \text{ and } B) = P(A) \cdot P(B|A)$. In this case, both the sample

space and the number of spades available will decrease by 1. The probability may be written as $P(A \text{ and } B) = \frac{13}{52} \cdot \frac{12}{51} = \frac{3}{51}$.

Difficulty level: Medium

32. **A.** The events are dependent since he does not replace the first card. The probability of dependent events A and B may be calculated using the formula $P(A \text{ and } B) = P(A) \cdot P(B|A)$. In this case, the sample space and the number of possible outcomes for event B will each decrease by 1. The probability may be written as $P(A \text{ and } B) = \frac{4}{52} \cdot \frac{3}{51}$, which equals $\frac{1}{221}$.

Difficulty level: Medium

33. **D.** The probability that an employee prefers espressos or takes the bus may be written as $P(E \text{ or } B) = P(E) + P(B) - P(E \text{ and } B)$. Thus, the probability may be written as $P(E \text{ or } B) = \frac{9}{61} + \frac{39}{61} - \frac{7}{61}$, which is approximately 67%.

Difficulty level: Medium

34. **A.** A standard normal distribution (or z-distribution) has a mean of 0 and a standard deviation of 1.

Difficulty level: Easy

35. **B.** The z-score can be interpreted as the number of standard deviations above or below a population mean. The z-score may be calculated using the formula $z = \frac{X - \mu}{\sigma}$, where X represents the individual score, μ represents the population mean, and σ represents the population standard deviation. Substituting the value of 18.9 for X, 19 for μ, and 0.1 for σ gives: $z = \frac{18.9 - 19}{0.1}$, which equals -1. Thus, the number of ounces contained in the sample bag is 1 standard deviation below the claimed number of ounces (or population mean).

Difficulty level: Medium

36. **E.** A z-distribution table shows a mean to z area of 0.4726, given a z-score of 1.92. Thus, the area under a normal curve between the given z-score and the mean is approximately 47%.

Difficulty level: Medium

37. **A.** A z-distribution table shows a mean to z area of 0.4983 for a z-score of 2.93. Since you are interested in the area to the right of this z-score, the area of 0.4983 should be subtracted from 0.5. Recall the area under a normal curve is 1. The area to the right of the z-score is equal to $0.5 - 0.4938$, or 0.0017, which is approximately 0.002. This area is also given as the "smaller portion" in a z-table providing such information.

Difficulty level: Medium

38. **E.** A z-distribution table shows a mean to z area of 0.4978 for a z-score of −2.85. The area above the mean is equal to 0.5, so the area above a score that is 2.85 standard deviations below the mean is equal to the sum of 0.4978 and 0.5, or 0.9978. Thus, the area under the curve that is above 2.85 standard deviations below the mean is 99.78%.

Difficulty level: Medium

39. **B.** The *t*-distribution should be used, since the population standard deviation is not known. The formula to use when comparing a sample mean to a population mean and only the sample standard deviation is known is $t = \dfrac{\overline{X} - \mu}{\left(\frac{s}{\sqrt{n}}\right)}$. Substituting 11.9 for the sample mean, 12 for the population mean, 0.1 for the sample standard deviation, and 50 for the sample size gives the following: $t = \dfrac{11.9 - 12}{\left(\frac{0.1}{\sqrt{50}}\right)}$, which is approximately −7.1. The critical *t*-value for 49 degrees of freedom, using a one-tailed test and alpha of 0.05, is approximately 1.68. Since the absolute value of −7.1 is greater than 1.68, the null hypothesis should be rejected. Thus, there is a significant difference between the mean of the sample and the population mean. A one-sample *t*-test may be calculated using a graphing calculator by choosing STAT, TESTS, and then T-TEST. For this one-directional test, you can choose $< \mu_0$. Click CALCULATE.

Difficulty level: Medium

40. **A.** The two sample means may be compared using a two-sample *t*-test. Choose STAT, TESTS, and then 2-SAMPT-TEST. Enter the sample mean,

sample standard deviation, and sample size for each sample. Choose a null hypothesis of no difference ($\neq \mu 2$) and a pooled variance. Notice that no pooled variance will also result in a p-value less than 0.001. A p-value less than 0.001 is considered significant; therefore, the null hypothesis will be rejected and a significant difference between the sample means may be declared.

Difficulty level: Hard

Section II, Part A: Free-Response Questions

1.

(a) Jason's score is 3 standard deviations below the SAT mean score: $z = \dfrac{1200 - 1500}{100}$, where $z = -3$.

(b) The percentage of test-takers who scored below Jason is 0.13%, or the difference of 0.5 and 0.4987 (the mean to z area).

(c) The percentage of test-takers whose score fell between the SAT mean and Jason's SAT score is 49.87%, or the mean to z area.

Difficulty level: Hard

2.

(a) The margin of error may be calculated using the formula $E = z_{\frac{\alpha}{2}} \cdot \dfrac{\sigma}{\sqrt{n}}$, where $z_{\frac{\alpha}{2}}$ represents the critical z-value for a specified degree of confidence. The critical z-value for a 95% level of confidence is 1.96. Thus, the margin of error may be written as $E = 1.96 \cdot \dfrac{0.2}{\sqrt{36}}$, which is approximately 0.065.

(b) The confidence interval for a 95% level of confidence may be written as $\overline{X} \pm 0.065$, where $\overline{X} = 22.5$. Thus, the confidence interval is approximately (22.435, 22.565).

(c) Since 22.5 lies within the 95% confidence interval, it is a likely possibility for the true number of ounces of cereal contained in each box.

Difficulty level: Hard

3. It is not likely that the company's claim is true (or correct) because the claimed number of ounces per jar, or 3, does not fall within a 95% confidence interval. The 95% confidence interval is approximately (2.871, 2.929). Since 3 ounces is larger than the upper limit of this interval, is it doubtful that the company's claim is correct.

   Difficulty level: Hard

4.

(a) There is a significant difference between the company's claim and the average annual salary shown by the sample. The problem calls for a *t*-test; the *t*-value has an absolute value greater than 5. The critical *t*-value for 29 degrees of freedom, for a two-tailed test, is approximately 2.045. Since 5 is greater than 2.045, the null hypothesis should be rejected and a significant difference should be declared.

(b) The *p*-value is less than 0.001.

   Difficulty level: Hard

5.

(a) The margin of error is equal to the product of the critical *z*-value for a desired level of confidence and the square root of the ratio of the product of $\hat{p}$ and $\hat{q}$ to the sample size, n, written as $E = z_{\frac{\alpha}{2}} \cdot \sqrt{\frac{\hat{p}\hat{q}}{n}}$, where $\hat{q} = 1 - \hat{p}$. The critical *z*-value for a 90% confidence level is 1.645. In this case, $\hat{p} = \frac{15}{50}$. Thus, the margin of error may be written as $E = 1.645 \cdot \sqrt{\frac{(0.3)(0.7)}{50}}$, or approximately 0.107.

(b) The confidence interval for a proportion is represented by the formula $C = \hat{p} \pm E$, where C represents the confidence interval, $\hat{p}$ represents the point estimate for the proportion, and E represents the margin of error. Substituting a value of 0.3 for the point estimate and 0.107 for the margin of error gives the following approximate confidence interval for the population proportion: (0.193, 0.407).

(c) Any percentage lying between the confidence limits is a possible true population proportion for Democrats. Thus, 20% is a likely true population proportion.

   Difficulty level: Hard

Section II, Part B: The Investigative Task

6.

(a) The chi-square statistic is approximately 0.044.

(b) Three degrees of freedom were used. The degrees of freedom are equal to $n - 1$, where n represents the number of categories being compared.

(c) The p-value lies above 0.995. The p-value was determined by locating the approximate chi-square statistic of 0.044 for 3 degrees of freedom and finding the corresponding probability. Since 0.044 lies below the chi-square statistic of 0.072 for 3 degrees of freedom, the probability lies above 0.995.

(d) No, there is not a significant difference between the number of inches of rainfall received per month by the city this year and the recorded average number of inches received per month. The probability value is greater than a level of significance of 0.05. Thus, the null hypothesis of no difference should not be rejected, and no significant difference should be declared.

(e) No, the declaration of no significant difference would remain. The p-value for 2 degrees of freedom for a chi-square statistic of approximately 0.042 is between 0.99 and 0.975. Such a p-value is larger than a level of significance of 0.05.

   Difficulty level: Hard

Glossary

Alternative Hypothesis: Hypothesis stating that a difference exists between the score and the population mean or between two means.

Analysis of Variance: A statistical test that determines whether there is a significant difference between two or more nominal groups. An analysis of variance may be one-way, meaning it includes only one independent variable, or factorial, meaning it includes more than one independent variable.

Back-to-Back Stem Plot: A graph that compares distributions of two or more data sets.

Bar Graph: A graph that represents the frequency of nominal or interval categories of a set of data.

Bimodal: Having two peaks (as a distribution).

Binomial Distribution: A probability distribution that represents the probability for x successes over n trials, given a particular probability of each success.

Bivariate Data: Data that represent two variables.

Blinding: A technique that hides the identity of individuals and/or products, methods, etc., included in a study.

Boxplot: A graph that represents univariate data. It represents the median, first, and third quartiles and upper and lower limits of a data set.

Case Study: A study involving one or more participants who freely discuss ideas without being constrained to a particular set of questions.

Causal-Comparative Study: A study in which researchers observe participants but look to past occurrences for possible causes of behavior. Also called *ex post facto study*.

Census: A survey that involves the entire population.

Central Limit Theorem: A theorem that states that the mean and standard deviation of the sampling distribution may be assumed to equal the mean and standard deviation of the population when given large sample sizes.

Chi-Square Test: A test that examines the significance of differences between observed and expected frequencies.

Cluster Sampling: A sampling technique that involves the random selection of groups of participants, not individuals.

Completely Randomized Design: A design with a random sample of size n, whereby each treatment is randomly assigned to the sample.

Compound Probability: Probability that involves two or more events.

Conditional Probability: Probability that one event will occur given that the other event has occurred.

Conditional Relative Frequencies: The frequencies for each category in a two-way relative frequency table.

Confidence Interval: An interval that likely contains the population mean or proportion. Also called *interval estimate*.

Confounding Variable: A variable that has not been accounted for in a study and may impact the outcomes of the study.

Control Group: A group in an experiment that does not receive a treatment.

Convenience Sampling: A sampling based on convenience involving groups that do not represent random samples and may be influenced by external variables.

Correlation: A relationship between two variables.

Cumulative Frequency Plot: A graph that represents cumulative frequencies as each subsequent interval range is added.

Decile: Measure of position that represents multiples of 10 percent of data.

Deductive Reasoning: Reasoning that follows given laws, rules, or other widely accepted principles.

Degree of Freedom: A value that is equal to the sample size minus 1.

Dependent Event: An event with a probability that is affected by another event. For example, the act of drawing two cards from a deck represents dependent events if the first card is not replaced.

Descriptive Statistics: A field of statistics that is not inferential and includes calculations of measures of center and spread and measures of position.

Directional: The direction is either above or below the mean or proportion.

Disjoint (Mutually Exclusive) Events: Events that cannot occur at the same time or that have no outcomes in common.

Dotplot: A graph of a number line with points plotted above appropriate values on the line.

Double Bar Graph: A technique for comparing the distributions of two variables in which the frequency is shown by the height of the bars.

Effective Survey: A survey that includes appropriately ordered questions that are nonleading, clear, and concise.

***Ex Post Facto* Study:** A study in which researchers simply observe participants but look to past occurrences for possible causes of behavior. Also called *causal-comparative study*.

Expected Value: The average of all possible values that may result from a trial. It is equal to the sum of the products of each value and the probability of obtaining that value.

Experiment: A procedure that involves treatments given to one or more groups of participants.

Experimental Probability: Probability that is derived from an experiment and may be represented as the ratio of the number of times an event occurs to the total number of trials.

Frequency Plot: A graph that represents the frequency of data falling within certain intervals. It connects frequencies with a line.

Frequency Table: A table that represents the frequencies of data.

Histogram: A graph that represents the frequency of data falling within certain intervals. The height of each bar represents the frequency.

Historical Research: Descriptive research that includes historical documents such as interviews, transcriptions, books, articles, and other media.

Hypothesis of No Difference: A hypothesis that states that no difference exists between the score and the population mean or between two means. Also called *null hypothesis*.

Independent Events: Events that do not influence each other.

Inductive Reasoning: Reasoning that moves from the general to the specific and is based on experience or observation.

Inferential Statistics: A field of statistics that includes hypothesis testing and analyses such as *t*-tests, analyses of variance, and regression analyses.

Interquartile Range: A measure of spread that looks at the middle 50 percent of a data set or the difference between the first and third quartiles of a data set.

Intersection: The probability that events A and B will occur. On a Venn diagram, this probability is represented by the overlapping portion of the two events.

Interval Data: Data that are measured along a scale for which the distance between any two pairs of values is equivalent in some way.

Interval Estimate: An interval that likely contains the population mean or proportion. Also called *confidence interval*.

Joint Frequency: A frequency for each category in a two-way frequency table.

Kurtosis: The steepness or flatness of a distribution.

Law of Large Numbers: A law that states that as the number of trials of an experiment increases, the relative frequency of the experimental probabilities of an event will begin to approximate the theoretical probability of the event.

Least-Squares Regression Line: A line that passes through the points of a scatterplot, while minimizing the average standard error, or average deviations from the line. The line may be used to predict the value of a dependent variable, based on the value of an independent variable.

Leptokurtic: Describes a steep distribution that indicates a lesser level of variability about the mean than a normal distribution.

Level of Significance: A level, also known as alpha, determined by the researcher, that acts as a reference point for rejection of the null hypothesis. For a resulting p-value less than the level of significance, the researcher may reject the null hypothesis and declare a statistically significant difference.

Linear Regression: A test that determines the correlation between one independent and one dependent variable.

Logarithmic Transformation: A type of transformation used to achieve linearity.

Longitudinal Research: Research that involves the examination and comparison of a group of participants over a long period. (See *longitudinal study*.)

Longitudinal Study: A study that examines the same subjects over a long period. (See *longitudinal research*.)

Margin of Error: A statistic that represents the estimated difference between the sample mean and the population mean or the sample proportion and population proportion.

Marginal Frequency: The total in the margins of a two-way frequency table.

Matched-Pairs Design: An experimental design in which participants are grouped by pairs according to an *a priori* factor or factors and then randomly assigned to the groups.

Mean: The average of a data set.

Median: The middle value in a data set that is arranged in ascending order.

Mesokurtic: Describes a normal distribution.

Modality: The number of peaks in a distribution.

Mode: The value that occurs most frequently in a data set.

Modified Replication: A study that makes slight or major changes to an existing study to compare the outcomes of the original study to those resulting from the modified study.

Multiple Regression: A test that examines the relationship between two or more independent variables and one dependent variable.

Negative Correlation: A correlation in which the y-values decrease as the x-values increase.

Negatively Skewed Distribution: A distribution with a greater number of higher scores or values.

No Correlation: No evident pattern, or relationship, exists between two variables.

Nominal Data: A set of data whose values can be assigned a code in the form of a number where the numbers are simply labels.

Nonexperimental Research: Research that does not involve any treatments.

Nonresponse Bias: Bias that occurs when individuals or groups of individuals cannot or will not respond to a given survey.

Normal Distribution: A distribution that is symmetric and unimodal wherein the frequencies of values increase and decrease at the same rate.

Null Hypothesis: A hypothesis that states that no difference exists between the score and the population mean or between two means. Also called *hypothesis of no difference*.

Observational Study: A type of nonexperimental research in which a group or groups of participants are studied without any interference from the researcher.

One-Way Relative Frequency Table: A table that represents the ratio of a frequency for a particular category to the total frequencies.

Outliers: Scores that differ markedly from the center of the distribution and are located in the tails of a distribution. They influence the mean but have no effect on the median.

Overlapping: Having one or more outcomes in common.

Parallel Boxplot: A graph that represents data from two distributions that are displayed on the same chart, using the same measurement scale.

Parameter: A data value that is gathered from an entire population.

Percentile: The position at which x percent of values falls below a certain value and includes quartiles, deciles, and other percentages.

Perfect Correlation: A correlation in which the least-squares regression line is the actual line passing through the points. The points represent solutions of the line.

Placebo Effect: A case in which an individual feels that a difference has occurred regardless of whether it actually did.

Platykurtic: Describes a flat distribution, indicating a higher level of variability about the mean than a normal distribution.

Point Estimate: A value used to approximate the population mean or population proportion.

Positive Correlation: A correlation in which the *y*-values increase as the *x*-values increase.

Positively Skewed Distribution: A distribution with a greater number of lower scores or values.

Power: The probability of accurately rejecting a null hypothesis. It is the probability of being able to find statistical significance.

Power Transformation: Raising the values of the *x*- or *y*-variable to a specified exponent, or power.

_p_-Value: The probability of rejecting the null hypothesis.

Qualitative Analysis: An analysis that includes constant comparison, content analysis, and grounded theory. It focuses on trends and patterns evidenced by written or spoken words.

Quantitative Analysis: An analysis that includes descriptive statistics, *t*-tests, analyses of variance, and linear or multiple regressions.

Quartile: A value that divides the data into groups of 25 percent. A data set will include a first quartile, median, and third quartile.

Quasi-Experimental Experiment: An experiment in which no random sampling is used.

Randomized Block Design: A design in which the random sample is created based on the similarity of the participants.

Range: A value equal to the difference between the maximum and minimum values in a data set.

Regression: A test that determines the correlation between two or more variables.

Reliable Survey: A survey that has consistent results over a specified period.

Repeated-Measures Design: A design that uses the same subjects for all aspects of the experiment via inclusion in the control and treatment groups.

Residual Plot: A graph that represents the difference between predicted y-values and actual y-values.

Sample: A group drawn from a population that is used to represent the whole population.

Sampling Bias: Bias that occurs when not all members of a population are represented.

Sampling Distribution: The distribution of means or n random samples.

Scatterplot: A graph that shows the correlation between two variables.

Simple Probability: The likelihood of a single event occurring.

Simple Random Sampling: A sampling technique that allows every person an equal chance of being chosen as a participant.

Spread: The variability around the center of a data set.

Standard Deviation: A statistic that represents the variability around the center of a data set. It is equal to the square root of the ratio of the sum of the squared deviations of the scores to the difference of the number of scores and 1.

Standard Normal Distribution: A distribution that includes standardized scores with a mean of 0 and a standard deviation of 1. It involves standardized (z-) scores, as opposed to raw scores.

Statistic: A data value that is gathered from a sample or samples.

Stem-and-Leaf Plot: A graph that represents univariate data. The stem portion of the plot represents the tens digits, and the leaf portion represents the ones digits.

Stratified Random Sampling: A sampling technique in which a population is divided into groups, and then a random sample is drawn from each stratum.

Strict Replication: All aspects of a study are replicated to the extent possible in which the same conditions, research questions, and methodology are used.

Strong Correlation: A correlation that is close to −1 or +1. It shows little deviation of data points from the least-squares regression line.

Survey: A type of instrument that determines the ideas and beliefs of a certain population or sample pertaining to certain topics.

Survey Bias: Bias that occurs when survey questions prompt participants to respond in a particular manner.

Systematic Sampling: A sampling technique in which every nth person on a list is chosen for participation.

t-Distribution: A distribution that is used when the population standard deviation is unknown.

Theoretical Probability: Probability that is based on theory and may be represented as the ratio of the number of possible outcomes for an event to the sample space for the event.

Treatment Group: A group that receives some treatment or intervention.

Trendline: A line drawn on a graph that best fits the data. It can be curved or straight.

True Experiment: An experiment in which participants are randomly selected for group placement.

t-Test: A statistical test that compares a sample mean to a population mean or compares two sample means. The test is used when the population standard deviation is not known.

Two-Way Frequency Table: A table that compares frequencies of data for two variables.

Type I Error: An error that results from the rejection of a null hypothesis when it should not be rejected.

Type II Error: An error that results from the failure to reject a null hypothesis.

Unimodal: Having one peak (as a distribution).

Union: The probability of events A or B occurring. On a Venn diagram, this probability is represented by the area, contained within the two circles, representing the events.

Univariate Data: Data that represent one variable.

Valid Survey: A survey that measures what it purports to measure.

Variance: A value that is equal to the square of the standard deviation. It is equal to the ratio of the sum of the squared deviations of the scores to the difference of the number of scores and 1. It is used to represent the variability in a data set, about the center.

Volunteerism: A source of sampling bias that occurs when individuals have a certain agenda when responding to a survey.

Weak Correlation: A correlation that is close to 0. It shows a large deviation of data points from the least-squares regression line.

z-Distribution: A distribution that is used when the population standard deviation is known.

z-Score: A standardized score that represents the number of standard deviations a score falls above or below a mean.

About the Authors

Amanda Ross, PhD, is an educational consultant in Flagstaff, Arizona. She writes and reviews mathematics curricula and assessment items, creates instructional design components, performs standards alignments, writes preparatory standardized test materials, authors grant proposals, and serves as an external evaluator. Prior to performing full-time consulting work, she served as a public school teacher, a lecturer, a research assistant, a professional development coordinator, and an instructional designer. She is currently writing a book on statistical analyses with a professor at Texas A&M University. Ross graduated from Texas A&M University in 2006 with a doctorate in curriculum and instruction in mathematics education.

Anne Collins has been involved in the writing and editing of multiple mathematics books in the My Max Score series. She is the author of numerous scholarly journal articles and enjoys both the research and teaching aspects of mathematics. She received her bachelor's degree in mathematics and physics from Bowling Green State University and subsequently went on to complete her doctorate in mathematics at Duke University in 2002. Collins has been teaching ever since. She currently teaches both mathematics and statistics and serves as the math assessment writer for Northeast Editing, Inc., in Jenkins Township, Pennsylvania.

Also Available

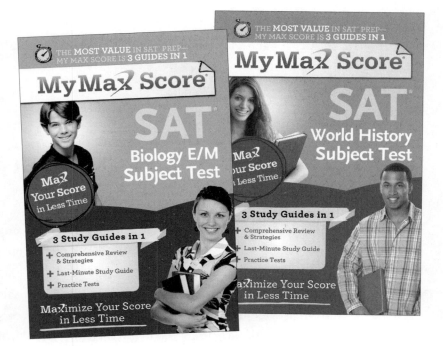

My Max Score SAT Biology E/M Subject Test
by Maria Malzone • 978-1-4022-7298-1

My Max Score SAT Literature Subject Test
by Steven Fox • 978-1-4022-5613-4

My Max Score SAT Math 1 and 2 Subject Test
by Chris Monahan • 978-1-4022-5601-1

My Max Score SAT U.S. History Subject Test
by Cara Cantarella • 978-1-4022-5604-2

My Max Score SAT World History Subject Test
by Northeast Editing, Inc. • 978-1-4022-7295-0

My Max Score ASVAB
by Angie Johnston and Amanda Ross, PhD • 978-1-4022-4492-6

$14.99 U.S./£9.99 UK

Also Available

My Max Score AP Biology
by Dr. Robert S. Stewart Jr. • 978-1-4022-4315-8

My Max Score AP Calculus AB/BC
by Carolyn Wheater • 978-1-4022-4313-4

My Max Score AP English Language and Composition
by Jocelyn Sisson • 978-1-4022-4312-7

My Max Score AP English Literature and Composition
by Tony Armstrong • 978-1-4022-4311-0

My Max Score AP European History
by Ira Shull and Mark Dziak • 978-1-4022-4318-9

My Max Score AP U.S. Government and Politics
by Del Franz • 978-1-4022-4314-1

My Max Score AP U.S. History
by Michael Romano • 978-1-4022-4310-3

My Max Score AP World History
by Kirby Whitehead • 978-1-4022-4317-2

$14.99 U.S./$17.99 CAN/£9.99 UK

To download additional AP practice tests and
learn more about My Max Score, visit mymaxscore.com.

My Max Score
AP* Study Guide Apps

Maximize Your Score in Less Time

**Our bestselling
AP Study Guides
are now interactive
and available in
the App Store.**

These iPad and iPhone
compatible apps contain
everything you need to
prepare for your AP exam.

The MyMaxScore AP Study Guide apps:

- ✔ Provide an interactive way to study for AP exams
- ✔ Allow you to track your time spent on each question
- ✔ Give you the opportunity to make notations and mark questions for further study
- ✔ Give you a personalized progress report
- ✔ Help you stay organized

It's never too early to start a complete review, but it's also never too late
for a score-boosting crash session.

Download these valuable AP test prep apps today:

- ✔ AP Calculus AB/BC
- ✔ AP U.S. History
- ✔ AP English Language and Composition
- ✔ AP English Literature and Composition
- ✔ AP U.S. Government and Politics

Go to MyMaxScore.com today to learn more about how you can max your score!

*AP is a registered trademark of the College Entrance Examination Board, which neither sponsors nor endorses this product.

Essentials from
Dr. Gary Gruber

and the creators of My Max Score

"Gruber can ring the bell on any number
of standardized exams."
—*Chicago Tribune*

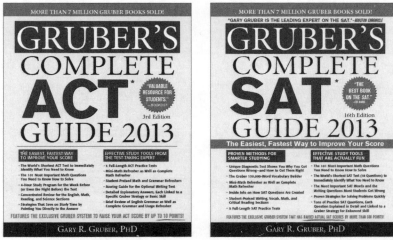

$19.99 U.S./£14.99 UK
978-1-4022-7301-8

$19.99 U.S./£14.99 UK
978-1-4022-6492-4

$16.99 U.S./$19.99 CAN/£11.99 UK
978-1-4022-4308-0

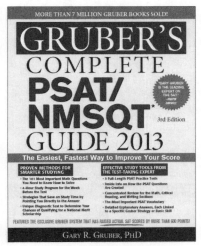

$13.99 U.S./£9.99 UK
978-1-4022-6495-5

"Gruber's methods make the questions
seem amazingly simple to solve."
—*Library Journal*

"Gary Gruber is the leading expert on the SAT."
—*Houston Chronicle*

$16.99 U.S./£11.99 UK
978-1-4022-5337-9

$14.99 U.S./£9.99 UK
978-1-4022-5340-9

$14.99 U.S./£9.99 UK
978-1-4022-5343-0

$12.99 U.S./£8.99 UK
978-1-4022-6072-8